François Rabelais

Other books by Donald M. Frame

Selections from the Essays of Montaigne
Edited and Translated by Donald M. Frame

Montaigne in France, 1812–1852

The Misanthrope and Other Plays
and
Tartuffe and Other Plays
by Molière
Translated by Donald M. Frame

Montaigne's Discovery of Man

Montaigne: A Biography

The Complete Works of Montaigne
Translated by Donald M. Frame

RABELAIS

Attributed to the French School, before 1694
Musée de Versailles; photo Musées Nationaux Paris

DONALD M. FRAME

François Rabelais

A Study

NEW YORK AND LONDON

HARCOURT BRACE JOVANOVICH

Printed in the United States of America

Library of Congress Cataloging in Publication Data

Frame, Donald Murdoch, 1911–
François Rabelais: a study.

Bibliography: p.
Includes index.
1. Rabelais, François, 1490 (ca.)–1553?
2. Authors, French—16th century—Biography.
PQ1693.F68   843'.3   [B]   76-62519
ISBN 0-15-133465-X

First edition

B C D E

To Kathleen

Toutes choses prenoit en bonne partie,
tout acte interpretoit à bien.

Abbreviations

BHR *Bibliothèque d'Humanisme et Renaissance*

ER *Etudes rabelaisiennes.* 13 vols. Geneva: Droz, 1956–76.

FR *François Rabelais: Ouvrage publié pour lo quatrième centenaire de sa mort. 1553–1953.* Geneva: Droz; Lille: Giard, 1953.

HR *Humanisme et Renaissance*

RER *Revue des Études Rabelaisiennes*

Prefatory Note

My hope for this book is the same one that I expressed a dozen years ago for my biography of Montaigne: that it may earn both the confidence of the scholar and the interest of the general reader. Thus I have offered as notes on the page only those that seemed necessary or important to an understanding of the text. All notes that are merely references will be found, designated by numbers, at the end of the book.

The quotations from Rabelais are given always in English translation, sometimes in the original French as well. While I think that Montaigne is adequately translatable into English, I feel less sure that Rabelais is, and when in doubt have offered his text in his own French as well as in translation. I find even the best English versions so fallible that the translations given here are my own.

D.M.F.

Introduction

François Rabelais is one of the most puzzling of the world's great writers. He wanted to be; he loved to play games with his readers, and he played them well.[1]* Moreover, his work speaks with many voices: to name but a few, those of Grandgousier, Gargantua, Frère Jean, Pantagruel, Panurge, Epistémon, Homenaz, Editus, and the narrator, known to us by the anagram Alcofribas Nasier. Each reader must decide for himself which of these voices speaks (or speak) for Rabelais, and at what time; each reader must often be wrong.

Modern Rabelais scholarship began around the turn of the century with Abel Lefranc and such fellow workers as Jean Plattard, Lazare Sainéan, and Jacques Boulenger. Lefranc's concern was historical: to relate the book to Rabelais's biography and to contemporary events.[2] More recently Lucien Febvre, V. L. Saulnier, M. A. Screech, Robert Marichal, A. J. Krailsheimer, and many others have sought the sense of Rabelais in his relation to the intellectual currents—mainly religious— of his time. In the last ten years such critics as Alfred Glauser, Jean Paris, and Floyd Gray have placed his stylistic creativity far above his ideas. Mikhail Bakhtin's Russian study *Rabelais and His World* has explained Rabelais as the supreme literary spokesman of the world of the carnival, in which the "official" values of the Middle Ages and Renaissance were turned upside down.

These and countless other scholars have traced many lines of his portrait, but much of it remains obscure. Besides the five books of *Gargantua and Pantagruel* (of which only the first four are certainly authentic), we have little of what Rabelais wrote: a few prognostica-

* Numbered notes are on pages 201–217.

xiii

tions and almanacs, a few dedicatory letters and about a half dozen others, and little else. In the books for which he is known and admired, he seems to have sought—successfully—to remain an enigma.

Although the voices in the story are many, two predominate. One is clear and easy to identify: that of Gargantua for the late chapters of his book, that of Pantagruel from late in *Book Two* on, and to some extent that of Grandgousier for a few chapters of *Book One*. This "angelic" voice, as Thomas M. Greene has called it,³ is that of an enlightened Christian sage, a philosopher-king; it is a constant in the last three books, and in the first two also, once the giants are educated. Stoical as well as Christian, it takes everything in good part and refuses to be disturbed by anything beyond man's control. This is Pantagruelism, which Rabelais clearly holds up to us as an ideal.

But Pantagruelism does not express the boisterous, irreverent gaiety of much of the book, which teems with an often lyrical obscenity, an unrestrained delight in eating, drinking, elimination, and copulation, and a fondness for practical jokes that are often cruel. Whereas Gargantua graciously frees a conquered aggressor army, Frère Jean slaughters the entire band that attacks the vineyard of Seuillé. Whereas the mature giants are courtly, and ladies are honored in the Abbey of Theleme, Panurge and Frère Jean regard women only as bedfellows, and Panurge plays a foul trick on a Paris lady who spurns his propositions. Whereas the ideal education of Gargantua is marked by sobriety, the Prologues are full of invitations to drink. This jovial, lusty, cruel world is the one we know as Rabelaisian; and A. C. Keller has pointed out that this "Rabelaisianism," as he calls it, marks more of the book than does Pantagruelism.⁴ Bakhtin's depiction of this "Rabelaisian" world leaves out Pantagruelism completely. We need to bring the two worlds together, as Rabelais did in his book.

Perhaps we also need another term for this "Rabelaisian" world; for to call it that is to imply that this is genuine Rabelais and that Pantagruelism is not. "Alcofribasism" will hardly do, nor even "Panurgism"; but we might speak of these two worlds and voices as those of Pantagruel on the one hand and of Alcofribas or Panurge on the other.

Usually Rabelais keeps the worlds and voices distinct. In Gargantua's letter to his son Pantagruel (II: 8),* in the account of Gargantua's own reformed education (I: 23–24), and in the description of the Abbey of

---

* Textual references will be given as follows: (Book) II: (chapter) 8, (page) 202. The edition of reference is the Pléiade edition of Rabelais's *Œuvres complètes*, eds. Jacques Boulenger and Lucien Scheler (Paris: Gallimard, 1959).

Theleme (I: 52–57), the voice of Alcofribas (or of Panurge) is rarely heard. At times, however, it succeeds that of Pantagruel with disconcerting suddenness. One example is Gargantua's lament for his wife Badebec, who died giving birth to Pantagruel:

Jamais je ne la verray, jamais je n'en recouvreray une telle; ce m'est une perte inestimable! O mon Dieu, que te avoys-je faict pour ainsi me punir? Que ne envoyas-tu la mort à moy premier que à elle? Car vivre sans elle ne m'est que languir. Ha, Badebec, ma mignonne, m'amye, mon petit con (toutefois elle en avoit bien troys arpents et deux sexterées). (II: 3, 181)

[Never shall I see her, never shall I find one like her; it's an inestimable loss to me! O my God, what had I done to you for you to punish me so? Why did you not send death to me earlier than to her? Ah, Badebec, my darling, my love, my little cunt (to be sure, hers was a good three acres and two sesterées in size).]

Another comes in the *Fourth Book*, where Pantagruel interprets Plutarch's story of the death of Pan as referring to that of Jesus, and speaks of him with apparent love and emotion. Then Rabelais continues:

Pantagruel, ce propous finy, resta en silence et profonde contemplation. Peu de temps après, nous veismes les larmes découller de ses œilz grosses comme œufz de austruche. Je me donne à Dieu, si n'en mens d'un seul mot. (IV: 28, 619)

[Pantagruel, having finished this story, remained in silence and profound contemplation. A short time after, we saw the tears flow from his eyes, big as ostrich eggs. God take me if a single word of that is a lie.]

These sudden changes of voice, from the lofty idealism of Pantagruel to the grotesque jocosity of Alcofribas, are a source not only of comedy but of puzzlement. In most writers the sudden comic touch cancels a serious part that precedes it, puts that too in a comic light. This, I think, was not Rabelais's intent, nor is it his effect on most readers. Neither voice cancels the other; both continue to sound in our inward ear. Ours to harmonize them as best we can; for the book includes them both.

To put it another way, Rabelais is not Panurge, or Frère Jean, or for that matter Pantagruel; he is all of them and much more. In Plato's terms, roughly, Panurge illustrates the appetitive function of the soul, Frère Jean the spirited, Pantagruel the rational.* The rational must rule—and Pantagruel does—but fairly, in harmony, for the greatest

* See for example their behavior in the tempest (IV: 19, 594), where Pantagruel prays and then helps, Frère Jean merely helps, and Panurge does little but defecate and blubber in his fear.

happiness of all three functions. The harmonious interplay of these three characters (as indeed of all the band), and that of the three functions and of the two dominant voices and worlds, is one of the marvelous qualities of Rabelais's book.

Contents

CONTENTS

François Rabelais

The Times

Born in 1483 or 1494, we believe, and dying in 1553, Rabelais lived in a time of ideological ferment. The discovery of the New World and the circumnavigation of the globe showed Europeans an expanding earth full of wonders, and a greater diversity in mankind than they had dreamed of, and shook their faith in earlier assumptions: had not Saint Augustine, for example, denied the existence of the Antipodes? The shock, however, was less great than we might suppose today; the Old World's main interest in the New involved trade, and chances to convert the heathen.

In Rabelais's time arabic numerals were still rarely used in France, arithmetic was rudimentary, and algebra virtually unknown. Watches and clocks were scarce, and accurate reckoning of time very rare. People believed in demons and sorcery; science as we know it (and trust it) remained undiscovered; and medicine was largely a branch of humanism. The distinction between the natural and the supernatural was rarely made, and the hand of God was seen everywhere in human affairs.[1]

For most of Rabelais's French contemporaries the supreme discovery was that of the Italian Renaissance. The Italian wars of the 1490s and early 1500s under Charles VIII, Louis XII, and Francis I were conquering expeditions in support of French claims to Naples and Milan, but resulted in the cultural conquest of France by Italy. Countless Frenchmen returned with visions of a beautiful rich life hitherto unknown in France, which was still recovering from the Hundred Years' War. Great works of art were brought to France, and also great artists—Leonardo, Cellini, and many more—to create new masterpieces in their new home. Printing presses multiplied, especially in Lyons and Paris; Rabelais was one of many who contrasted their divine inspiration with the diabolical one of firearms. Although steeped in medieval ways and fascinated by them,[2] Rabelais looked on the recent past as Gothic darkness now giving way to a golden age of learning. Although the term Renaissance was not yet used, the idea of a cultural rebirth, a return to the glorious days of Greece and Rome, was a heady commonplace, especially after the coronation of that great patron of the new arts, letters, and ideas, Francis I.

Politically the period was tense and troubled, especially after Charles V of Spain—from 1517 on Emperor of the Holy Roman Empire in spite of the costly competition of Francis I—embarked on his long and constant struggle with the French king for European hegemony, while Henry VIII of England generally sought to keep a balance between the two great continental powers. After the battle of Pavia in 1525, Francis I was a prisoner of Charles V for a year, and his three sons for three years after that; in 1536, France was invaded by the Imperial forces. Politics affected religion, and vice versa: Francis I generally sought the help of the Turks, a threat to the Empire from the east, and of that thorn in the side of Charles V, the German Protestant princedoms. Cold war generally prevailed when open warfare did not.

The central controversy of the age, religious reform, was not new. Earlier it had centered mainly on the ignorance and corruption of the clergy—to which issues the critical spirit of Renaissance and Reform now added others. Knowledge of Greek and Hebrew gave the humanists access to the original texts of the New and Old Testaments and led them to challenge the Latin Vulgate and thus the authority of the Church. Most Reformists, militant or peaceful, denied the scriptural basis of five of the seven sacraments: marriage, ordination, penance, extreme unction, and confirmation. Baptism and communion, unchallenged as institutions, were questioned as to mode and meaning. Most reformers, by translating Scripture into the vernacular, sought to substitute the Bible itself (as they saw it), or as understood by the individual believer, for the Bible as interpreted by the Church. Militant reform—not new in Western Europe after John Hus, Wycliffe, and others—flared up as never before with Luther in 1517, Zwingli a little later, Calvin in 1536, and a host of others.

It was peaceful reform, reform within the Church without schism, that attracted the best French writers of the early sixteenth century. The great precursor was Laurentius Valla (1407–57), who exposed the fraudulence of the so-called Donation of Constantine and published critical annotations on the New Testament. The great leader in Rabelais's time was an admirer of Valla's, the Dutchman Desiderius Erasmus (1469?–1536), known for his *Handbook of the Christian Soldier, Adages, Praise of Folly, Colloquies,* and a Latin edition of the New Testament published in 1516. His Biblical exegesis challenged many accepted views; his learned and witty satire exposed folly and ignorance. Rabelais, like many contemporaries, looked to him as his intellectual father—and mother—and stated that whatever he was he owed to him. Another more mystical and metaphysical leader was Jacques Lefevre d'Etaples (Faber Stapulensis, circa 1460–1536). The peaceful Reformists were often called "Evangéliques" [Evangelicals] for their unswerving allegiance to the Bible and their eagerness to reveal it to all believers by putting it into the vernacular. Their main patroness was the King's highly cultivated and influential older sister, Queen Margaret of Navarre (1492–1549), whose mystical credo involved union in love with God through Christ. Rabelais was to dedicate his *Third Book* to her.

The opposition to all Reformists centered in the Sorbonne—the dominant Faculty of Theology of the University of Paris led by their syndic Noël Béda. Obscurantist scholastics in the eyes of the avant-garde, but usually supported by the conservative Parlement of Paris, they furiously attacked all innovators, often with success. Burning at the stake was not infrequent.

When Rabelais began to write his stories, a prime target of the Sorbonne was the Collège des Lecteurs Royaux [College of the Royal Lecturers], the future Collège de France, founded in 1530 by Francis I after years of urging by Guillaume Budé. It was the first nontheological institution of higher learning in France, where leading scholars taught such subjects as Greek and Hebrew without tuition. The Sorbonne was outraged to see students without its theological training given the tools to criticize the Vulgate by examining the Bible in the original. In chapter 8 of *Pantagruel* Rabelais shows his delight in the new golden age of learning thus opened up. Not a religious man, Francis I was long influenced by his sister Margaret and hostile to the Sorbonne; he protected the academy he had founded even after he turned against the Evangelicals.

His change in attitude was caused by the Affair of the Placards, in which, on the night of October 17–18, 1534, posters attacking the mass and other "Papist abuses" were put up in the main squares of Paris and even on the King's chamber door in Amboise. From then on Francis I regarded even peaceful Reformists as potential rebels against his authority, and—with some vacillation—began a persecution that grew even harsher under his son, Henry II (1547–59). Two years after the Placards, Calvin emerged in Geneva as the leader of militant Protestant authoritarianism, which had no more use or tolerance for the Evangelicals than had the Sorbonne. It is no wonder that the exuberant optimism of Rabelais's first two books, *Gargantua* and *Pantagruel*, written before the Placards, is absent from the last three.

Rabelais wrote at a time when the oral tradition was only beginning to lose ground to the printing press.[3] He writes in 1552 of learning from Chastillon how King Francis had his book read aloud to him; and the book abounds in a "spoken" dialogue with the reader. Even if in the modern sense, as some have said, there are no real characters in Rabelais, there emphatically are voices—many, distinct, and varied. The oral storyteller is always there, and we are never far from the human voice.[4]

Most writers have little or no choice of the language they write in; not so Rabelais. He wrote Latin fluently and with apparent ease. It was, of course, still *the* international language of the learned; French was disdained by many as a kind of slang, unfit for serious ideas; no important work of philosophy or theology had yet even been attempted in it. Change was in the air, to be sure; three linguistic milestones were soon to come: the Edict of Villers-Cotterets (1539), which made French the language of the law courts; Calvin's translation of his own *Institutes of the Christian Religion* from Latin into French (1541); and the emergence of the Pléiade poets, notably Ronsard and Joachim du Bellay, with the latter's manifesto for learning from the ancients but writing in French, *Deffence et Illustration de la langue françoyse* [*Defense and Illustration of the French Language*] (1549). However, Du Bellay himself lists only two learned Frenchmen besides Rabelais—Budé and Lazare de Baïf—who at that date had not scorned to write in French.

For the writer in Latin there was a further choice. The medieval Latin of the schools had remained viable by adopting many French expressions and allowing many departures from the classical norms. The humanists denounced this Gallicized speech as unworthy of an educated man; Rabelais ridicules it in the speech of the Sorbonicole Janotus de Bragmardo (I: 19–20). The extreme purists condemned any word or expression not found in Cicero. Others, like Erasmus—and Rabelais after him, in the few Latin writings he has left—practiced a Latin that combined expressiveness with purity.

But Rabelais chose to write his book in French, and did not tell us his reasons. One of these is surely the genre in which he wrote, the comic tale of gigantic feats, which appealed to the larger group of readers who could handle French easily, but Latin with difficulty if at all. (The genre, to be sure, became more learned with the *Third Book*; but by then his readers must have counted on reading him in French.) Another probable reason is a desire for popularity and money. But there is probably a more important reason still. Rabelais's love of his language, his delight in exploiting—and creating—its resources, is apparent on every page. He revels not only in the savory speech of the people and the market place but also in dialects, archaisms, and new coinages of his own, from Hebrew and Greek as well as from Latin and French. Far more than the younger Pléiade poets, he illustrated, amplified, and adorned the French language. His words, endowed with their own life, constantly take us from reality into fantasy.[5] Although he can tell a story crisply when he wants to, he usually disdains economy and rarely settles for two words when six—or sixty—are available. One critic has written aptly of his "ivresse lexicographique" [lexicographical intoxication]. Inadequate though it is, the evidence suggests that this intoxicating freedom to play with words—shared later by James Joyce—was something Rabelais felt not in Latin but only in French. For all his love of Greek and Latin, his great gift for writing was in his native tongue—and he knew it.

The Life

(1494? – 1553)

The gaps in our knowledge of Rabelais's life are enormous.[1] We do not know when he was born, or consequently his age at any point; anything about his childhood; what woman or women bore the three illegitimate children of his that we know of; how he regarded and got on with his sexual partner or partners; or why he entered and later left the monastic life.

What we do know, however, holds together pretty well. The fourth child of Antoine Rabelais, an eminent lawyer in the old town of Chinon, which rises up a hillside on the Vienne just south of the Loire, he was probably born in the neat stone farmhouse of La Devinière in the fields a few miles away. He had two older brothers, Antoine and Jamet, and an older sister Françoise. Though he may have studied with the Franciscans of nearby La Baumette or in the university town of Angers, home of his mother's family, we know nothing of his early years.

When was he born? The only clear evidence is an entry in a Paris church, made over a century later, that says he died in 1553 at the age of seventy. This would mean, however, that he entered orders at about thirty, left no record of his existence until he was thirty-seven, fathered three illegitimate children in his mid-forties and late fifties, and was almost fifty—a ripe age at the time—when he started to write his book, almost seventy when he finished it. A later birth date such as 1494, which some scholars have suggested, seems a good deal likelier.[2]

Our first glimpse of Rabelais is provided by a letter of his dated March 4, 1521, from the Franciscan monastery of Le Puy Saint-Martin at Fontenay-le-Comte in Vendée, to the great Hellenist Guillaume

Budé, secretary to the King. From this and from Budé's reply a month later[3] we learn that Rabelais was by that time not only a monk but a priest (which means he had probably already been in orders for six or seven years as novice and then scholastic);[4] that his friend Pierre Amy or Lamy—a fervently religious man versed in Greek, who had probably helped him learn it,[5] and who was already in correspondence with Budé—had urged Rabelais to write him and introduce himself; and that he had done so, diffidently, with a Greek epistle in verse, now lost, that Budé had acknowledged. The two men exchanged more letters in 1522 and 1523.

Rabelais and Amy found other humanist friends in two distinguished jurists of Fontenay-le-Comte, Amaury Bouchard and André Tiraqueau. These two men engaged in a literary exchange—Tiraqueau as critic, Bouchard as defender—on the nature of women and their proper place in marriage, of which one document, the second edition (1524) of Tiraqueau's *De Legibus Connubialibus* [On the Laws of Marriage], mentions that Rabelais is translating into Latin Book II of Herodotus' *Persian Wars*—a fascinating link, eight years before *Pantagruel*, between two great storytellers.

Late in 1523, however, came a harsh interruption of Rabelais's studies. Reacting against the work and popularity of Lefèvre and especially Erasmus, the Sorbonne banned the study of Greek in France, and the superiors of Rabelais and Amy confiscated their books. Amy fled to a Benedictine monastery less submissive to the Sorbonne, and later turned Protestant. Rabelais stayed on until his books were returned a few months later, and then, with papal permission (an indult from Pope Clement VII), transferred to the nearby Benedictine monastery of Saint-Pierre de Maillezais, whose abbot Geoffroy d'Estissac, bishop of Maillezais, became his first patron.

Rabelais served as his secretary and may have tutored his nephew Louis. From his headquarters in the priory of Ligugé, one September 6 (between 1524 and 1527), he addressed a French verse epistle to his friend Jean Bouchet, an important lawyer of Poitiers, who later published it with his own verse.[6] Fluent and erudite but otherwise undistinguished, the epistle is a reminder that in his day Rabelais was highly regarded as a poet—one whom Clément Marot mentioned as a friend and François Sagon as a foe in their poetic quarrel of 1537–38. His inscription over the gate to Theleme (I: 54) shows his great skill at intricate rhyme in the style of the still popular Grands Rhétoriqueurs.

From these years in Poitou, presumably, dates his decision to leave the monastic life and become a doctor. Medicine was not a new interest for him. He had apparently been involved in it from as early as 1521[7] in his monastery, where, as in many others, it presumably was practiced out of Christian charity. In the town of Fontenay his friend Tiraqueau shared his informed interest in it.[8] It was probably in 1527 or 1528 that he gave up the monk's robe and residence, and went to Paris to prepare for his new career.[9]

Still basically a humanistic study, medicine was then encyclopedic in its range of interest and philosophical in its implications. Between his part-time study of it and his monastic life Rabelais seems for some time to have found no grave conflict. The confiscation of his Greek books in 1523, however, may have prepared him to make the break. (He may have studied some law in Paris as well; his books show a considerable knowledge of it.) Although he had no love for the monastic life, what led him to leave it without permission as he did was presumably less a distaste for it than an eagerness for the more useful work he anticipated in medicine. These Paris years—1527 or 1528 to 1530—are most likely the time when he fathered two of his illegitimate children, François and Junie, probably both by a widow about whom we know nothing else.*

On September 17, 1530, Rabelais enrolled in the Faculty of Medicine of Montpellier, which, with that of Paris, was the best in France. Three months later, only six weeks after the courses started, he became a bachelor in medicine. This normally took two years, but many students—Rabelais presumably was one—did much of their preparation elsewhere and then took their degree at Montpellier.[10] Medicine was of course not the experimental science it is today, but was still chiefly concerned with interpreting such ancients as Plato, Aristotle, Hippocrates, and Galen. At Montpellier the new bachelors did most of the explication of the masters. Rabelais explained two of the principal texts of Greek medicine, Hippocrates' *Aphorisms* and Galen's *Small Art of Medicine* (the *Ars Medica*, then often also called the *Ars Parva*). As the first to do so from the original, he had great success; his lectures helped bring Greek medicine into favor over that of the Arabs. He was in Montpellier from September 1530 to October 1531, April to May 1537, October 1537 to April 1538, in August 1539, and probably much more than this.[11] His colleagues there included Guil-

---

* We learn of them through their successful request to Pope Paul III on January 9, 1540, for legitimation. The son is probably the François Rabelais who, five years after Rabelais's death, was convicted, with two others, of robbing a servant of the widow of a counselor in the Paris Parlement, and sentenced by the Parlement (September 12, 1558) to be beaten and whipped naked. See J. Lesellier, "Deux enfants naturels de Rabelais légitimés par le Pape Paul III," *HR* 5: 549–70, 1938.

laume Rondelet (probably the model of Rondibilis in the *Third Book*), Scurron, Sylvius (Dubois), and Nostradamus.[12] With some of them, in October 1531, he acted in *The Comedy of the Man Who Married a Dumb Wife* (see III: 34). In 1537 we learn from his friend Etienne Dolet of his public dissection of a cadaver, which showed a still unusual concern for experiment. His writings, however, reveal mainly a distinguished humanist whose excellent Greek helped him get back to the original texts of the masters.

By the spring of 1532 Rabelais was in the flourishing city of Lyons, situated on the road to Italy and exposed to the Italian Renaissance—a rival to Paris as capital of French arts and letters. An able scholar probably low in funds, he worked for leading printers, editing for Sebastian Grieff (Gryphius) a volume (II) of Giovanni Manardi's Latin letters on medicine with Rabelais's own Latin preface (dated June 3, 1532), dedicating the work to his friend Tiraqueau.[13] A month later (July 15) he dedicated to Geoffroy d'Estissac another Gryphius volume, his edition of Hippocrates' *Aphorisms*, prepared, he says, the year before at Montpellier (pp. 959–62). the Greek text and a Latin translation (not his own) on facing pages, with his own corrections and commentaries. These last show mainly his concern for a correct version; in his preface to Manardi he had attacked the old "Gothic darkness" and the complacent self-love (*philautia*) of those who cling to false science (*pseudologia*) instead of seeking, with the humanists, a better understanding of the ancient texts.

Both editions probably helped bring about Rabelais's appointment on November 1, 1532, to the prestigious but modestly paid post of doctor to an extremely old hospital in Lyons, the Hôtel-Dieu de Notre-Dame-de-Pitié du Pont-du-Rhône, which he held until early 1535.* Already that September he had edited, again for Gryphius, a document supposed to be an ancient Roman will but proven not long after to be a recent fabrication, *The Will of Lucius Cuspidius*, with a dedication (pp. 962–64) to his friend Amaury Bouchard, who had admired it.

Later that autumn (November 30, 1532) he wrote to Erasmus, sending him a book he had heard he wanted and hailing him most warmly as his spiritual father and mother, the source of all he knows:

Patrem te dixi, matrem etiam dicerem, si per indulgentiam mihi id tuam liceret. . . . quidquid sum et valeo, tibi id uni acceptum. . . . Salve itaque

---

* One researcher, Dr. Drivon—as cited by Jean Plattard, *François Rabelais* (Paris: Boivin, 1932), p. 134—has shown that there was a slight drop in the mortality rate there during Rabelais's tenure as doctor.

etiam atque etiam, Pater amantissime, pater decusque patriae, litterarum adsertor ἀλεξίκακος, veritatis propugnator invictissime. (p. 965; cf. pp. 964–67)

[I have called you father, I would even call you mother if I were allowed to by your indulgence. . . . Whatever I am and am worth, I have received from you alone. . . . Therefore I hail you again and again, most loving father, father and ornament of the fatherland, savior of letters who protects them from evil, invincible champion of the truth.]

Although humanists normally addressed friends and enemies in extravagant praise or abuse, this is more than formula. As Lucien Febvre has shown,[14] Rabelais's greatest debt in religion and humanism is to Erasmus.

Late that summer of 1532, or early that fall, an anonymous work appeared in Lyons, bearing no date or publisher's name, which was to lead Rabelais to try his hand at storytelling: *Les Grandes et inestimables cronicques du grant et enorme geant Gargantua* [The Great and Inestimable Chronicles of the Great and Enormous Giant Gargantua].[15] The story was in the air in oral tradition; other versions were published around the same time.[16] Although clumsy and only moderately comic, the little book was a big success. It told of a family of giants created by Merlin to serve King Arthur. Grant-Gosier [Bigthroat] and Galemelle are born magically; they have the child Gargantua; the three travel through France to join Arthur; but the parents die at Mont-Saint-Michel for lack of a purgative. Merlin transports Gargantua to Arthur on a cloud; fighting for Arthur, Gargantua conquers the Gos and Magos, the Dutch and the Irish, and a twelve-cubit giant in single combat. Finally, after two hundred years, he is translated to fairyland by Morgan and Melusine.

In various forms the name Gargantua and stories about him had abounded in France for centuries.[17] Pantagruel had appeared in a mystery play a half century before (Simon Gréban's *Mystère des actes des Apôtres*) as a little devil who gathered salt from the seashores and poured it down the throats of drunkards. The terrible drought of 1532 made thirst a timely topic. Often in Rabelais's day, and in his book, "Pantagruel" was used to mean a thirst-provoking irritation of the throat.

It was these *Cronicques de Gargantua* whose success impelled Rabelais to bring out in the fall of 1532, with the printer of popular books Claude Nourry in Lyons, under the anagrammatic pseudonym Alcofribas Nasier, the first of his storybooks, his *Pantagruel*. The hero is another giant, son of the popular Gargantua, and spreads thirst all around him. The story is in the old tradition of the romances of great deeds, of which Rabelais mentions three in his Prologue. Rabelais borrows some of the devices of the *Cronicques*, such as the comic precision of the measurements of the giants' food, drink, and dress (later, in *Gargantua*, it will be the giant's adorning his mare with the bells of Notre-Dame), as he does a few ideas from the macaronic poem *Baldus* of the Italian monk Teofilo Folengo ("Merlin Coccai"). However, his book was new, his own, and an immediate hit. Two editions were sold out in no time, and pirating began. Capitalizing on its popularity, Rabelais promptly published a volume of comical predictions for the next year (1533) under the title *Pantagruéline Prognostication*. Late that year a speaker in the Sorbonne criticized *Pantagruel* as obscene; but no action against it is known to have been taken this early.*

It was probably that summer of 1533, when the King was in Lyons with his court for the marriage of his eldest son, the future Henry II, to Catherine de' Medici, that Rabelais met one of his greatest protectors, Jean du Bellay. Then in his forties, Du Bellay was Bishop of Paris, and in time would become an archbishop and cardinal: an able, highly cultivated diplomat sympathetic to peaceful Church reform and highly esteemed by the King. Soon afterward Du Bellay passed through Lyons again on his way to Rome.† Suffering so badly from sciatica that he could hardly endure the trip even by litter, he invited Rabelais to come with him as his doctor, and Rabelais accepted. They left Lyons in January 1534, reached Rome by early February, and stayed about two months. Rabelais vainly sought absolution for having given up the monastic robe and residence without authorization.[18] He had planned to do three other things in Rome: study Italian herbs and drugs, meet learned men, and draw up a topography of ancient Rome from an on-the-spot study of ancient texts. Disappointed in his first two aims, he fared better with the topography, with support from Du Bellay and help from two of his staff, Nicolas Leroy and Claude

---

* It is sometimes stated that the book was then condemned by the entire Sorbonne; but the speaker, Nicolas Le Clerc, as quoted by Calvin in a letter, spoke for himself but not for the whole faculty. See Febvre, *Le Problème de l'incroyance*, p. 108; and Marcel de Grève, *L'Interprétation de Rabelais au XVIe siècle*, ER III (1961), pp. 16–17. However, Le Clerc was in charge of such matters at the time; see Jean Plattard, "L'Écriture Sainte et la littérature scripturaire dans l'œuvre de Rabelais," *RER* 8:290–91, 1910.
† Francis I sent him there to urge Pope Clement VII to change his plans to excommunicate Henry VIII of England for divorcing Catherine of Aragon. Du Bellay pleaded ably, it appears, but in vain.

Lyons—Dolet, Jean Visagier, Nicolas Bourbon, Rabelais, and others—who had little choice but to conform, at least overtly.

In late 1539 or early 1540 Rabelais again went to Italy, this time to Piedmont, in the retinue of Jean du Bellay's older brother Guillaume, seigneur de Langey, who was first assisting, then acting lieutenant general, working to strengthen the shaky French outpost in Turin. Except for six months in France in 1541–42, Rabelais remained there until early 1543. Langey did wonders to improve justice and increase the food supply, putting himself heavily in debt by paying for provisions himself. Rabelais presumably was one of his doctors, and may also have been in charge of his library, for Langey loved letters. Once again Rabelais got into trouble, this time for discussing his master's views in a letter to one La Fosse, a former friend of Langey who had changed sides. It is around this time that we learn, from the Latin verses of his friend Guillaume Boyssonné, of the death in Lyons of Rabelais's third illegitimate child, his son Théodule, whose loss he felt deeply.

In November 1541 Rabelais returned from Turin with Langey and, with François Juste in Lyons, brought out a new edition of *Gargantua and Pantagruel* (the definitive one, the last one he corrected), in which he tempered his gibes against the conservatives, removing the long list of "Sorbillans, Sorbonagres, . . . Borsonisans, Saniborsans" (II: 18) and changing "théologien" to "sophiste" and "scolastique" to "sophistique" throughout. At about the same time, however, his supposed friend Etienne Dolet re-edited both books in the original version. Rabelais broke with him and attacked him violently in his note to the reader for a new edition of *Gargantua and Pantagruel* published by the successor to François Juste, Pierre de Tours. However, the Sorbonne officially condemned both editions on March 2, 1543, thus forbidding their sale or possession. Meanwhile Gryphius published a work now lost, the *Stratagèmes, c'est-à-dire prouesses et ruses de guerre du pieux et très célèbre chevalier de Langey,* "traduit du Latin de Fr. Rabelais par Claude Massuau" [Stratagems, that is to say Warlike Exploits and Ruses of the Pious and Very Famous Lord of Langey, "translated from the Latin of Fr. Rabelais by Claude Massuau"]. Rabelais returned to Turin in May 1542.

Late that year Langey, mortally ill, started back home but died on the way, near Tarare in France, on January 9, 1543, amid his despairing retinue. His will allotted some money to Rabelais, but Langey's debts swallowed this up. Rabelais and others accompanied the body to Le Mans and took part in the funeral. The death of Langey, whom Rabelais idolized,[21] was soon followed by that of Geoffroy d'Estissac and by the condemnation of his books. However, he was apparently in the King's good graces.[22] In the next year (1544), under another anagrammatic pseudonym, Seraphino Calbarsy, he published in Paris, with Jehan Real, a *Grande et Vraye Prognostication nouvelle pour l'an 1544* [Great and True New Prognostication for the Year 1544]. And on September 19, 1545, although persecution was growing, he obtained the King's permission to publish the sequel to *Gargantua and Pantagruel*, his *Tiers Livre*, which came out early in 1546, as well as the remaining "heroic deeds and sayings" of Pantagruel.

The *Third Book* is very different from the first two. Published by Christian Wechel in Paris, in the new humanistic type rather than the Gothic, it is signed with Rabelais's own name, given an unsensational title, and dedicated to Queen Margaret of Navarre. Completely devoid of giantism, it is addressed to a more learned public, and is less outspoken than *Gargantua*.[23] Its theme is Panurge's wish to marry and his many consultations about his prospects as a husband, which all inform him that he will be cuckolded, beaten, and robbed by his wife. At last he determines to cross the seas and consult the oracle of the Divine Bottle.

Rabelais lets himself go a few times against monks, the Sorbonne, and heresy-sniffers; but mostly he seems tired of trouble and hopeful to have his work taken in good part. However, the time was very bad; later in 1546 Etienne Dolet was burned at the stake mainly for translating the pseudo-Platonic dialogue *Axiochus*, in which the immortality of the soul is denied. The Sorbonne condemned the *Third Book* in late December; but already in March Rabelais had left the country.*

Although he thought of going on to Strasbourg—where he knew a friend of the Du Bellays, Jean Sturm—he settled in Metz, an imperial town, in a house owned by his friend Saint-Ayl, and served the city as a doctor or more probably as a counselor. Once again, however, he found himself short of funds, and wrote Jean du Bellay early in 1547 to implore his help.

Later that year the new King of France, Henry II, sent Du Bellay to Rome to be in charge of all the French cardinals. Rabelais either went with him or, more likely, joined him there at Du Bellay's request in the first half of 1548.[24] Meanwhile he either sent to Lyons or left there on his way to Rome, for Pierre de Tours to publish, an almanac or prog-

---

* This may have been a flight, as has often been said; but it may have been a secret mission. The best account of this period in Rabelais's life is by R. Marichal, "Le Quart Livre de 1548," in *ER* IX (1971), pp. 131–50, especially pp. 138–40.

nostication for 1548, and the so-called partial edition of the *Quart Livre,* apparently written in Metz, in eleven chapters that correspond to most of the first twenty-five of the complete edition of 1552. These tell of Medamothi, Dindenault, the Chiquanous, and the tempest, and end abruptly just after that.

On this visit to Rome Rabelais spent his time mainly in meeting humanists and looking after the ailing cardinal. When Du Bellay gave a great festival in March 1549 to celebrate the birth of the King's second son, Rabelais wrote an account to Cardinal de Guise; then, on his return to France with Du Bellay later that year, he had it published in Lyons by Gryphius as *La Sciomachie* [The Simulated Combat].

As Rabelais grew more famous, attacks from both sides became more violent. Boisterous though he could be, he was not thick-skinned; his complaints against malicious critics mark his Prologues from the *Third Book* on.[25] In 1549 he was blasted (among others) as a licentious enemy of religion in the Latin *Theotimus* of a Fontevrault monk with a doctorate from the Sorbonne, Gabriel Dupuyherbault (Putherbeus).[26] A year later Calvin attacked him—with some provocation[27] —in *De Scandalis,* listing him with Gouvéa, Des Périers, and others as a renegade who had tasted the good doctrine but then turned his back on it. Rabelais answered both men when he listed them (IV: 32, 629) among the descendants of Antiphysie (Antinature) as "les Démoniacles Calvins, imposteurs de Genève, les enraigéz Putherbes, . . . et aultres monstres difformes et contrefaicts en despit de Nature" [the demoniacal Calvins, impostors of Geneva, the mad Putherbes, . . . and other monsters deformed and ill-made in despite of Nature]. Rabelais's letter of January 28, 1552 (pp. 517–22) dedicating the *Fourth Book* to a new protector, Cardinal Odet de Chastillon,* speaks eloquently of his weariness of abuse and readiness to give up storytelling rather than endure more, but says that the cardinal himself, and the encouragement he elicited from the King, persuaded him to continue. At all events, on August 6, 1550, Chastillon got him the royal privilege to reprint his earlier works, in their original form but revised and corrected, and also the sequels, "ceulx qu'il délibère de nouvel mettre en lumière" (p. 317) [those that he plans to bring out new]. Heartened by this, Rabelais completed his *Fourth Book* late in 1551.

In that same year Du Bellay made him curate of Saint-Martin de

---

* A liberal young prelate, later a Protestant, whose brother Gaspard de Coligny, Protestant leader and adviser to King Charles IX, was murdered in the Saint Bartholomew's Day Massacre of 1572.

Meudon and Saint-Christophe-du-Jambet. Rabelais did not reside at either, but "farmed them out"—as was often done—and probably stayed mainly in Paris.

The *Fourth Book* continues the *Third* by telling of the trip to seek the Divine Bottle, but again is new in many ways. Its unity is in the voyage; its main interest in the strange characters, creatures, and places that the friends encounter. The longest of the books, it is also the closest to a fantasy. Quietly but firmly Evangelical at first, it grows more aggressive from Chapter 30 on and very Gallican in the chapters on Papimania.

It appeared in February 1552. When Rabelais was completing it a few months before, his Gallicanism seemed likely to please King Henry II, then embroiled in a bitter quarrel with Pope Julius III. When it appeared, however, the quarrel was on the mend; once again Rabelais's timing was unfortunate. The Sorbonne censured the book; on March 1, 1552, while the King was away from Paris, the publisher, Michel Fezandat of Paris, was forbidden to sell it; but on the King's return in May the ban was lifted.

Little is known of Rabelais's last year. Late in 1552 a friend in Lyons heard he was in prison, but later wrote that he was not sure. In January 1553, for reasons unknown to us, he resigned his two curacies. His death came probably in mid-1553. Stories of such last words as "seeking the great Perhaps" and "Lower the curtain. The farce is over" are nothing but legends. He was buried in Saint-Paul's Cemetery in Paris, rue des Jardins.

His four books continued to be published after his death. In 1562 there appeared, without publisher's name, *L'Isle sonante* [The Ringing Island] by M. Françoys Rabelays, a version of Chapters 1–16 of the *Fifth Book*. The entire book came out in 1564 as *Le Cinquiesme et dernier livre des faicts et dicts héroïques du bon Pantagruel* [The Fifth and Last Book of the Heroic Deeds and Sayings of the Good Pantagruel], again ascribed to Rabelais, again with no publisher's name. An undated but contemporary manuscript in the Bibliothèque Nationale in Paris offers a third reading that some prefer to the others. The book completes the voyage to the land and oracle of the Dive Bouteille [Divine Bottle], gives the oracle's pronouncement, TRINCH [Drink], tells how happily Panurge (eager at last to marry) and the others received it, and leaves the party ready to sail back home. The problem of the book's authenticity will be discussed in chapter 7.

Pantagruel: Book Two

(1532)

As we have noted, Rabelais's first giant story was published by a printer of popular books (Claude Nourry of Lyons), signed Alcofribas Nasier, and related to the anonymous *Chronicles of Gargantua* by its own horrific title: *Pantagruel. Les Horribles et Espouventables Faicts et Prouesses du tresrenommé Pantagruel, Roy des Dipsodes, filz du grand geant Gargantua* [Pantagruel. The Horrible and Frightful Deeds and Exploits of the Very Renowned Pantagruel, King of the Dipsodes, Son of the Great Giant Gargantua]. It is presented, in other words, in the tradition of the comic giant story as a sequel to its popular predecessor. In his first venture into this form, Rabelais is not yet ready to make it his own.

It was a venture that might bring him not only general popularity but also the scorn of other humanists. (Later, with such writers as Bonaventure des Périers, Noël du Fail, Margaret of Navarre, and Henri Estienne, the telling of fairly bawdy tales in the vernacular was to become an accepted recreation for the learned; but this was partly due to Rabelais himself.) Probably Rabelais needed money. Almost certainly he felt compelled to try his hand at comic storytelling. Furthermore, for any book sympathetic to Evangelical humanism, the moment seemed propitious. Yet in this one, Rabelais rarely shows his sympathy for such causes; he seems to feel limited by the genre in which he has chosen to write.

Since standard editions give the final (1542) version of *Pantagruel* that Rabelais corrected, let us look at it as it first appeared. The differences, though not great, are worth noting. The significant passages that disappeared are one in which Panurge boasts that female theologians and crucifix-kissers are among his Parisian sexual conquests (16, 236); one in which he refers to David, when he conquered Goliath, as a "petit chiart" (29, 289) [little shit-in-his-breeches]; and three rather mild references to the Sorbonne (10, 214; 16, 238, 239). Not in the first edition were the introductory *dizain* by Hugues Salel; the crack at Calvin in the Prologue (p. 168): "prestinateurs, emposteurs" [predestinators, impostors]; and the sequence (appearing in 1534–37) on the contentious disputants of the Sorbonne, which Spitzer found so horrifying[1] and which defy translation: "Sorbillans, Sorbonagres, Sorbonigènes, Sorbonicoles, Sorboniformes, Sorbonisecques, Niborcisans, Borsonisans, Saniborsans" (18, 253). Finally, most of the last two pages of the book (34, 312–13), with their violent attacks on calumniators, and the prediction of Panurge's cuckoldry earlier in the chapter, date from 1534 and 1533 respectively. The other changes are not very significant.

The primary sources of *Pantagruel*, the *Chronicles of Gargantua*, supply only the incentive, the idea, the skeleton of a plot, and some details of comic gigantic precision. Nor is Rabelais's debt great toward the poem *Baldus* (in Italian and Latin) by Merlin Coccai, from which he takes mainly the ideas of a brave comic scamp as companion to his giant hero; of four other companions having specific powers, as do Rabelais's Carpalim (the swift), Eusthenes (the strong), Gymnaste (the agile), and Epistémon (the knowing or understanding); and of the sheep merchant and the tempest, which Rabelais picks up in the *Fourth Book*.

Nonetheless, *Pantagruel* may be seen as a redo of the *Chronicles of Gargantua*, the enormously successful model (far outselling that best seller the Bible, says Rabelais in his Prologue) that he set out to improve upon in his first venture in the genre. With the gigantic details he takes the basic structure—birth, travels, exploits—but adds to these a whole comic world that makes the book his own: in the first quarter of his book alone, the Prologue, the genealogy, the Limousin student, the Library of Saint-Victor, the letter on education, and Panurge.

The book as a whole may be divided into three parts: genealogy, birth, childhood, episodes (chapters 1–8); Panurge (9–24); the war and what follows (25–34). In part one, the first three rubrics fill the first five chapters; then come the Limousin student who speaks only

Latinized French (6), the Library of Saint-Victor with its wildly comic titles (7), and the letter on education from Gargantua to Pantagruel (8). At this point Pantagruel's retinue are still all anonymous except his tutor Epistémon (5, 188); but now Rabelais seems to need someone to carry along the story and the comedy. Hence chapter 9 is entitled "Comment Pantagruel trouva Panurge, lequel il ayma toute sa vie" [How Pantagruel Found Panurge, Whom He Loved All His Life]. For most of the next sixteen chapters Panurge takes center stage, while Pantagruel and Alcofribas feed him lines. To be sure, chapters 10–13 center on Pantagruel as he judges, with inspired nonsense, the nonsense lawsuit of Lords Baisecul and Humevesne [Kissass and Sniffshit].[2] Then come Panurge's escape from the Turks, plans for building the walls of Paris, tricks, ways of getting pardons cheap, and (18–20) his wondrous replacement of Pantagruel in the debate in sign language with the English scholar Thaumaste. Chapters 21–22 relate the cruel trick he plays on the Paris lady who spurned his advances; 23–24, the call to Pantagruel to return, since his father has been translated to fairyland, to defend his homeland of the Amaurotes against the invading Dipsodes, and also Panurge's solution of the riddle of the ring that a forlorn Paris lady sent to her wayward lover Pantagruel. In short, almost all this central section of the book (chapters 9, 14–24) finds Panurge in the spotlight; and he will remain there, or close to it, in the ten final chapters.

This third part brings Pantagruel and his friends back to defend his country; relates the conquest of the Dipsodes (25–29), and its sequels (30–31): Epistémon's visit to hell and restoration to life by Panurge, and the consequences of victory; and moves on to two unrelated giant episodes: the world in Pantagruel's mouth, visited by the narrator (32), and the mining expedition into Pantagruel's bowels to cure his constipation (33); and to what was originally a very brief conclusion (34) promising more to come—none of which, as he promised it, ever came. Much of the plot is episodic: one incident follows another without being brought on by it. The deeds of young Pantagruel (ch. 5) precede the meeting with the Limousin student (6) but do not lead to it; nor does 6 lead to 7 (the Library of Saint-Victor), 7 to 8 (Gargantua's letter), 8 to 9 (Pantagruel meets Panurge), or 9 to 10 (the Baisecul-Humevesne trial). There are inconsistencies (which were never to worry Rabelais): at the end of chapter 8 Pantagruel becomes an excellent student; yet in 9 he shows no sign of understanding Panurge speaking in Latin, the language of the schools.

Nevertheless certain characteristic patterns emerge: the recurrence of trickery, riddles, and mystification; the theatrical presentation that always surrounds the speaker or actor by a group, much as in a play; surprise and shock; and grotesque inflation followed by comic and humiliating deflation.[3] Gérard Defaux finds the book unified by Rabelais's opposition to the sophists, who are typified by Panurge and a temptation to Pantagruel.[4] Episodic in plot, *Pantagruel* even so has a solid thematic unity.

The spirit of the carnival, which Mikhail Bakhtin has studied so rewardingly in Rabelais, is at its most abundant in this book, with much joyous banqueting (ch. 20, 25, 26) and jovial obscenity. In this last especially Panurge is central, with his plan to rebuild the walls of Paris out of female genitalia; with his stories: the lion, the fox, and the problem of filling the old woman's vagina; and the man carrying his two infant daughters and doubting their virginity (ch. 15); his plans for paying poor men to copulate with ugly old women (17); his arranging to have dogs mount the lady of Paris who rejected his advances (21, 22); his explanation why a league is shorter in France than in Brittany or Germany (23); his plans for the 150,000 beautiful camp followers of Anarche's army (26); and so on. Pantagruel himself is not above this spirit, as he will be from the *Third Book* on; even after growing from a lusty uncouth infant—who once eats a live bear and most of a cow (ch. 4)—into an enlightened king, he is still involved in scatological humor, as when a fart of his engenders a nation of dwarfs (27), the excrement has to be mined out of him (33), and he talks to the narrator Alcofribas, who has just spent six months in his throat, as follows:

"—Voire, mais (dist-il [Pantagruel]), où chioys-tu?
—En vostre gorge, Monsieur, dis-je.
—Ha, ha, tu es gentil compaignon! (dist-il)." (32, 308)

["Right," said he [Pantagruel], "but where did you shit?"
"In your throat, sir," said I.
"Ha, ha, you're a good fellow!" said he.]

When Epistémon returns from hell (30, 295–96), he marks the event by breathing, opening his eyes, yawning, sneezing, and then releasing "a big household fart," which tells Panurge that he is cured. And so it goes.

Although less frequent than later, there is occasional satire in *Pantagruel*: in chapter 10, which opens the Baisecul-Humevesne trial, of the accumulation of legal papers when witnesses are alive to testify; in the next three chapters, of incoherent pleading; in the Thaumaste episode (ch. 18–20), of the idea that signs can express more than words. Most striking is the catalogue of the books in the Library of Saint-Victor (ch. 7), whose targets include a few jurists but mainly theologians, notably scholastics: the Sorbonne and other opponents of Reuchlin and Luther. Here in translation are a few titles, of which some in the original are in Latin, some in French: "The Codpieces of the Law." "A Most Subtle Question, whether a Chimera Bombinating in the Void Can Devour Second Intentions; and It Was Debated for Ten Weeks in the Council of Constance." "The Agitations of the Doctors of Cologne against Reuchlin." "Cuntatorium of Hypocrisy, author Jacobus Hoch-strates, Master of Hereticometrics." "The Crutches (?) of Gaietan." "The Ways of Sweeping Furnaces, by Master Eccium." "Béda, Of the Excellence of Tripes."*

The satire in *Pantagruel*, mainly parodistic and comic, is not copious but telling.

At the same time, Rabelais's concern with the serious and the good appears as Pantagruel develops from an uncouth child into a hero. Where in chapter 6 he had scared the Limousin student literally shit-less, he is kind to Panurge (from 9 on), to Baisecul and Humevesne (10–13), and to Thaumaste (18–20), and generous to his Dipsode pris-oner, refusing ransom because, he says, all he wants is to enrich the vanquished and reform them in total freedom (28). He takes in good part Alcofribas's liberty in defecating in his throat. In chapter 33, for the first time, Rabelais speaks of him as "le bon Pantagruel" (p. 309). His prayer to God before his combat with Loup Garou (29) is a model of Evangelical piety. By the end of the book he is on his way to becoming the ideal king that he will be in the last three books.

However, the serious parts of *Pantagruel* are only two: the letter from Gargantua (8) and Pantagruel's prayer before combat (29). Let us examine them more closely.

Gargantua's letter comes out of the blue. In the lofty Ciceronian style that Rabelais reserves for serious utterances, Gargantua starts by

---

* Reuchlin was a humanistic Hebrew scholar attacked by the conservatives in Cologne, including Hoogstraeten, and later by the Sorbonne. Cajetan and Eck were adversaries of Luther. Noël Béda, syndic and leader of the Sorbonne, was known for his potbelly.

praising God for giving man a sort of immortality through his posterity, claims to have lived not without sin but without reproach, and urges his son to grasp the opportunities that his day offers. In his own childhood, he says, "The time was still dark and smacking of the infelicity and calamity of the Goths, who had destroyed all good literature" (8, 204). Now, however, all disciplines are restored, the essential languages are taught: Greek ("without which it is shameful for a person to call himself learned"), Hebrew, Chaldean, Latin; printing is in flower; it is a true golden age; Gargantua himself, reputed the most learned man of his time, would barely be accepted among beginning students. Therefore, he tells his son, use your chance and learn well: first languages—Greek, Latin, Hebrew, Chaldean, and Arabic; then history and geography; geometry, arithmetic, and music (I have started you on these, he says; "poursuys la reste" [pursue the rest]); civil law; all but astrology and the sophistry of Raymond Lully; the facts of nature: fish, birds, trees and bushes, herbs, metals, and precious stones; medicine, through wide reading and dissection; and of course the New Testament in Greek and the Old in Hebrew. In Gargantua's famous summarizing phrase, "que je voy un abysme de science" (p. 206) [let me see an abyss of knowledge].

In a brief moral conclusion, since "science sans conscience n'est que ruine de l'âme" (p. 206) [knowledge without conscience is but ruin of the soul], Gargantua urges his son to avoid abuses, to love and help his neighbor, revere his preceptors, shun evil company, and above all serve, love, and fear God and be joined to Him "par foy formée de charité" [by faith formed of charity]. Finally, he says, having learned and done all this, come home to receive my blessing before I die.

This letter, long accepted by all as a serious statement of Rabelais's, has struck several recent readers—Gerard J. Brault, Jean Paris, and Gérard Defaux—as a parody. Brault's case, made ten years ago,[5] was picked up by Paris soon after[6] and further strengthened by Defaux[7] when he added, to the main argument of the other two—that the letter is preceded and followed by comic episodes—his view that the author of the letter, Gargantua, is established from chapter 3 on as a comic figure, "a Limousin schoolboy who has come late to the study of good letters and has had his head turned by culture."[8] Even Defaux, however, leans heavily on the notion that the ideal of encyclopedic learning was not only medieval but basically antihumanist and thus foreign to Rabelais, apparently defining humanism largely by Socrates and Erasmus, who surely were rather ideals than types. Even Defaux, in my judgment, has not made a truly convincing case for the theory that this is parody.

The letter, after all, fits perfectly with what elsewhere appear clearly to be some of Rabelais's strongest convictions, and specifically with the ideas on education that he expresses in *Gargantua*, ideas whose seriousness has not to my knowledge been questioned. Everywhere else where he appears to be speaking in earnest it seems almost certain that he is. In short, I see the letter as a hymn of gratitude for the golden age of knowledge inaugurated by the newly founded Collège des Lecteurs Royaux, and as a program of encyclopedic learning, largely but not solely bookish, plus a brief and rather unrelated—but, I think, sincere—exhortation to virtue and piety.[9] For the early French Renaissance love of learning it remains a classic text.

When Pantagruel is about to fight the formidable giant Loup Garou [Werewolf] with his unbreakable steel club, he prays to God in his distress, noting, like many Reformists, that God forbids the use of force in matters of faith, and promising Evangelical reform if God grants him His help. I quote in part:

"Seigneur Dieu . . . Rien icy ne me amène, sinon zèle naturel, ainsi comme tu as octoyé ès humains de garder et défendre soy, leurs femmes, enfans, pays et famille, en cas que ne seroit ton négoce propre qui est la foy; car en tel affaire tu ne veulx coadjuteur, sinon de confession catholicque et service de ta parolle, et nous as défendu toutes armes et défences. . . . Doncques, s'il te plaist à ceste heure me estre en ayde, comme en toy seul est ma totale confiance et espoir, je te fais vœu que, par toutes contrées, tant de ce pays de Utopie que d'ailleurs, où je auray puissance et auctorité, je feray prescher ton sainct Evangile purement, simplement et entièrement, si que les abus d'un tas de papelars et faulx prophètes, qui ont par constitutions humaines et inventions dépravées envenimé tout le monde, seront d'entour moy exterminéz."

Alors feut ouye une voix du ciel, disant *"Hoc fac et vinces,"* c'est à dire: Fais ainsi, et tu auras victoire. (II: 29, 290–91)

["Lord God . . . Nothing brings me here but natural zeal, even as Thou hast granted to humans to guard and defend themselves, their wives, children, country, and family, unless the issue were Thine own affair, which is faith; for in such a matter Thou wantest no collaborator, unless that of Catholic confession and the service of Thy word, and hast forbidden us all weapons and defenses. . . . Thus, if it please Thee to help me in this hour, since in Thee alone is my entire confidence and hope, I make Thee a vow that throughout all lands, both of this country, Utopia, and elsewhere, where I shall have power and authority, I shall have Thy Holy Gospel preached purely, simply, and in its entirety, so that the abuses of a pile of fake pietists and false prophets, who by human institutions and depraved inventions have envenomed everyone, shall be exiled from around me."

Then was heard a voice from Heaven saying *"Hoc fac et vinces,"* that is to say, Do thus, and thou shalt conquer.]

These few serious pages (the letter and the prayer) occupy only about four percent of the book, but express sympathies that Rabelais clearly felt: the insatiable love of learning, especially book learning; the stress on languages (the indispensable tools), with Hebrew and Greek as keys to the original texts of the Bible; the earnest piety; the reliance on prayer—prayer direct to God; the rejection of force in matters of faith; the Reformist insistence on preaching the Gospel pure and entire, with no human institutions and inventions. Rabelais does not yet speak out much; but when he does, he speaks out clear.

This first of Rabelais's fictions offers only two real characters, Pantagruel and Panurge, and it is Panurge who dominates. (Defaux sees him as a sophist who, rather like Diderot's Jacques the Fatalist, leads his master and almost wins him over.) Primarily he is an unfailing source of bawdy stories, tricks, and rough practical jokes in the manner of the time. Although in dealing with the lady of Paris he is said to fear blows, he is courageous as well as resourceful in the war. As a literary creation, however, he remains in this book not yet fully a man of flesh and blood but somewhat two-dimensional, a stock figure of an aging student scamp reminiscent of Till Eulenspiegel, Folengo's Cingar, the already legendary François Villon, and many others.

He is most human in his relation to Pantagruel, which will change radically in the later books. Now he outshines his lord and master. In all their scenes together Pantagruel plays straight man to his comic lead, as Panurge tells his jokes and stories and solves the riddle of the lady's ring. His resourcefulness puts Pantagruel to shame: he defeats the learned Thaumaste in the debate by signs (18–20); destroys the 660 enemy horsemen in the first encounter of the war (25); matches Pantagruel in impromptu verse (27); miraculously restores Epistémon to life (30); marries off the conquered king Anarche to an old whore, and makes him a hawker of green sauce.

More striking yet, he often acts as a protector, almost an elder brother, to his young king. When he finds him worrying all night about the debate with Thaumaste, he sends him to bed lest he catch a fever from excessive thinking, offers to take his place, and is gladly accepted. In Utopia he is the first who volunteers to reconnoiter (24).

When they see the enemy horsemen approaching and Pantagruel tells them all to wait in the ship while he disposes of the enemy, Panurge countermands his order and, with help only from Carpalim, Eusthenes, and Epistémon, ropes and roasts them all but one. When even Pantagruel hesitates to take on Loup Garou and his three hundred giants alone, citing the caution of Hercules, Panurge tells him he is stronger and smarter than Hercules and sends his master into action (29). Finally when Epistémon is thought to be dead, "Pantagruel was so grief-stricken that he wanted to kill himself"; but Panurge reassures him, helps find the dead body, and then restores Epistémon to life. This mature, resourceful, protective Panurge appears only in this, Rabelais's first storybook.

Although *Pantagruel* is still more a comic giant story than the later books, rather episodic, less venturesome in ideas, and less masterly in treatment of character, it is already full of vintage Rabelais. Starting in this vein at nearly forty (or fifty), from the Prologue on he displays enormous zest and skill in the games he plays with—and on—the reader. The drolly pointed book titles in the Library of Saint-Victor; the stately letter on education from Gargantua; the inspired nonsense of the Baisecul-Humevesne trial; the verve of the story of the lion, the fox, and the old woman; the ingenuity of the debate in signs; the moving prayer of Pantagruel before battle; the topsy-turvy world that Epistémon finds in hell; the strange new world in Pantagruel's mouth: these are surely among the highlights of the entire five books. Each reader will have his own favorites, but will probably agree that there are many parts to cherish.

Pantagruel was a well-deserved success and a considerable venture. In his next book Rabelais was to venture much further still.

Gargantua: Book One

(1534)

The traditionally accepted publication date of *Gargantua*, late summer or early autumn of 1534, has been seriously challenged of late, mainly by M. A. Screech, who once accepted it[1] but now holds for the summer of 1535,[2] and by Gérard Defaux, who believes that the book was composed relatively early in 1533 and published early in 1534.[3] Screech's main arguments (which have convinced Marcel Françon[4]) are two: the resemblance of some of Picrochole's plans for world conquest (ch. 33), notably those involving Barbarossa and Tunis, to some of Charles V's stunning victories and rumored plans in the summer of 1535; and the pessimistic outlook for the Evangelicals expressed in the prophetic enigma (ch. 58), which he believes could not have preceded the Placards. Defaux finds a close relation between the bells of Notre-Dame (taken by Gargantua for his mare), and Béda and the other Sorbonne theologians exiled from Paris by Francis I in May 1533.[5] The references to Barbarossa and to Tunis lead V. L. Saulnier to a conclusion wholly different from Screech's.[6] Robert Marichal examines the theories of both Screech and Defaux at length and considers the traditional date still the likeliest.[7]

I find Marichal's arguments convincing. As he notes (p. viii), Defaux's case depends partly on identifying Béda with a bell. I have two main qualms about Screech's theory: first, that the enigma (58, 161, line 12) points clearly to the coming winter ("cest hyver prochain"), not the past one, as the time of trouble; and second, that the allusions to Barbarossa and to Tunis do not seem to me necessarily to refer to Charles V's conquests, and even if they do refer to them, are not very clear as factors in dating. I still find the traditional date the likeliest that has been proposed.

What we know about the reception of *Pantagruel* is scanty but consistent.[8] Like its successors, it was an instant best seller.[9] The inventory of his books by a Parisian bourgeois aptly named Jacques Le Gros lists it among the novels and adventure stories—by implication, as nothing serious. John Calvin wrote his friend François Daniel about an assembly of the faculties of the University of Paris in October 1533 at which Nicolas Le Clerc of the Faculty of Theology, defending himself and his colleagues against the King's charge of having condemned as heretical Margaret of Navarre's anonymous *Miroir de l'ame pecheresse* [Mirror of the Sinful Soul], made it clear that his real condemnation was of such obscene books as *Pantagruel*. (A charge of mere obscenity by a confirmed Sorbonagre is virtually a clean bill of health in point of ideas, whether Evangelical or humanistic or both.) Most striking is the testimony of Nicolas Bourbon, a neo-Latin poet and friend from Champagne, in the poem "In Rabellum"[10] in his *Nugae* [Trifles] of 1533. He castigates Rabelais for diverting students from their proper task, the study of good letters and the sacred texts, to waste their youth on money-grubbing frivolities. What are you doing, he asks? Fear the Muses and their condign revenge.

Frail as it is, this evidence suggests that Rabelais's readers found *Pantagruel* rather trivial and that some friends were disappointed. Marcel de Grève fails to use one piece of evidence which I think makes his theory indisputable. When in 1534 Rabelais republished *Pantagruel*, the first thing he added to the conclusion was this: "If you say to me: 'Master, it would seem that you were not very wise to write us these funny stories and amusing jests,' I answer that you are hardly more so to spend your time reading them" (II: 34, 312).

This suggests that Rabelais felt keenly the criticism of his humanist and Evangelical friends for writing such a frivolous book, and responded to it in 1534 with such additions to the *Pantagruel* as the "Sorbillans, Sorbonagres, Sorbonigènes, Sorbonicoles . . ." (II: 18, 253) and most of all with his new and outspoken *Gargantua*.[11]

In short, it appears that *Pantagruel* was received simply as a comic giant story; that Rabelais's friends deplored this "waste" of his learning and talent; and that his reaction, his need for self-expression, and the temper of the time—still generally favorable to Reformists—led him to write a second book (in the fiction the first) that was to be, among other things, a redo of his first.

Rabelais's first Prologue, to *Pantagruel*, was a relatively simple account of the success of the *Chronicles of Gargantua* and their curative virtues, claiming the same virtues plus absolute veracity for his own book, and invoking picturesque afflictions on any reader who doubted a word of it. The Prologue to *Gargantua* is more complex.

Rabelais opens by paraphrasing Alcibiades' comparison, in Plato's *Symposium*, of Socrates to a Silenus, a box with a comical outside and precious stones or drugs within; for Socrates' homely exterior contained one of the wisest and noblest souls that ever was. Turning to his book, he warns his readers not to be misled by its comical appearance but to open it and ponder carefully what is inside; for the substance is not as frivolous as the title suggests. Did you ever, he asks, see a dog with a marrowbone? Like him you should break the bone and "sugcer la sustantificque mouelle" [suck out the substantific marrow]; and he explains:

C'est à dire ce que j'entends par ces symboles Pythagoricques avecques espoir certain d'estre faictz escors et preux à ladicte lecture: car en icelle bien aultre goust trouverez et doctrine plus absconce, laquelle vous révélera de très haultz sacremens et mystères horrificques, tant en ce que concerne nostre religion que aussi l'estat politicq et vie œconomicque. (p. 5)

[That is to say what I mean by these Pythagorean symbols, with the certain hope of being made astute and brave by the said reading: for in it you will find quite another taste and a more abstruse teaching, which will reveal to you some very lofty sacraments and horrific mysteries, as regards both our religion and also civil and domestic life.][12]

Having given the reader pause by this bombast, Rabelais goes on virtually to deny all he has just said. Do you really believe, he asks, that Homer meant all the allegories read into him by Plutarch, Heraclides Ponticus, and others? Or that Ovid's *Metamorphoses* announce the sacraments of the Church, as some have claimed? If you do, you and I are miles apart.

Si ne le croiez, quelle cause est pourquoy autant n'en ferez de ces joyeuses et nouvelles chronicques, combien que, les dictans, n'y pensasse en plus que vous, qui par adventure beviez comme moy? (p. 5)

[If you don't believe it, why don't you believe the same sort of thing about these joyous new chronicles, even though, as I dictated them, I was not thinking about such matters any more than you, who perchance were drinking, like me?]

Here obviously Rabelais is playing a game. First he offers us a theory of hidden meaning, of substantific marrow within the bone of the book; then he casts that theory in doubt by his overelaborate claims; finally he denies any intent to put such meaning there. Now the serious ideas in the book are clear; no plausible cryptic meanings have been found; the notion of the substantific marrow fits the last three books better than it does *Gargantua*. What are we to make of all this?[13]

I think Rabelais offers us two ways of reading the book and invites us to choose the second, but without canceling the first. The rich similes of the Silenus and the dog with the marrowbone remain in our mind even after Rabelais has denied their validity. The possible relation of this tactic to *Gargantua* as a redo of *Pantagruel* is not to be lightly dismissed. Many readers over the years have taken the Prologue as a statement of hidden meaning and nothing more. This I think is wrong. Its effect is to put an idea into our head and then take it away. It leaves us with the hint of a hint, but mainly with the freedom to make of the book what we will and can.

The fifty-eight chapters of *Gargantua* may be divided as follows: 1–13, genealogy, birth, childhood; 14–15 and 21–24, education; 16–20, arrival in Paris, the bells of Notre-Dame, Janotus de Bragmardo; 25–51, the war against the aggressor Picrochole; 52–57, the Abbey of Theleme; 58, the prophetic enigma.

Even this outline shows that twelve chapters (as against one plus of *Pantagruel*) are devoted to serious ideas: education and Theleme; it does not show the book's richness in humanistic and Evangelical views. In the war, for example, we come to know the gay, fearless antimonk Frère Jean des Entommeures [Friar John of the Hashes]; we learn how it is that although a monk, he is still a nice guy, and what is wrong with monks; we meet a group of simple pilgrims and hear Grandgousier's wise advice to them. Even the taking of the bells, borrowed from the *Grandes Cronicques*, is used to ridicule the Sorbonne.

Gargantua is much less episodic, more coherent, than *Pantagruel*. Gargantua's invention of the perfect ass-wipe (ch. 13) leads directly to his education and trip to Paris. The war comes in abruptly, but wars often do; it leads to Frère Jean (27) and his exploits, to Grandgousier's appeal for help to Gargantua, Gargantua's harangue to the vanquished (50), and the Abbey of Theleme (52–57).

The carnivalesque element is still prominent, less than in *Pantagruel* but more than in the later books, especially in the early chapters: how Gargantua was carried eleven months in his mother's belly (3); how his pregnant mother Gargamelle ate plenty of tripes (4); the talk of the topers (5); how Gargantua was born through his mother's ear (6); how he got his name, and inhaled the good red wine (7). It appears again in 13 with his invention of the ass-wipe; in 17, when he pays for his welcome by flooding the Parisians with his urine "par ryz" [for a laugh]; in the banquet with Janotus (20); in his games (22); in much of the action involving Frère Jean (especially 27 and 39); and in the account of Theleme (52–57). At most, however, this spirit informs about one third of the book, as against almost half of *Pantagruel*. The obscenity is less frequent; Frère Jean keeps it alive but does not harp on it—or dominate the book—as does Panurge in *Pantagruel*. Satiric and serious ideas hold a far larger place.

The "voice of Pantagruel"—Rabelais speaking of the serious and the good—is now more frequent and outspoken. There is the kindness of Gargantua and his friends to Janotus (18–20); the education of Gargantua (23–24); the reluctance of Grandgousier to wage even defensive war (28), his concern to do God's will in combating Picrochole (29), and his earnest attempts to appease him (30–32); his wise kindness to the pilgrims (45); Gargantua's clemency to the vanquished (50–51), and the conviction that such clemency pays; the asylum for the Evangelical preachers in Theleme (54); and the whole concept of Theleme as a place where "Do What You Will" leads to virtue and happiness. All these illustrate a benevolent optimism about human nature that is one of the charms of *Gargantua*.

Like its predecessor, the book has just two leading characters: Gargantua and Frère Jean. The latter is to my mind Rabelais's livest creation. One scholar[14] has found him Evangelical; I see him primarily as an antimonk. To be sure, when he first appears, Rabelais stresses his "regular" monkishness: in his mistrust of study and learning, and as a "cloistered monk, . . . young, lusty, natty, good humored, very adroit, bold, adventurous, determined, tall, thin, with a wide open throat and a very advantageous nose, a fine dispatcher of prayer books, a fine hastener of masses, a fine cleaner-upper of vigils; to sum it all up, a real monk if ever there was one since the monking world has been monking in monkishness; moreover a cleric to the teeth in breviary matter" (27, 83–84).

He stands out, however, by his contrast with other monks. When we first meet him (ch. 27), his Abbey of Seuillé and its vineyard are under attack by Picrochole's soldiers, who kill and ravage as they go. While his colleagues chant prayers for protection, Frère Jean, concerned for the wine, with just a stout stick (the shaft used to hold the cross in processions) takes on Picrochole's hordes singlehanded and routs them with horrendous slaughter. When he meets Grandgousier, Gargantua, and their company (39–40), a main question is why everyone loathes most monks but likes Frère Jean, and monks are compared with monkeys for their uselessness. Here is Gargantua's summary:

Likewise a monk (I mean one of these idle monks) does not till the soil like the peasant, does not guard his country like the soldier, does not cure the sick like the doctor, does not preach to and indoctrinate people like the good educational Evangelical preacher, does not transport commodities and things necessary to the commonwealth like the merchant. That is the reason why they are hooted at and abhorred by all. (40, 118)

And when the more conservative Grandgousier protests that monks do pray to God for us, Gargantua—for the only time in the book—flatly contradicts his father.

It is apparently Gargantua who goes on to brand monks' prayers as self-serving; to state that all true Christians pray to God, Who receives their prayers with favor; and to include Frère Jean in their company in contrast with most monks: "Now such [a true Christian] is our Frère Jean. Therefore everyone wants him in his company. He is not a bigot; he is not slovenly; he is nice, joyous, determined, a good companion; he works; he tills; he defends the oppressed; he comforts the afflicted; he provides for the suffering; he guards the abbey's vineyard" (40, 119).*

Rabelais continues to contrast Frère Jean with ordinary monks in his heroic exploits during the war (42–44) and when Gargantua founds the complete antimonastery, Theleme, for him to administer (52 ff.). His only part in this, however, comes in chapter 52, where he helps Gargantua shape it.

Frère Jean reveals his character—lusty, dynamic, restless, impulsive—every time he opens his mouth. His speech is like no one else's. Here is a sample:†

Hon, que je ne suis roy de France pour quatre vingtz ou cent ans! Par Dieu, je vous metroys en chien courtault les fuyards de Pavye!‡ Leur fiebvre quartaine! Pourquoy ne mouroient-ilz là plustost que laisser leur bon prince

* The book does not show Frère Jean tilling the soil, comforting the afflicted, or providing for the suffering (unless we count the pilgrims in 44). These alleged activities seem to be mentioned because presumably few monks engage in them.
† 39, 116–17. This is one continuous passage; the ellipses (. . .) are not mine but in the text.
‡ The soldiers who fled at the battle of Pavia (1525), when the French were defeated and Francis I captured by the Imperial army.

en ceste nécessité? N'est-il meilleur et plus honorable mourir vertueusement bataillant que vivre fuyant villainement? . . . Nous ne mangerons guères d'oysons ceste année . . . Ha, mon amy, baille de ce cochon . . . Diavol! il n'y a plus de moust: *germinavit radix Jesse.** Je renye ma vie, je meurs de soif . . . Ce vin n'est des pires. Quel vin beuviez-vous à Paris? Je me donne au diable si je n'y tins plus de six moys pour un temps maison ouverte à tous venens! . . . Congnoissez-vous Frère Claude des Haulx Barrois? O le bon compaignon que c'est! Mais quelle mousche l'a picqué? Il ne faict rien que estudier depuis je ne sçay quand. Je n'estudie poinct, de ma part. En nostre abbaye nous ne estudions jamais, de peur des auripeaux. Nostre feu abbé disoit que c'est chose monstrueuse veoir un moyne sçavant. Par Dieu, Monsieur mon amy, *magis magnos clericos non sunt magis magnos sapientes*† . . . Vous ne veistes oncques tant de lièvres comme il y en a ceste année.

[Ha! if I were only King of France for eighty or a hundred years! By God, I'd fix those runaways from Pavia like cropped dogs! Bad cess to them! Why didn't they die there rather than leave their good prince in such a plight? Isn't it better and more honorable to die fighting like a man than to live fleeing ignominiously? . . . We shan't have many goslings to eat this year . . . Ah, my friend, give me some of that roast pig . . . Devil take it, there's no more must: the root of Jesse has grown. I renounce my life, I'm dying of thirst . . . This wine could be worse. What wine did you use to drink in Paris? Devil take me if I didn't keep a house there open to all comers for six months once upon a time! . . . Do you know Friar Claude des Haulx Barrois? O what a good companion he is! But what's got into him? He's been doing nothing but study for I don't know how long. As for me, I don't study. In our abbey we never study, for fear of the mumps. Our late abbot used to say that it's a monstrous thing to see a learned monk. By God, my friend, the greatest clerics are not the most intelligent . . . You never saw so many hares as there are this year.]

Even in his talk Frère Jean is always a man of action.

Grandgousier and Gargantua develop in similar ways from comic giants into wise and benevolent kings. Grandgousier is first presented as "a good joker in his day, loving to drink them down as much as any man then alive" (3, 12), jesting with Gargamelle about his penis and what it has wrought, then going off to drink while she is in labor (6, 22). He rejoices in his son's inventiveness in discovering the perfect asswipe, sees to his education, learns from his initial mistake in this area and corrects it (14–15). When he next appears (28), lamenting Picrochole's unprovoked attack, his age makes him somewhat pathetic,

* "The root of Jesse has grown." From the breviary, recalling Isaiah 11:1, and possibly making a bawdy pun on "moust" and "mou" (soft, suggesting a soft penis).
† Frère Jean's Latin is of course monkishly bad.

but he is piously resolved to appease the aggressor if possible. From then on he is always admirable: in his letter to Gargantua (29); his remonstrance to Picrochole (through his envoy Ulrich Gallet: 30–31); his return of the cakes (32); his welcome to Gargantua, Frère Jean, and the others (39–40); his advice to the pilgrims (45); his humanity to his prisoner Toucquedillon; and his Christian condemnation of all aggressive war (46). He lacks the youth, vigor, education, and prowess of his son and grandson; his piety is more old-fashioned, less Evangelical; but like them he is an exemplary king.

Gargantua starts out as a carnivalesque comic giant, with his name (already traditional, meaning "big throat," just like his father's); his horrific cry at birth, "Give me drink! drink! drink!"; his eighteen chins; his habit of beshitting his breeches (7, 25); his other uncleanly ways as a child (11, 37–38); his vigorous penis, which his nurses adore and love to play with (11, 39); his practical joke about the stables (12); his choice of the ass-wipe as a research project (13); his inability to answer young Eudémon (15); his naming of the region of Beauce (16); his flooding Paris with his urine, and taking the bells of Notre-Dame for his mare (17); his lazy, gluttonous life—at first—as a student (21); and his games (22). For him the change comes with his good education under Ponocrates (23–24) and is confirmed in the war. There he is sometimes still gigantic—combing the cannon balls out of his hair (37), eating six pilgrims in his salad (38), and flooding the countryside with his urine (38, 113)—but rarely comic in any other way; the exception is when Frère Jean puts him—and himself—to sleep by reading him psalms (41). Once educated, he is not only erudite (39, 115; 45, 132–33; 50, 142–45) but exemplary: in his condemnation of most monks and statement of what they should be (40), his clemency to the vanquished (50), his statutes for Theleme, and his interpretation of the prophetic enigma (58). By the end of the book he is a model like his father, and like his son Pantagruel in the last three books.

The war in *Pantagruel* was a series of ingenious exploits by Panurge and his companions in a fantasy nowhere-land, Utopia, with only one serious part, Pantagruel's prayer. The war in *Gargantua* is very different. The scene is Rabelais's home district around Chinon. The value of discipline is stressed (27, 43, 48). Rabelais's treatment abounds in satiric and serious ideas expressed mainly by his characters.

Clearly satiric is his account of the trivial origin of the war—in a harmless dispute between a few of Grandgousier's shepherds and Picrochole's cakemakers. Satiric too is his portrait of the aggressor king Picrochole [Bitter Bile]: his refusal to hear any but one side of the story (26); his conviction that Grandgousier's peace overtures are prompted by fear (32); his council of war (33) and the megalomania it reveals in and around him. More serious is Rabelais's analysis, expressed by Grandgousier and Ulrich Gallet, of the cause of Picrochole's aggressiveness. Despite his name, Picrochole is an old friend and ally of Grandgousier, and the latter tries to understand what has come over him. Here is Grandgousier's first explanation (28, 89):

For him to have outraged me so in this matter can only be the devil's work. Good God, Thou knowest my heart, for from Thee nothing can be hidden; if by chance he had gone mad and if, to restore his brain, Thou hadst sent him here to me, give me the power and the wit to return him by good teaching to the yoke of Thy holy will.

When he writes to Gargantua soon after, Grandgousier appears to understand Picrochole's affliction when he says of his own vain efforts to appease him: "Whence I knew that eternal God has abandoned him to the rudder of his own sense and free will [de son franc aibitre et propre sens], which can only be wicked unless it is continually guided by divine grace, and, to contain him in his duty and lead him back to understanding, has sent him here to me under hostile colors" (29, 90). Still later (32, 95), when Ulrich Gallet returns from his embassy to Picrochole, his explanation is about the same: "Cest homme est du tout hors du sens et délaissé de Dieu" [This man is completely out of his mind and abandoned by God].

Rabelais's theory seems to be this: led astray by the devil, Picrochole has put his trust in his own sense and free will, which without God's grace and guidance can only be evil.* Once he has abandoned God, God in turn has abandoned him; but God may still arrange for him to be restored to his right mind. When a good man goes bad, Rabelais seems to be saying, this is how it happens.

Other serious ideas are the strong condemnation of aggressive war by Grandgousier in chapter 46; his exemplary treatment of his prisoner Toucquedillon (also 46); and above all the clemency of Gargantua to the vanquished.

Addressing them in a dignified speech, he tells how his ancestors

* The relation of this to the trust in free will in Theleme will be discussed later in this chapter.

have always preferred "the lively remembrance of men acquired by liberality" (50, 142), the trophies erected by grace in the hearts of the vanquished, to the standard trophies of stone. His prime example is the way Grandgousier treated the defeated Alpharbal, king of Canarre, whom he handled kindly and sent home loaded with gifts, and the enormous tribute that Alpharbal and the Canarrians paid year after year—far more than could have been exacted—until soon Grandgousier may have to forbid it. And he draws the moral: "This is the nature of a free gift; for time, which erodes and diminishes all things, augments and increases benefits, because a good turn liberally done to a man of reason grows continually by noble thought and remembrance" (50, 144). To be sure, he sentences a number of "war criminals" to work at his new printing press; but this mild sentence is pronounced as a deterrent in the interest of justice.

The clear message—that clemency pays—contrasts with the then recent views of Machiavelli and marks the highest point of Rabelais's optimism about human nature; for the "man of reason," whose gratitude will constantly grow, by implication includes all Picrochole's army except the bad leaders and advisers.

Gargantua has six chapters on education (14–15, 21–24) where *Pantagruel* had one (8). In *Pantagruel*, Gargantua encouraged his son to study and outlined what he was to learn. In *Gargantua*, Rabelais sets forth his program for the best use of the working day: how to learn everything worth learning without spending a lifetime at it. Here we see not only the good new education but also the bad old, and not only intellectual but also physical and general education: arts, crafts, trades, professions. Between the two presentations I find no change in views, but a completion of the first by the second.

Chapter 14 tells how Grandgousier, wanting to have his promising son educated by "some learned man," entrusts him to a theologian, Maistre Thubal Holoferne, who reads him medieval commentaries on *De Modis Significandi* (which Gargantua learns by heart, backward as well as forward), and who teaches him to write Gothic script, at which he spends fifty-three years, ten months, and two weeks, whereupon Thubal dies of the pox and is succeeded by "another old cougher," Jobelin Bridé, who gives Gargantua more of the same—presumably for about the same length of time. Thanks to all this pointless memorization of stupid texts, the young giant becomes "crazy, silly, all dreamy and stupid" (15, 49), wholly unable to make any reply to the gracious salutation of young Eudémon. So Grandgousier sends him to Paris to learn under Ponocrates [Toil-Resistant], who first has him study in his accustomed way so that he (Ponocrates) may see why Gargantua is such an idiot, and finds that he eats, drinks, and sleeps a lot, hears a lot of masses, and studies perhaps one meager half hour a day—with his eyes on his book but his soul in the kitchen (21, 64). He has him purged with hellebore (against madness) and sets him to work "in such training that he did not lose an hour of the day" (23, 68; cf. 23, 69).

This chapter title (for such it is) is one of the keys to the good, strenuous new education that ensues. Now Gargantua rises at four instead of eight or nine. Every moment is put to good use. Scripture is read to him during his morning rubdown and explained even while he goes to the toilet. While he is being dressed he hears the lessons of the previous day repeated, learns them by heart, and applies them to real-life situations. For three hours he is read to; then "they" (presumably he and Ponocrates) go out for physical sport, discussing the readings as they go; they exercise only until they either tire or sweat. Discussion continues as they wait for the frugal lunch that keeps them fit for the afternoon's work. A story is read to him at lunch and followed by discussion—full of ancient medical lore—of the properties of the foods they eat. Cards and dice serve the study of arithmetic; while digesting their lunch they play games of geometry and astronomy, and practice instrumental as well as vocal music.

After lunch, three more hours of study, rehearsing the morning's lesson and going further, lead to an elaborate program of physical exercise, this time explicitly practical, to prepare the young giant prince (as Machiavelli had prescribed) for any hazard of war by making him expert in the use of all weapons and in swimming, boating, climbing, gymnastics, and weight-lifting. On their way back they study trees and plants, comparing their findings with those of the ancients; during supper (the only big meal) they review the day's lessons; later their recreation is in singing, playing instruments, cards, or dice, or sometimes going to visit men of letters or travelers who know foreign lands. Before retiring they observe the stars, again go over the day's lessons, and offer grateful prayers to God. "Ce faict, entroient en leur repous" (23, 75) [This done, they entered upon their rest].

Their rainy-day activities substitute, for the outdoor sport, useful household jobs such as splitting and sawing wood and beating sheaves;

arts such as painting and sculpture; and a wide variety of what today we might call field trips: learning about trades by watching artisans at work; going to hear public lectures, declamations, the pleas of good lawyers, and the like, not forgetting "the speeches of the Evangelical preachers" (24, 76). Gargantua also becomes an expert fencer, visits apothecaries' shops, observes mountebanks and listens to their "beau parler" (24, 77).

Once a month, when the weather is good, Ponocrates takes Gargantua to the country for a day of relaxation without books; but even then much of their sport is reciting favorite Latin poetry and translating it into French verse.

Obviously Rabelais's program of education seeks to produce a "Renaissance man" vigorous in mind and body, expert in a wide range of activities. But is it merely an arduous means to a desirable end? Will the student have any fun at all? The answer is clear as we note the phrases that stud Rabelais's account (23, 70–71): "liberty," "entertaining story," "talk joyously," "beautiful canticles," "nice things," "affection," "pleasantly," "joyous instruments," "entertained themselves by singing," and the like. It is even clearer when he tells how much Gargantua profited from this training, "which, although at the beginning it seemed difficult, as it continued was so sweet, light, and delightful, that it was more like a king's pastime than a student's study" (24, 77).

Inevitably, Rabelais's views on education are often contrasted with those that Montaigne proposed a half century later. Similar in their Renaissance concern with the whole man and optimism about what good education can do, they differ in Rabelais's overriding emphasis on learning and Montaigne's on judgment. Yet even this contrast is often overstated. Rabelais condemns mere memorization and requires his student to digest and apply all he learns; while Montaigne provides for an early inculcation in which the student is *told* such essentials as the purpose of study, the nature of justice and contentment, the motives of men, and in short, what serves to make him wiser and better.[15] Each man is representative of his moment: Rabelais, of the excited wonder at the new golden age; Montaigne, of the later disillusionment at the sight of learned fools. Had their times been reversed, many of their emphases might have been as well.

The culmination of *Gargantua* is in the six nearly final chapters (52–57) on the Abbey of Theleme. Although much is clear about it, much is not, partly at least because it starts to be an antimonastery but ends up as a general utopia, at times almost a pipe dream.

The name comes ultimately from the Greek verb ἐθέλω ("to wish, be fain, implying purpose or design, whereas Βούλομαι denotes mere willingness or desire"[16]), and more immediately from the noun θέλημα, which, as Per Nykrog has shown,[17] is used in the New Testament to designate the will of God, and which in humans denotes a will that is not reflective but rather spontaneous. The name means "Abbey of One's Will," and its single rule, "Fay ce que vouldras," means "Do what you will." For a man with Rabelais's experience of monasteries and hatred of constraint, it is a natural beginning.

It is built to reward Frère Jean for his exploits in the war. He turns down the direction of his own Abbey of Seuillé, asking how he could govern others when he cannot govern himself, and instead requests to found an abbey of his own design. Gargantua agrees, and in chapter 52—after which Frère Jean disappears for the rest of the book—they plan it as the opposite of a regular abbey: no walls, no clocks or bells, no men without women or women without men, no restriction on leaving; in place of the vows of chastity, poverty, and obedience, "It was decreed that there people could be honorably married, that everyone should be rich and should live in freedom" (52, 149). The endowment, needless to say, is Gargantuan, the building a Renaissance château "a hundred times more magnificent than Bonivet, Chambord, or Chantilly" (53, 150).

With the inscription over the great gate (ch. 54), a complication arises. In ninety-eight intricately rhymed verses in the old tradition of the Grands Rhétoriqueurs, Rabelais tells us who is to be kept out and who admitted. Unwanted are hypocrites, cheats, abusers of the people, persecutors, and in general all men of ill will. Invited are attractive men and attractive women, preferably of noble lineage,[18] and the Evangelical preachers: "vous, qui le sainct Evangile/ En sens agile annoncez, quoy qu'on gronde" (54, 154) [you who announce the holy Gospel in its true sense, despite complaints]. What they are doing in Theleme is a fair question.

Chapters 53, 55, and 56 are devoted mainly to the magnificent grounds, lodgings, and clothes of the Thelemites.[19] The ladies originally dressed just as they liked ("à leur plaisir et arbitre"), but later chose freely to reform ("par leur franc vouloir") and all to dress alike (56, 156). Such was the sympathy between them all that the men dressed to match the women (56, 158).

Chapter 57 brings us to the heart of Theleme. All the residents' life was spent "not by laws, statutes, or rules, but according to their will and free choice" (57, 159). They did whatever they wanted whenever they wanted; thus it was established.

En leur reigle n'estoit que ceste clause:

FAY CE QUE VOULDRAS,

parce que gens libères, bien néz, bien* instruictz, conversans en compaignies honnestes, ont par nature un instinct et aguillon, qui tousjours les poulse à faictz vertueux et retire de vice, lequel ilz nommoient honneur. Iceulx, quand par vile subjection et contraincte sont déprimez et asserviz, détournent la noble affection, par laquelle à vertuz franchement tendoient, à déposer et enfraindre ce joug de servitude: car nous entreprenons tousjours choses défendues et convoitons ce que nous est dénié. (57, 159–60)
[In their rule was only this clause:

DO WHAT YOU WILL,

because people who are free, well born, well taught, frequenting decent company, have by nature an instinct and spur which always impels them to virtuous deeds and holds them back from vice, which they called honor. These same people, when they are oppressed and enslaved by vile subjection and constraint, turn aside the noble affection by which they freely tended toward virtue, to depose and infringe this yoke of servitude: for we always undertake forbidden things and covet what is denied us.]

Their freedom, Rabelais goes on, led all to want to do whatever anyone wanted to do: drink, play, exercise, hunt, or whatever. All were so nobly taught (by whom and when, we have no idea) that they could read, write, sing, play musical instruments, and speak and write verse and prose in five or six languages. Never were there such gallant and attractive men and women. Whereas earlier (52, 149) they could be married in Theleme, now (57, 160) they can leave and be married; and their marriages normally turn out well.

Theleme poses many problems. Why does Frère Jean appear at the outset and then disappear? Is he brought in, as Screech argues, only as an afterthought to try to connect Theleme with the rest of the book? (This seems quite possible to me.) What is he doing in his "abbey" with all the gallant, learned, sumptuously dressed, and apparently fastidious young men and women?[20] What are the Evangelical preachers doing there—except being protected from persecution? Women are admitted between the ages of ten and fifteen, men between twelve and eighteen; how many preachers would qualify? How many would speak five or six languages, play instruments, and spend their time

* The Pléiade text wrongly reads "bain."

composing foreign verse and prose? Where and how do the residents learn their many skills and many languages, the girls by age ten and the boys by age twelve? Are people married in Theleme or not? These are only some of the many problems and questions.[21]

To account for all the puzzles, I think we must posit a Rabelais whose many frustrations made him ready to daydream even in print. An antimonastery for him is already a bit of a Utopia; why not make it one in every sense? Whatever the chronology, the account of the abbey develops from one thing to the other.

The optimism of Theleme is obvious but less extreme, in my judgment, than that of Gargantua's speech to the vanquished (ch. 50), and not always clear in degree. One recent critic, Henri Busson, finds it irreligious;[22] but this seems exaggerated. However, the trust in man's free will on which it rests needs to be reconciled with Rabelais's apparent mistrust of it in his account of Picrochole (28, 29, 32) in some such way as the following. Obviously he knows that the world includes bad people as well as good. The bad, he seems to believe, have abandoned God's guidance for their own, and have in turn been abandoned by God; whereas the Thelemites, although not conspicuous in their dedication to worship or their consciousness of God, are presumably still under His guidance. For Rabelais, in this book at least, most humans, unless ill-born or somehow perverted (as by bad training or bad company), are naturally likely to be decent people who in the main do God's will. In this he is of course at the opposite pole from his contemporary and enemy John Calvin.

We have noted Rabelais's remarks about monks. To fill out the picture of his religious views in *Gargantua*, let us turn to those on pilgrimages, the Sorbonne, and Evangelical preachers.

The six pilgrims, led by Lasdaller—"Wearybones," in J. M. Cohen's translation—appear comically in chapter 38 to be eaten by Gargantua in a salad, removed by his toothpick when one of them hits the nerve of a tooth with his stave, have their road blocked by his urine, and explain their misadventure in the words of Psalm 124. In chapter 44 Frère Jean delivers them from Picrochole's army, and in 45 they appear before Grandgousier. Following a superstition common in their day, that various saints may cause, and protect against, various ailments, they have been to Saint-Sébastian near Nantes to pray for protection from the plague. When Grandgousier learns that their preachers are responsible, he denounces them as false prophets; tells how he punished one in his own kingdom "although he called me a heretic" (45, 131) and thus rid the country of them; and concludes: "The plague kills only the body, but such impostors poison souls."

Frère Jean warns the pilgrims that monks will have made their wives pregnant in their absence. When Lasdaller answers that no one would be tempted by *his* wife, Frère Jean retorts that a good workman uses any material and that they will indeed find their wives with child when they get home, "for even the shadow of an abbey bell tower is fertile" [car seulement l'ombre du clochier d'une abbaye est féconde] (45, 132). Then Grandgousier dismisses them with the advice of genuine piety, which they receive with admiration and delight:

"Go your way, you poor folk, in the name of God the Creator; may He ever be your guide; and henceforth do not be easy marks for these idle and useless trips. Support your families, work, each man in his vocation, educate your children, and live as the good apostle Saint Paul teaches you to. So doing, you will have the protection of God, the angels, and the saints with you, and there will be no plague or ill that will do you harm." (45, 132)

As the repressive enemy of the new humanistic and religious ideas, the Sorbonne comes in for criticism and ridicule. (It was in 1534 that Rabelais added to *Pantagruel* [18, 253] the horrific variations on names for its members: "Sorbillans, Sorbonagres, Sorbonigènes," and so on.) Throughout the *Gargantua* of 1534 the characters later labeled "sophists" were still "theologians": the stupid tutor Thubal Holoferne (and presumably his successor Jobelin Bridé) and Janotus de Bragmardo. When the Parisians gather in dismay at Gargantua's taking the bells of Notre-Dame, the place where they do so, in the original editions, is not Nesle (as later), but the Sorbonne, of which Rabelais writes confidently (or at least hopefully): "where then used to be, now no longer is, the oracle of Paris" (17, 55). His main satire of the Sorbonne follows when Maistre Janotus de Bragmardo comes to Gargantua's lodging, well attended and well wined, to plead for the return of the bells. Gargantua decides to return the bells without his knowledge and then have the fun of listening to his plea, which proves to be made up largely of simple proverbial French, much clearing of the throat, and much kitchen Latin. Here is a sample, which I will not attempt to translate: "*Omnis clocha clochabilis, in clocherio clochando, clochans clochativo clochare facit clochabiliter clochantes. Parisius habet clochas. Ergo gluc*" (19, 58). Ponocrates and Eudémon burst into uncontrollable laughter; Janotus joins them; they give him plenty to drink, and also the hose and sausages promised by his colleagues if the bells were restored. With these he returns to the Sorbonne and asks for the promised sausages and hose. His colleagues refuse, saying "that he should be contented with reason" [qu'il se contentast de raison], since Gargantua has already given him the same reward. Here, well set up by Rabelais, is Janotus' reply:

> "Reason," said Janotus, "we use none of that in here. Wretched traitors, you are good for nothing; earth bears no people wickeder than you are, I know that well. Don't limp in front of the lame; I've practiced wickedness with you. God's spleen! I'll notify the King of the enormous abuses that are fabricated in here and by your doing, and may I be a leper if he doesn't have you all burned alive as buggers, traitors, heretics, and seducers, enemies of God and of virtue!" (20, 61)

And with this triumphant accusation from the lips of one of its own, Rabelais takes his leave of the Sorbonne.

The good Evangelical preachers are often singled out for favorable mention. When Gargantua arrives in Paris everyone turns out to wonder at his size, for (explains Rabelais) the people of Paris are such stupid rubbernecks that more of them will gather to watch a juggler, a relic-bearer, a mule with cymbals, or a hurdy-gurdy player, than to hear a good Evangelical preacher (17, 53). In the good education under Ponocrates, one of the rainy-day activities is to go to hear the discussions of the Evangelical preachers (24, 76). When Gargantua explains why monks are in bad odor (40, 118), one reason is that they do not preach and indoctrinate like the good educational Evangelical preacher. Finally, as we noted, the Evangelical preachers (not so named but clearly designated) form the rather unlikely third group of people who join the attractive young men and women in Theleme (54, 154). Rabelais rarely misses a chance to show his admiration for this group.

Gargantua ends with an "Enigme en prophétie" [Prophetic Enigma] which, with its interpretation, fills the final chapter 58. It consists of 108 verses in rhymed couplets, of which all but the last ten were later published in the posthumous collected works of Mellin de Saint-Gelais. The rest of the poem is generally assigned to Saint-Gelais, but to me Rabelais seems just as likely to be the author.[23] The enigma tells of a swarm of troublemakers who will appear "this coming winter" and raise havoc in the land, setting subject against noble, son against father.

deeds of the good Pantagruel" (p. 316). But the times were bad. In 1545 several thousand Waldensians (Vaudois) in southeastern France were slaughtered as heretics. In the following year Etienne Dolet was burned at the stake. Rabelais's *Third Book* was to be condemned less than a year after it appeared. We may smile at his formula "jusques au feu exclusivement" [up to but not including the stake], but to him this was not just a joke.

The *Third Book* is very different from its predecessors. Even the title announces this; instead of horrific deeds, it is *The Third Book of the Heroic Deeds and Sayings of the Good Pantagruel* [Le Tiers Livre des faicts et dicts heroïcques du bon Pantagruel]. It is signed no longer by an anagram but by "M. Fran. Rabelais docteur en medicine." Full of his vast erudition, it aims at a more learned public than do the first two books; its Evangelism is more covert than that of the outspoken *Gargantua*. The giant story is completely abandoned; at no time does Pantagruel—or Gargantua—appear as other than normal size. Pantagruel, now rarely involved in the comedy, stands above the others and apart as an ideal Christian philosopher-king. Despite the title, there are no heroic deeds, and indeed almost no plot; instead, there is a series of thirteen consultations by Panurge on whether or not he should marry.

In his Prologue (pp. 326–27) Rabelais shows his concern over the reception awaiting such a book. He tells how King Ptolemy, son of Lagus, sought to delight his Egyptian subjects by showing them an all-black Bactrian camel and a slave whose skin was part white, part black; but their reaction to these monsters was fright, indignation, and abomination. He draws the moral: "This example makes me vacillate between hope and fear, fearing that in place of anticipated happiness I may encounter what I abhor, my treasure may be coals, in place of Venus I score Barbet the dog,* instead of serving them I anger them, instead of amusing them I offend them, instead of pleasing them I displease." To be sure, he goes on to say emphatically that this will not happen; but I think his uneasiness is real.

The book has three main parts: five chapters on Panurge's debts, followed by a transitional one; forty-one (7–47) on Panurge's marriage, all but the first two presenting consultations, and one against clandestine marriages; and four chapters (49–52) on the herb Panta-

* In place of the best score in the game of knucklebones (*osselets*, *tales*), I make the worst.

gruelion. The main problems it offers are the meaning of the Prologue and its relation to the book itself; the relation of the first part (on debts) to the rest; the meaning of the last part (Pantagruelion) and its relation to the rest.

The prevailing view for many years was that of Abel Lefranc, stated in his Introduction to the *Tiers Livre* in the critical edition in 1931. For him the book was a part of the Querelle des Femmes, which in the early French Renaissance, and especially in the 1540s and 1550s, opposed the idealizers of women—Platonic, courtly, and Petrarchan—to their condemners in the medieval monastic and *gaulois* traditions. Rabelais's principal spokesman, Lefranc argues, is the doctor, Rondibilis, who is clearly an antifeminist. The Prologue reveals Rabelais as a royal publicist calling the nation to defensive war against the threatening enemy, Charles V. The chapters on Pantagruelion relate simply to Rabelais's main sources, notably Pliny the Elder.

In the last twenty years this view has been superseded. V. L. Saulnier shows the *Third Book* as a quest for ready-made authority in a dangerous and difficult time—a quest that in the *Fourth Book* will become a personal voyage of inquiry; to him it is rather antifeminist but not primarily so.[2] *Hésuchisme*, or crypto-Evangelism, is for him an important message of the book as a whole and the key to the enigma of the Pantagruelion.[3] He finds Panurge more sympathetic than do many (of whom I am one), relatively free of *philautie* [self-love], not just glib in his praise of debts, often right against his advisers, almost an Everyman figure. To him the advisers are mere *conseilleurs*, not *conseillers*, limited by professional deformations. The problem of the book is decision-making in a dangerous period.

M. A. Screech agrees with Saulnier that the Querelle des Femmes is not central and that decision-making is, but in other ways sees it quite differently.[4] He finds it feminist and strongly philogamic; sees Panurge as a fool who cannot accept not having things all his own way; and sees Bridoye, the judge, as a Christian fool whose folly may be wisdom before God, in contrast with the born fool-madman Triboullet and the self-made fool Panurge. For him the counselors are often right and Panurge often if not always wrong. Pantagruel, whose wise attitude toward marriage contrasts explicitly with that of Panurge, is the perfect ruler and friend, Evangelical and Stoical in thought, the "idea and exemplar of all joyous perfection," as Rabelais calls him (III: 52, 506). For Screech the parts on debts and Pantagruelion are primarily parodies of inflated rhetoric.

Walter Kaiser's view of the *Third Book* is close to Screech's reading, while emphasizing Rabelais's debt to Erasmus.[5] He finds a certain "perfect" folly in Pantagruel[6] and, like Saulnier, some sense in Panurge.[7] He sees the Prologue as clearly antiwar; the praise of debts as much like *The Praise of Folly;* and the Pantagruelion as an emblem of the goal of the quest, corresponding to Diogenes' barrel in the Prologue.

Of these four views of the *Third Book*, I am most indebted to that of Screech.

I find the Prologue clear in some ways, cryptic in others, and the conclusion for the most part cryptic. The opening chapters (in praise of debts) are related to the consultations by the conclusion of chapter 4 (p. 346) on "le debvoir de mariage" [the duty of marriage] and by Panurge's later coupling of the two ideas (9, 359): "quitte et non marié" [out of debt and unmarried]. The consultations interweave those with friends—Pantagruel (9–11), Epistémon (24), and Frère Jean (26–28)—with the others that precede the quartet. Pantagruel is naturally the first; Frère Jean, the last of these, leaves Panurge discouraged. Apart from these we start with nonpersons (Virgilian lots, dreams), then move to fantastic people (the Sibyl, the mute), and to the impressive dying poet Raminagrobis and the pompous dealer in "mantics," Her Trippa. Then Pantagruel proposes the quartet: the theologian Hippothadée, Doctor Rondibilis, Judge Bridoye, and—almost as an afterthought—the philosopher Trouillogan, who is there to resolve all doubts but does not. All but Bridoye are consulted, and Panurge is left like a trapped mouse. Pantagruel suggests that, since he is not satisfied with the answers of the wise, they should consult a fool (37, 461); they talk of the court fool Triboullet, see and hear the Christian fool Judge Bridoye (39–44), then consult Triboullet, whose "answer" suggests—like the rest, but more specifically—that if Panurge marries he will be cuckolded, beaten, and robbed (46, 490). Triboullet's return of the emptied wine bottle prompts Panurge to decide that he must consult the Divine Bottle (47, 492); this leads to the plans for Pantagruel's marriage, the preparations for the trip, and the Pantagruelion.

Following Lucian, the Prologue starts with Diogenes at the siege of Corinth by Philip of Macedon. Seeing everyone busy with preparations for defense[8] and lacking suitable employment, he drives his barrel up Mount Cranion and down again, so as not to be the only one idle. Rabelais says that he himself, finding his compatriots all preparing for battle, will do the same by serving both defenders and counter-attackers with "un guallant tiercin et consécutivement un joyeulx quart de sentences pantagruelicques" (pp. 325–26)—in other words, the *Third* and *Fourth Books*—drawn from the wine in his Diogenic tub.

As he thinks of Ptolemy, son of Lagus, however, he fears at first for the reception of his book; but then he claims to recognize in all his readers "a specific form and individual property, which our ancestors called Pantagruelism, by means of which they will never take in bad part things of any sort which they know issue from a good, frank, and honest heart" (p. 327). These are the only ones invited to read his book; for the censors and persecutors he has only curses and adjurations to leave it alone.

Critics disagree whether the Prologue is meant to be prowar or ironically antiwar. It appears prowar on the face of it; but this seems to involve an unlikely rejection of Erasmus (for his "Dulce Bellum Inexpertis" in the *Adages*) as one of "certains repetasseurs de vieilles ferrailles latines" [certain botching menders of old Latin iron tools] (p. 323). I lean slightly to the antiwar reading; but I do not believe with Kaiser (pp. 118–19) that Rabelais, who in *Gargantua* and *Pantagruel* rejects wars of aggression but favors those of defense, might not still approve of defensive war; or that the contemptuous phrase clearly must refer to Erasmus rather than to one of his sources. In any case, this question does not seem to me critical for the reading of the entire *Third Book*.

After an introductory chapter on how Pantagruel kept the conquered Dipsodes loyal by colonizing part of their land with Amaurotes, we learn how in less than two weeks Panurge has spent three years' advance revenue from his castleship of Salmiguondin and thus gone deeply into debt. The reaction of Pantagruel, now a genial, untroubled Stoical Christian, is described in loving detail (2, 335):

Pantagruel, adverty de l'affaire, n'en feust en soy aulcunement indigné, fasché ne marry. Je vous ay jà dict et encores rediz que c'estoit le meilleur petit et grand bonhomet, que oncques ceigneit espéc; toutes choses prenoit en bonne partie, tout acte interprétoit à bien; jamais ne se tourmentoit, jamais ne se scandalizoit; aussi eust-il esté bien forissu du déificque manoir de raison, si aultrement se feust contristé ou altéré, car tous les biens que le ciel couvre et que la terre contient en toutes ses dimensions: hauteur, profondité, longitude et latitude, ne sont dignes d'esmouvoir nos affections et troubler nos sens et espritz.

Seulement tira Panurge à part et doulcettement luy remonstra que, si ainsi vouloit vivre et n'estre aultrement mesnagier, impossible seroit, ou pour le moins bien difficile, le faire jamais riche.

[Pantagruel, advised of the matter, was not at all indignant, angered, or saddened by it inside. I have already told you, and I tell you again, that he was the best little and big good man who ever girded on a sword; he took all things in good part, interpreted every act favorably, never tormented himself, never was scandalized; and indeed he would have departed far from the deific manor of reason if contrariwise he had become saddened or changed; for all the good things that the sky covers and that the earth contains in all its dimensions—height, depth, length, and breadth—are not worthy to move our affections and trouble our senses and minds.

Only he drew Panurge aside and gently pointed out to him that if he wanted to live thus and not husband his property differently, it would be impossible, or at least very difficult, ever to make him rich.]

Panurge replies to Pantagruel that he has no concern with being rich, and launches into his praise of debts. He claims to be following the Sorbonne and practicing the four cardinal virtues (prudence, justice, strength, temperance); rejoices in the good will and abundance of his creditors (ch. 3); and shows the need for what he calls debts in the heavens, the earth, and the microcosm, man.[9] In chapter 4 he ecstatically proclaims the converse: the joy and harmony of the universe, earth, and man wherever debts are the rule.

Most of Panurge's praise is not really of debts but of *caritas*, the Christian love that leads people to help one another. From the debtless world of chapter 3, he proclaims, "will be banished Faith, Hope, Charity, for men are born to aid and succor men" (p. 342); but in the happy world of debts "Charity alone [will] rule, be regent, dominate, triumph" (4, 344). Hence some critics, like Saulnier (*Le Dessein*, pp. 51–53), have seen a serious and beautiful message in Panurge's rhetoric. However, I follow Screech in seeing the function of the episode (apart from its eloquent comedy) as depicting the new Panurge as glib, ingenious, erudite, but incurably wrongheaded and ruled by *philautia*.

The main evidence for this is in chapter 5, where Pantagruel at last answers Panurge (p. 347): " 'I understand,' replied Pantagruel, 'and you seem to me a good pleader and devoted to your cause. But you may preach and plead from now to Whitsuntide, in the end you will be amazed how you will have persuaded me of nothing, and by your fine talk you will never get me to go into debt. Owe nothing to anyone, says the holy apostle [Saint Paul], except love and mutual affection.' " Reasonably, he recognizes that lending and owing are sometimes proper, and states when this is so. Then he urges that they change the subject, saying that he will deliver Panurge from his past (p. 348). When Panurge then asks him to let him keep at least a few debts to avoid the dangers that confront him without them, Pantagruel finally shuts him up on the subject for good (p. 349).

In short, once the new Pantagruel is established as a Stoically Christian sage, the new Panurge is established as a delightful master of specious eloquence, then gently but firmly squelched by the calm reason of his young prince and master.

After Panurge decides to marry, to dress strangely, and to give up wearing his magnificent codpiece until he marries (ch. 7–8), come the thirteen consultations (ch. 9–47), of which the first and largest group of nine (ch. 9–28) are with friends, nonpersons, and four persons credited with the power of divination. These start with one (Pantagruel) who makes no prediction at all, continue with six that (except for Raminagrobis) point toward cuckoldry, and end with two (Her Trippa, Frère Jean) which make that prediction emphatically.

We start with Pantagruel (ch. 9–10) for three good reasons: (1) at that point he is the only character besides Panurge (Frère Jean and the others appear only from ch. 13–14 on); (2) he is Panurge's prince and master, whom it is natural and proper for him to consult first; and (3) as the sage of the book, he is the man needed to show how Panurge should approach marriage but does not. Chapter 9, in which Pantagruel begins each answer with the last words or sounds of Panurge's previous remark ("poinct-poinct, Pourpoinct-poinct, mariez-mariez, m'auriez-mariez, mal riez-mariez), shows Panurge's complete inability to make up his mind. His remarks go back and forth between desire for marriage and fear of its consequences. His reproach to Pantagruel at the start of chapter 10 for giving contradictory advice sums up his problem: he wants Pantagruel to make up his (Panurge's) mind. Pantagruel's reply is a central statement of the *Third Book*:

"Aussi (respondit Pantagruel) en vos propositions tant y a de si et de mais, que je n'y sçaurois rien fonder ne rien résoudre. N'estez-vous asceuré de vostre vouloir? Le poinct principal y gist: tout le reste est fortuit et dépendent des fatales dispositions du ciel." (III: 10, 361)

["Accordingly," replied Pantagruel, "in your propositions there are so many 'ifs' and 'buts' that I cannot base or resolve anything upon them. Are you not certain of your own will? The principal point lies there: all the rest is fortuitous and dependent on the fatal dispositions of heaven."]

Pantagruel goes on to say that marriage can be a heaven or a hell, and to state how a person must go into it if he wants to marry: "One should go into it as a chance, eyes bandaged, head bowed, kissing the earth and commending oneself to God for the rest, since one has once for all decided to go into it. I could not possibly give you any other assurance about it."

Now that we know that Panurge must, but cannot, make up his mind to run the risks of marriage, we are ready for the first two inquiries, by Virgilian lots and by dreams. These set the pattern for the rest by predicting—though not yet clearly and explicitly—that if Panurge marries he will be cuckolded, robbed, and beaten by his wife. Panurge, now as later, shows his specious ingenuity by interpreting the predictions in his own favor. Likewise with the first consultation with someone other than a friend, the picturesque Sibyl of Panzoust (ch. 16–18), whose ingeniously ambiguous verses seem to predict disaster for Panurge but may just possibly mean the opposite. There follows the wordless consultation with Nazdecabre the mute (ch. 19–20)—not unlike Panurge's debate with Thaumaste in *Pantagruel*; again the mute's gestures leave a little latitude for interpretation, and Panurge uses it.

Raminagrobis, the dying poet of chapter 21, who is visited by Panurge, Epistémon, and Frère Jean, anticipates the philosopher Trouillogan as, in a rondeau adapted from Guillaume Crétin, he tells Panurge "Take her, do not take her," and that either way he will do well. He is clearer when, following the lead of Erasmus,[10] he tells of a swarm of ugly and pestilential beasts (who could be insects, or more likely monks), who have pestered him on his deathbed, disturbing his serene contemplation of death, until he drove them away. This leads to a debate among Panurge, Epistémon, and Frère Jean that reveals Panurge as a suspicious heresy-sniffer.

Epistémon, consulted in chapter 24, ridicules Panurge for his outlandish accouterment but pronounces his fate in marriage too difficult a question for him to resolve. Her Trippa, however, who presumably represents Cornelius Agrippa and whom Panurge pronounces a notable cuckold himself, cites over thirty "mancies" or divinations, from pyromancy and acromancy (by fire, by air) to necromancy and sciomancy (by the dead, by ghosts), to show that Panurge will suffer the triple fate predicted by the others (ch. 25). His fiendish emphasis on

Panurge's prospective cuckoldry leads to the consultation with Frère Jean (ch. 26–28), who gaily points to the advantages of wearing horns. He twits Panurge about his advancing years, though in the fiction he himself is a generation older; and Panurge, for the only time in Rabelais, admits that all the consultations have foretold cuckoldry for him (28, 429):

> I fear that during some long absence of our king Pantagruel, whom I must accompany even if he should go to all the devils, my wife will make me a cuckold. That is the decisive word: for all I have spoken to about it threaten me with it and affirm that it is thus predestined for me by the heavens.

With Frère Jean's advice to wear the ring of Hans Carvel to secure his wife's chastity (the ring being her vagina), the three friends return to Pantagruel (29, 434), who hails Raminagrobis' verses as the best of advice and draws this lesson: "I have not yet seen an answer that I like more. It means in summary that in the undertaking of marriage each person must be the arbiter of his own thoughts and take counsel of himself. Such has always been my opinion, and I told you as much the first time you spoke to me about it. But you were tacitly making fun of my opinion, I remember, and I recognize that *philautia* and self-love is deceiving you."

With this reminder the first group of consultations ends. Panurge is still resistant to good advice. All that has changed is that his fate if he marries is now clearer.

The main group of consultations is announced when Pantagruel goes on to suggest a change of course. All we are and have, he says, consists of soul, body, and property (29, 434). Theologians act to conserve our souls, doctors our bodies, jurists our property, so let us bring one of each to dinner Sunday and discuss your perplexity.

Panurge objects that most theologians are heretics, doctors loathe medications, and lawyers never sue one another; but Pantagruel contradicts him on theologians and praises the other two professions for not using their skills for themselves, and then, to resolve any doubts, proposes a foursome for Sunday dinner: the theologian Hippothadée, the doctor Rondibilis, the jurist Bridoye, and the philosopher Trouillogan. As it turns out, Bridoye is not consulted but saved for another role.

Hippothadée, the theologian, answers Panurge's question—"Should I marry or not?"—"with incredible modesty" (30, 436). Like Pantagruel, he insists that Panurge must make up his own mind, and like an Evangelical preacher he declares that continence is a *special gift* and that it *far* better to marry than to burn *with lust*:[11]

> "My friend, you ask us for advice, but first you must advise yourself. Do you feel importunately in your body the pricks of the flesh?"
>
> "Very strongly," replied Panurge; "no offense, Father."
>
> "No offense, my friend," said Hippothadée. "But in this problem, do you have from God the gift and special grace of continence?"
>
> "Faith, no," replied Panurge.
>
> "Then marry, my friend," said Hippothadée, "for it is far better to marry than to burn in the fire of concupiscence." (30, 436–37)

Panurge, of course, is delighted with this answer, and invites Hippothadée to his wedding. But a point occurs to him that he trusts is minimal: Shall I not be cuckolded? " 'No indeed, my friend,' replied Hippothadée, 'if it please God.' " This drives Panurge wild; he claims that it sends him to God's privy council, and takes back the invitation to the wedding. But Hippothadée, undismayed, points out that his answer merely leaves to God what belongs to God, Who has revealed His holy pleasures in the Bible. All Panurge must do is marry a good woman of good family trained in virtue, keeping good company (cf. Theleme), loving and fearing God and eager to keep His commandments (which forbid adultery); and himself be a virtuous husband to her, constantly imploring God's grace for his protection. Panurge, of course, can only reply that such a woman never existed; he wants no part of such an equitable arrangement; and here the chapter and the consultation end. Hippothadée shows the patience of a Pantagruel, reads Panurge like a book, and gives him excellent advice—which Panurge's *philautia* will not let him take.

Rondibilis, the doctor, whose consultation follows (ch. 31–34), is very different though not contradictory. Although he has heard Panurge and Hippothadée, he is not a good listener; in effect he gives a lecture with scant attention to questions or interruptions. Medically, he sides with Plato against Galen, notably on the nature and action of the uterus. He starts with Panurge's concupiscence and the five means offered by Platonic authorities to check it: wine taken intemperately, certain drugs and plants, heavy physical labor, fervent study, and finally the venereal act itself. " 'I was waiting for you there,' said Panurge, 'and take that for myself. Let whoever wants to, use the preceding ones' " (31, 443). Rondibilis encourages him to marry, as one fit to have fine children if he finds a suitable wife.

But when Panurge asks about his possible cuckoldry (32, 444), Rondibilis is appalled at his even raising the question. Cuckoldry, he says, naturally follows marriage; it is rightly said of any married man that " 'he is, or has been, or will be, or may be a cuckold.' " In the most misogynistic chapter of the book, he goes on to deplore the fragility, inconstancy, and imperfection of women, whom Nature seems to have created by some mistake, not for any perfection of their own, but only to give man company and perpetuate the race. Their inward parts demand satisfaction, at the risk of their health; great is the credit of those who have been able to "bring this unruly animal to obedience to reason" (32, 447). For men the usual consequence is of course cuckoldry.

Rondibilis then tells how Jupiter at first forgot to assign a feast day to "that poor devil Cuckoldry," but then gave him a share of Jealousy's (ch. 33–34). To forbid a woman to do anything, he explains, is infallibly to make her do it. The examples that follow lead to the "moral comedy" of the man who married a mute wife, in which it appears that Rabelais himself once played at Montpellier; and the consultation ends with a Moliéresque scene in which Rondibilis pretends to refuse, but is careful to take, the money Panurge offers him in payment.

The philosopher Trouillogan is absolutely noncommittal (ch. 35–36). His answers to Panurge's repeated question "Shall I marry or not?" are all in effect "Either, neither, or both." His first such replies prompt comments by Gargantua, Rondibilis, and especially Hippothadée and Pantagruel, who again are of much the same mind. Hippothadée quotes Saint Paul (1 Corinthians 7:29), saying, "they that have wives be as though they had none"; and Pantagruel offers this interpretation, which may well be Rabelais's own, about the proper place of the wife in married life:

To have a wife is to have her for such use as Nature created her for, which is for the aid, pleasure, and society of man; not to have a wife is not to laze about her, not to contaminate for her sake that unique and supreme affection that man owes to God, not to give up the services that he owes naturally to his fatherland, to the commonwealth, to his friends, not to be heedless of his studies and business affairs in order continually to please his wife. (35, 456)

At one point Trouillogan sums up his advice in a way reminiscent of both Pantagruel's counsel and the rule of Theleme. When Panurge asks him " 'But for the love of mercy, advise me: what should I do?' " (36, 457), he answers, " 'What you will' " [Ce que vouldrez]. When asked whether he himself was ever cuckolded, his answer—" 'No, unless it was predestined' "—remains equally, and comically, elusive.

Since Rabelais brings Gargantua back for just this consultation and one later chapter, and gives him the last word, that word (36, 459–60) is worth noting. He marvels that since he left this world (translated to fairyland in II: 23, 267), "le monde est devenu beau filz" [people have become sharp], and the most learned and prudent philosophers have joined the Pyrrhonists and other skeptics. Lions, he says, may be caught by their mane, also horses; oxen by their horns (and so on for a list of seven); "but never will such philosophers be caught by their words." Twice he praises God for the change He hath wrought; but his tone seems to be one of ruefully amused resignation.

Here end the consultations with the experts. From Pantagruel's advice in chapter 10 we have come full circle. Panurge must make up his mind, but cannot; he must do what he wills, but he cannot achieve a firm and resolute will.

Now comes Pantagruel's question to Panurge: Since you don't like the answers of the wise, why don't you try a fool? When Panurge agrees, they decide on Triboullet and discuss him at length. Then, however, they go on to the Parlement of Myrelingues, where, Pantagruel has learned, his old friend Judge Bridoye may be in trouble. For six chapters (39–44) Triboullet is forgotten while we listen to Judge Bridoye, who is not consulted at all; then we return for the consultation with Triboullet.[12]

Bridoye had been mentioned already as Pantagruel's friend (29, 435), as a widower, and as one of the original three authorities. Later (36, 460) we learn that he had been summoned to the Parlement of Myrelingues to defend a sentence given by him and appealed, and that over four thousand of his sentences have been definitive, 2,309 appealed—and all sustained. Pantagruel, noting that justice needs help in these bad times, plans to go to his aid. For four chapters (39–42) Bridoye explains that, "like you gentlemen" [comme vous aultres, Messieurs], he makes his decisions by rolling dice (alea judiciorum: the dice, or hazards, of justice), and that his eyesight, weakened by age, leads him now to make mistakes about the number of dots on the dice—all this with countless Latin references to well-known legal authorities—and then tells how, and why, lawsuits must ripen before they are settled.

The next two chapters (43–44) are puzzling in their final form. In 43

Pantagruel sees God's hand in this, and asks the Parlement to pardon Bridoye and give him a younger man to help him, or else let himself, Pantagruel, put him to use. Then in 44 he tells the story of a complex problem of justice involving a woman of Smyrna, which even the Areopagus postponed for a hundred years. It might, he says, have been decided just as well by dice; but Bridoye's continued success astonishes him. Then Epistémon (pp. 485–86) explains Bridoye's case as one of Christian folly. This obviously makes no sense: Pantagruel at first understands this, then does not and must have it explained to him.

Walter Kaiser has shown that to make sense of this we need to follow the original reading of 1546 (not that of the "definitive" edition of 1552), in which it was Epistémon, not Pantagruel, who told the story of the woman of Smyrna, and then Pantagruel, not Epistémon, who more fully explained Bridoye as a Christian fool.[13] Since it seems clear that Rabelais (or conceivably his printer) nodded when he made the change, I shall follow the first edition.

Two statements show Bridoye as a Christian fool. In the first, Pantagruel tells the court: "And it seems to me that there is something—I know not what—of God in this [je ne sçay quoy de Dieu], Who has ordered and dispensed that in these judgments by lot all the preceding sentences have been found good in this venerable and sovereign court of yours—God Who, as you know, often wants His glory to appear in the stupefaction of the wise, in the lowering of the mighty, and in the elevation of the simple and humble" (43, 483). The other statement (44, 485–86), which is more complex and longer—too long to quote in full—belonged to Pantagruel until reassigned to Epistémon in 1552. He credits Bridoye's good fortune in judging to the benevolent regard of the heavens and the favor of the moving intelligences, which considered the "simplicity and sincere affection" of Bridoye, his mistrust of his own knowledge and capacity, his understanding of the Devil's wiles, and the fact that he in his perplexity "would commend himself humbly to God the just judge, invoke the aid of celestial grace, put his trust in the sacrosanct spirit for the chance and perplexity of the definitive sentence and, by this lot, would explore its decree and good pleasure." In all this, he finds, "there is no harm, but in the anxiety and doubt of humans, the divine will is manifested by lot."

The comedy of Bridoye rests largely in his complete assurance that in rolling dice to settle his cases he is acting like everyone else, and in the strings of abbreviated legal sources that he so readily rattles off.[14]

There remains the consultation with the court fool Triboullet, which takes up only a page (487) but leads to several pages of inter-pretation. Panurge gives him an inflated hog's bladder containing some peas (both items presumably dried), a gilded wooden sword, a little game pouch made of a tortoise shell, a wicker-covered bottle full of Breton wine, and a quarter pound of apples. Triboullet puts on the sword, eats some of the apples, drinks all the wine; then, before Pan-urge has finished explaining his problem, he hits him between the shoulders, gives him back the bottle, raps his nose with the bladder, and says, shaking his head: "Par Dieu, Dieu, fol enraigé, guare moine! cornemuse de Buzançay!" ["By God, God, mad fool, beware monk! Buzançais bagpipe!"]. He then goes off, plays with the bladder, refuses to utter another word, and threatens Panurge with his wooden sword when he tries to question him further.

Panurge brands Triboullet a fool, and a greater fool the one (Car-palim) who brought him (45, 488). Pantagruel pronounces Triboul-let's head shaking a sign of divine inspiration (45–46, 488–90) and this prophecy the worst yet for Panurge, since it shows not only that he will be cuckolded but why and by whom:

"He says that you are a fool? And what kind of fool? A crazy fool, who in your old age want to bind and enslave yourself in marriage. He says to you 'Beware monk!' On my honor, that by some monk you will be made a cuckold. I pledge my honor to it. . . . Note how much I defer to our foolish-wise Triboullet. The other oracles and replies have resolved you peacefully cuckolded, but had not yet openly expressed by whom your wife would be adulterous and yourself cuckolded. This noble Triboullet tells you. And the cuckoldry will be infamous and most scandalous. Must your con-jugal bed be defiled and contaminated by monkery?
"He says further that you will be the bagpipe [cornemuse] of Buzançais, that is to say well horned in every way [corné, cornard et cornu]. . . .
"Note further that he rapped your nose with the bladder, and hit you on the spine with his fist: that predicts that by her you will be beaten, tweaked in the nose, and robbed." (45–46, 488–90)

Panurge, of course, takes the opposite view. Although he admits that he belongs among the fools and that everything is foolish (or mad), he explains the "Beware monk!" [Guare moine!] as a reference to a spar-row [moineau], as with Catullus' Lesbia; the "cornemuse de Buzan-çay" as an allusion to his preference for rustic amours; and his blow on the spine and rapping of the nose as innocent fooleries, the first by Triboullet, the second between himself and his wife. With that we are ready for the end of the *Third Book* and for the two remaining books.

———

Triboullet's return of the empty bottle prompts Panurge to seek the word of the Divine Bottle and to urge Pantagruel to make the voyage with him (47, 492). Pantagruel agrees, provided he has his father's consent. Gargantua readily approves but says he would like to see his son married. He notes Panurge's undecidedness and tells Pantagruel to speak for himself. His son's answer seems clearly to have Rabelais's approval. " 'Most gracious father, . . . I hadn't yet thought about it: for all that business I was relying on your good will and paternal command. I pray to God rather to be seen stone dead at your feet to your displeasure than, without your pleasure, to be seen alive and married. I have never heard that by any law, whether sacred or profane and barbaric, it has been within the free choice of children to marry without the consent, will, and promotion of their fathers, mothers, and close relatives" (48, 494-95). In a long and violent diatribe that follows against clandestine marriages arranged by priests without the consent of the parents, Gargantua advocates killing the priests and grooms who thus steal daughters from their parents. Then he tells Pantagruel to take all he needs for his voyage and let him, Gargantua, arrange his marriage.

Two points are worth noting in this chapter 48. The violence of Gargantua, who presumably speaks for Rabelais, is very bold. As Screech has shown,[15] it condemns the Church's official view (that marriage is primarily the Church's affair and parental consent not indispensable but merely desirable), and takes a position far stronger than that of Erasmus and close to that of the Lutherans, favoring Imperial over canon law. The other point is that now for the first time we are dealing with two marriages, Pantagruel's as well as Panurge's. Panurge seems to be quite alone in the world; since no mention is ever made of any parents or relatives, we may assume that he has none. Nevertheless, the contrast is striking between Pantagruel's trusting acceptance of a marriage to be arranged by his father, and Panurge's frantic determination to marry on his own terms and inability to make up his mind to do so. The additional viewpoint it gives us on Panurge is scarcely to his credit.

The Pantagruelion enigma, which concludes the *Third Book* (ch. 49-52), is one of the most baffling passages in Rabelais. Twenty-odd years ago V. L. Saulnier distinguished eight moments in the history of its interpretation: Pantagruelion is (1) hemp; (2) the tie (rope) of hanged Protestants; (3) an apologia of human industry; (4) a souvenir of the region; (5) a technical enigma designed for the learned; (6) a prophecy of aviation; (7) literary advertising; (8) once again, a piece in praise of work. To these Saulnier adds a ninth, *hésuchisme*, or crypto-Evangelism.[16]

At least four more interpretations have been advanced, mainly since then: Pantagruelion is (10) a parody of the rhetorical eulogy (Screech); (11) hashish (Boulenger, Jean-Louis Barrault); (12) truth (Kaiser); and (13) the male reproductive power, or more specifically the male member (Morgan).[17]

Only numbers 2 and 4 through 7 of these, in my judgment, may be dismissed lightly; 8 repeats 3; which leaves seven theories: 1, 3 (and 8), and 9–13.* Mindful that any summary is also an interpretation, let us see what is in the four chapters.

Chapter 49, "How Pantagruel Made His Preparations for Going to Sea, and of the Herb Named Pantagruelion," describes hemp (*cannabis sativa*) and linen (asbestos will be added later) treated as a single plant, following mainly Pliny the Elder but also Charles Estienne.[18] The title of chapter 50 explains its subject: "How the Famous Pantagruelion Is to Be Prepared and Put to Use." Its discussion of how plants have been named continues into chapter 51, "Why It Is Called Pantagruelion, and of Its Admirable Virtues." One reason is that Pantagruel was the inventor (51, 505), not of the plant itself, but of its use to hang robbers. Another is resemblance (51, 506), for Pantagruel at birth was about the size of Pantagruelion. Yet another is its virtues:

> For, as Pantagruel was the idea and exemplar of all joyous perfection (I think that not one of you drinkers doubts it), so in Pantagruelion I recognize so many virtues, so much energy, so many perfections, so many admirable effects, that if it had been known in its qualities when the trees (by the account of the prophet† elected a wooden king to rule and dominate them, it would doubtless have won the plurality of the votes and suffrages. (51, 506)

Rabelais goes on to detail its virtues—medicinal, vestimentary, and general: partly of linen, mainly of hemp. On these last depends our ability to sail, and thus for all parts of the earth to meet and form one

---

* Roland Antonioli offers what might be counted as a fourteenth theory when he finds two images of the Pantagruelion jointly dominant in the episode: "that of the beneficent plant which places the hidden energies of Nature at the service of man, and that of the truth destined to germinate and spread about some day in the world." *Rabelais et la médecine, ER* XII (1976), p. 301.
† Jotham, in Judges 9:8 ff.

world. This frightens "the celestial intelligences, the Gods of the sea as well as of the earth" (51, 509), and the Olympian gods as well. They know that Pantagruel will soon marry and have children; this is destined by the Fates and cannot be stopped. His children, they fear, may invent an herb of similar energy and use it to visit the sources of hail, rain, and lightning; to invade the regions of the moon and lodge in the territory of the celestial signs; to " 'sit at table with us and take our goddesses for wives, which are the only means of being deified' " (51, 509). So they deliberate about what to do.

Chapter 52, "How a Certain Kind of Pantagruelion Cannot Be Consumed by Fire," brings in asbestos as another form of the herb; tells how this can only be purified by fire, though what it encloses may be entirely consumed; and rejects the comparison of the salamander, emblem of Francis I (still alive), who had once been the protector, then the persecutor, of the Evangelicals: "To be sure, I confess that a little straw fire invigorates and delights it. But I assure you that in a great furnace it is, like any other living creature, suffocated and consumed. We have seen the test of this" (52, 511).

For resistance to fire, Rabelais rejects the comparison with other plants, including larix, which is ultimately consumed by a raging blaze, whereas "asbestine Pantagruelion is rather renewed and cleansed in it than corrupted or altered" (52, 513). Therefore, Rabelais concludes the chapter and the book,

> Indes, cessez, Arabes, Sabiens,
> Tant collauder vos myrrhe, encent, ébène.
> Venez icy recongnoistre nos biens,
> Et emportez de nostre herbe la grène;
> Puys, si chez vous peut croistre en bonne estrène,
> Grâces rendez ès cieulx un million,
> Et affermez de France heureux le règne
> Onquel provient Pantagruelion. (52, 513-14)

> [Stop, Indes, Sabians, and Arabies,
> Such praise of ebony, incense, and myrrh;
> No, come to us our goods to recognize,
> And carry back the grain from our own herb;
> Then if a good present can grow with you,
> Give thanks to heaven by the million,
> And praise the happy rule as France's due
> In which there came Pantagruelion.]

To return to the theories. The first one listed by Saulnier, that Pantagruelion is hemp, seems only partly true (it is also linen, asbestos

—and Pantagruelion) and not productive; surely there is more to the enigma than that. The hashish theory rests on the identity with *cannabis sativa*, but seems to me unsupported by the text. That of Pantagruelion as representing the male reproductive power, perhaps the male member, is supported by some of the description and fits the concern with marriage and reproduction. That of a parody of a rhetorical eulogy balances the conclusion nicely with the opening praise of debts and seems compatible with the three other theories, but also seems to leave much unaccounted for.

Saulnier's theory of crypto-Evangelism is well supported by the last two chapters (51–52). (However, if asbestos represents *hésuchisme*, I should think the egg enclosed in asbestos—p. 511—would represent the believer; but clearly such an egg emerges from the fire fully cooked and burned.) For the robbers hanged (read: the persecutors) and the salamander (read: Francis I) this theory works perfectly. It makes the enigma a fit ending for the book and relates the entire book to the *Fourth*, and this episode to the many in which Saulnier finds this meaning. Kaiser's theory that Pantagruelion is truth offers some of the same advantages.

The view that Pantagruelion represents an apologia of human industry and progress seems to me the most solid of all, clearly suggested by the concluding part of chapter 51. Surely this is the message conveyed by the praise of what man has achieved thanks to linen and especially to hemp, bringing together distant parts of the globe, and by the fear of his accomplishments among the Olympian gods. This view could, I think, be reconciled with Screech's parody of the rhetorical eulogy; but it seems closer to Rabelais's serious manner. Whatever else this enigma means, I think it clearly means that.

In short, I have no new theory of the Pantagruelion; I find several beguiling but none quite able to account for all the text. I suspect that the enigma contains more than one key idea, perhaps several. I see no incompatibility between the theories of *hésuchisme*, or truth, and of praise of human industry, or between these and a parodistic element; they all seem justified by parts of the text and might be parts of Rabelais's message.

On the other hand, this may be one of the many episodes in Rabelais that we do not yet understand.

Though the Pantagruelion remains cryptic, the plan and sense of the book seem clear. The specific issue is Panurge's desire to marry and his inability to make up his mind; but broader issues are marriage itself, how to approach it, and how to make a decision whose results are unpredictable. Pantagruel deplores Panurge's indecisiveness and blames it on self-love, stubbornness, and the seduction of the Devil; by the end of the book Rabelais contrasts it with Pantagruel's acceptance of his father's will. The advisers, who include friends, random magicians, learned authorities, and a fool, are by no means all misguided or professionally deformed: Rondibilis and Trouillogan, and even more so Raminagrobis and Hippothadée, tell Panurge just what he needs—but cannot use. (The last three come close to the wise advice of Pantagruel himself.) The fault is with Panurge. Where Bridoye is the Christian fool, and Triboullet the professional fool, Panurge—engaging as he is—is the fool *tout court*, the plain self-made human fool.

Saulnier's theory that the *Third Book* tells of consulting ready-made authorities, and the *Fourth* of "the itinerary of a conscience making its way toward the truth amid the ambushes of the world" (*Le Dessein*, p. 39), seems, for all its elegance, too kind to Panurge, in whom I see no clear sign of such self-searching. (Think of him in the tempest or off Ganabin.) I think we must settle—at least for now—for the simpler, obvious relationship: Panurge, in the *Third Book*, is dissatisfied with all his consultations and their unfavorable answers; he must have the answer of the Divine Bottle, which the comrades travel to seek, and find at last at the end of the *Fifth Book*. If there is more independence in Panurge's search later, he is still seeking someone else's ready-made answer. As it turns out, it will be cryptic and require his own interpretation; but nothing suggests that he knows or even suspects this in advance. What he wants is a ready-made answer that will please him. In the end, in the *Fifth Book*, he will get it—or think he gets it.

The *Fourth Book*
(1548–1552)

The *Fourth*, Rabelais's longest, tells of part of the voyage, announced in the *Third Book*, to consult the oracle of the Divine Bottle. It appeared in two installments, a partial edition (eleven chapters) in 1548 and the complete one (sixty-seven chapters) in 1552. The partial one comprises about the first thirty percent of the complete one; its eleven chapters, later subdivided, became chapters 1, 5–12, 16–24, and part of 25; it ends abruptly just after the account of the tempest.

After the appearance of the *Third Book* early in 1546 and its prompt censure by the Sorbonne, Rabelais had gone to Metz—perhaps in flight, perhaps as an agent—and found employment presumably as a counselor. It was probably there that he composed the partial edition of the *Fourth Book*, as well as an *Almanach* since lost. Probably late in 1547, on his way to Rome again as doctor to Cardinal Jean du Bellay, he left both manuscripts with Pierre de Tours in Lyons for publication. Certain inconsistencies in the partial edition, and its abrupt ending, suggest that Rabelais was in a hurry and may have needed money, as we know he did earlier that year.

He left Rome with Du Bellay on September 22, 1549, and in early November was in Lyons. He was probably with the cardinal in Saint-Maur late in 1550, and possibly for longer. On August 6, 1550, another influential protector, Cardinal Odet de Chastillon, got him the royal privilege to reprint his earlier works and print the sequel. Thus encouraged, he completed the *Fourth Book* late in 1551.

The encouragement and protection were needed. Besides having his works condemned by the Sorbonne, Rabelais had been violently attacked from both sides: in 1549 by the Sorbonagre Dupuyherbault

(Putherbeus) and in 1550 by John Calvin. The Prologue to the incomplete *Fourth Book* and the letter dedicating the complete book to Chastillon tell of his heartsickness at such attacks.

Meanwhile the Council of Trent had been meeting since December 1545, tightening Catholic doctrine, confirming the split with the Protestants, and fostering the Counter Reformation. Henry II of France, finding the Council dominated by Italians, threatened to convoke a Gallican council instead as the true one. Rabelais refers to Trent as the "national council of Fools" (35, 636) and blames it for the tempest that threatens Pantagruel's ships and company. His Gallican sympathies are especially manifest in the episode of the Papimanes [Papimaniacs].

Although it continues the *Third Book*, the *Fourth* is very different. Where attention earlier had centered on the characters, now much of it goes to the strange people and creatures whom the voyagers meet. The story is that of the encounters; and the pattern of these—with some exceptions such as Quaresmeprenant [Lent-Observer] and the Andouilles [Chitterlings], the Papefigues [Pope-Figgers] and the Papimaniacs—is less clear than in the earlier books, the plot more episodic. Three main sources of Rabelais's fantasy may be partly responsible for this: Lucian's *True History* for the incredible voyage; the macaronic *Baldus* of Merlin Coccai (Teofilo Folengo) for three episodes: the sheep merchant, the tempest, and the whale; and the anonymous (and undistinguished) *Disciple de Pantagruel* of 1538 (also known as *Les Navigations de Panurge*) for Bringuenarilles the windmill-eater, the battle with the Andouilles, and the island of Ruach [Wind or Spirit]. A more general source is the accounts of contemporary voyages of discovery, notably that of Jacques Cartier. In every case, however, Rabelais's comic inventiveness makes his treatment fully his own.

Less important than in the *Third Book*, the characters in the *Fourth* are more sharply defined, sometimes almost typed: the blasphemously courageous and often reckless man of action, Frère Jean; the superstitious, heresy-sniffing, cowardly man of words, Panurge; the pious, idealized, effective philosopher-king, Pantagruel. Like the *Third Book*, the *Fourth* is full of learning, displayed mostly—often at great length —by Pantagruel, as incident after incident puts him in mind of classical analogues. The strength of the book lies mainly in Rabelais's fantasy and in the ways he uses it to veil, and to reveal, serious ideas, mostly Gallican and Evangelical.

Both editions of the *Fourth Book* are signed "M. François Rabelais,

Docteur en Médicine." The partial edition is preceded by the "Old Prologue," addressed to "most illustrious drinkers and you, most precious pockified blades" (p. 730), who, says Rabelais, have sent him word that they are ready and willing to judge his case: "Vous donnez, vous dictes, vous adjugez" (You give, you say, you adjudicate).* What they give, he answers, is a fine ample breviary. By this he presumably means a flask in the form of a breviary; and this leads him rather deviously to the origin of the phrase "crocquer pie" ("drink hearty"; literally, "eat magpie") in a horrendous battle between the jays and the magpies, which resulted in vast slaughter of magpies and in the cry of one triumphant pet jay to the guests whom, as before, he invited to drink), which now became "crocquez pie." The upshot is that by their "giving" they are inviting the narrator to drink; and he readily accepts.

"You say," he then goes on, "that I have not angered you in any way by all my earlier books, and that the wine of the *Third Book* was to your taste." For this he thanks them and recognizes them as good people [gens de bien].

"You adjudicate," he continues, "all the old quarters of the moon" (the marks of lunacy) to the "caphards, cagotz" (p. 733), and other such loathsome monsters; and for almost four pages he goes on to denounce "the calumniators of my writings." They might better be called devils; they spoil good food by "spitting in the basin" that contains it. They have done this to my books so as to keep them for themselves alone, denying them to the invalids for whom I had composed them in the hope of helping more patients than I could personally treat, by "the pleasure and joyous pastime, without offense to God, to the King, or to any other, that they take in my absence by hearing the reading of these joyous books" (pp. 734–35).

He concludes with the story of Timon of Athens telling his ungrateful fellow Athenians of his handsome fig tree, from which many had hanged themselves, warning them that he plans to cut it down in a week, and urging them to hang themselves from it before it is gone. Rabelais invites his calumniators to do the same and offers to supply the halters.

In this long counterattack against his critics, Rabelais goes further

* Robert Marichal, in his Textes Littéraires Français edition of the *Quart Livre* (1947), explains that this was the formula of the Roman praetor: "do judicem" [I designate such-and-such a judge], "dico jus" [I expose the plaintiff's claim, the juridical act], "addico litem" [I assign the object to litigation, giving the judge the power to absolve or to condemn] (p. 286, fn. 13).

than in the Prologue to the *Third Book*, but in the same direction. And here for the first time he offers his explanation that his books are written to make the sick merry and thus to improve their health.

Worth noting are some of the changes in the chapters that appeared in both 1548 and 1552. In chapter 1 (p. 542) he corrects one boner, his statement that the entire voyage was made safely and in fair weather. In chapter 6, when Panurge is preparing to play his deadly trick on the sheep merchant Dindenault, in 1548 he calls on Pantagruel and Frère Jean to witness the sport, and they do so. In 1552, not wanting to involve Pantagruel in so cruel a game even as a witness, Rabelais has Panurge invite Frère Jean and Epistémon; and he adds Frère Jean's concluding rebuke to Panurge (8, 561): "You are damning yourself like an old devil. It is written: Vengeance is mine, etc. Breviary matter."

Most striking are the changes in the account of the tempest, especially at the start (19, 594). Rabelais had originally described the action thus:

Pantagruel (par l'advis du Pillot) tenoit l'arbre fort et ferme. Frère Jean s'estoit mis en pourpoinct, pour secourir les Nauchers, aussi estoient Epistemon, Ponocrates, et les autres. Panurge restoit de cul sur le tillac, plourant et lamentant.[1]

[Pantagruel, on the advice of the pilot, held the mast strong and firm. Frère Jean had stripped to his doublet to help the sailors; so had Epistémon, Ponocrates, and the others. Panurge stayed on his ass on the deck, crying and lamenting.]

In 1552 Rabelais adds, directly after "Pantagruel," "préalablement avoir imploré l'ayde du grand Dieu Servateur et faicte oraison publicque en fervente dévotion" [after first having implored the help of great God the Savior, and having offered public prayer in fervent devotion]. Here mere action is replaced by prayer followed by action, and Pantagruel is set apart not only from Panurge but also from Frère Jean and the others; for he is the only one who prays. Of the many other 1552 additions (of which several make Frère Jean even more irreverent), two are similar: Pantagruel's cry "May good God the Savior come to our aid" (20, 599), and his even more pious prayer (21, 601): "Then was heard a piteous exclamation by Pantagruel, saying aloud: 'Lord God, save us: we perish! However, let it not happen according to our desires; but Thy holy will be done!' "[2]

The same spirit prompts one significant deletion. In the 1548 version, after the tempest had passed, Epistémon said that the way we die is "partly in the will of the gods, partly in our own";[3] in 1552 Rabelais changes this to read simply "in the holy will of God" (23, 606).

All these changes show Rabelais's stress in 1551–52 on the piety of Pantagruel, in incidental contrast with the impiety of Frère Jean.

Excellent Rabelais, the partial edition includes two of his finest episodes, the sheep merchant and the tempest. I find it closer to the *Third Book* than the rest of the *Fourth*, by virtue of the focus on Panurge and the infrequency of religious satire, found only in the reference to Trent as the "concile de Chesil" (18, 591). The account of the lay sermon, prayer, and psalm singing (1, 540–41) is Evangelical, but hardly polemical or satirical.

The complete edition of 1552 is accompanied by three other texts: the letter to Chastillon, the New Prologue, and—in certain copies and in the 1553 edition—the ten-page "Briefve Declaration" [Brief Declaration of Some of the More Obscure Expressions Contained in the Fourth Book of the Heroic Deeds and Sayings of Pantagruel] (pp. 737–46). Composed just before Marc-Antoine Muret's commentary on Ronsard's *Amours*, the Declaration explains some difficult terms, especially early in the book. It has generally been attributed (with some hesitation) to Rabelais and printed with his works. In recent years however, discrepancies between the sense of certain words as Rabelais uses them in the text of the *Fourth Book* and the definitions given for them in the "Brief Declaration" have led one scholar to question Rabelais's authorship and, more recently, another scholar to flatly deny it.[4]

More interesting is the dedicatory letter "To the Very Illustrious Prince and Most Reverend Lord Odet, Cardinal de Chastillon" (pp. 517–22) of January 28, 1552. Oldest of the noble Coligny family, elder brother of Gaspard de Coligny, the future Protestant leader who was to die in the St. Bartholomew's Day Massacre, Odet had been a cardinal (hence a "prince") since 1533, at the age of eighteen, and was soon to turn Protestant. Highly regarded in councils of state, he was Rabelais's last protector and one of his stanchest.

Whereas in 1548 Rabelais had complained of his calumniators in his Old Prologue, now in 1552 he does so solely in his letter to Chastillon. He says he has been asked to continue his "mythologies Pantagruelicques" [fabulous Pantagruelic narratives], especially since they make the sick better, and gives his now customary reply that they were written for that. He enlarges on the importance for the patient of the cheerful bearing of the doctor. Then, less fiercely than before, he turns to his calumniators:

But the calumny of certain cannibals, misanthropes, never-laughers, against me had been so atrocious and unreasonable that it had conquered my patience, and I was resolved not to write one iota more of these books. For one of the least of the slanders they used was that such books were all stuffed with various heresies (however, they could not point out a single one in any place); with gay lunacies, without offense to God or to the King, plenty: that is the sole subject and theme of these books; with heresies none, unless perversely and against all use of reason and of ordinary speech they interpreted what, on pain of dying a thousand times, if that were possible, I would not want to have thought: as if someone should interpret bread as stone, fish as snake, egg as scorpion. Once, complaining of this in your presence, I said to you freely that if I did not consider myself a better Christian than they show themselves to be for their part, and if in my life, writings, words, indeed even thoughts, I recognized any scintilla of heresy, they would not fall so detestably into the snares of the calumniating spirit, that is, the Devil, who by their ministry raises such a crime against me: by myself, like the phoenix, would the kindling be piled up and the fire lit to burn myself in it. (p. 520)

Chastillon, Rabelais goes on, replied that the late King Francis I, notified of these calumnies, had Rabelais's books read to him and found nothing suspect; likewise his son Henry II, who at Chastillon's request had granted Rabelais his royal privilege and protection, as Chastillon had told Rabelais both in Paris and while visiting his good friend Jean du Bellay at Saint-Maur.

Accordingly, says Rabelais, "now, free from all intimidation, I trust my pen to the wind" (p. 521), confident in Chastillon's continued protection. Whatever I write it will be thanks to you: "For by your so honorable exhortation, you have given me both courage and inventiveness; and without you my heart had failed, and the fountain of my animal spirits remained dried up" (p. 522).

Even if we allow for exaggeration in a dedicatory letter, I think we may take this as expressing Rabelais's feelings. For the existence of the *Fourth* and *Fifth Books* we are probably much in debt to Chastillon.

The new Prologue to the complete *Fourth Book*, Rabelais's longest, is free of personal problems. It contains his final definition of Pantagruelism (p. 523), as "a certain gaiety of spirit pickled in disdain for fortuitous things,"* which sums up its cheerful acceptance of modera-

---

* Reminiscent not only of Stoicism in general but of a book by Rabelais's late friend Budé, *De Contemptu Rerum Fortuitarum* [Of the Disdain for Fortuitous Things] (1522).

tion [médiocrité]. It dwells on the theme "God's will be done" (pp. 523, 525, 537), and suggests that a moderate wish for oneself (such as for health) may be in accord with God's will. When he wrote it, Rabelais had probably less than two years to live and may have been very ill.

The main part of the Prologue tells the story (taken from Aesop, perhaps via the *Adages* of Erasmus) of Couillatris and his lost ax (pp. 526–27, 533–37). There is a long interruption (527–33) in which Jupiter, hearing the wails of Couillatris, complains of being interrupted from settling the affairs of the world and asks Priapus what to do about the quarrel over Aristotle between Peter Ramus (anti) and Pierre Galland (pro). Priapus first suggests that he turn them both to stone (Peter, Pierre), then discourses on the meanings of *coingnée* [ax, or screwed] and tells of a host of recent musicians singing bawdy songs on related matters; then we return to Couillatris.

Couillatris was a country woodchopper whose meager living depended on his ax. One day he lost it, and he screamed to Jupiter to give it back. Tired of the racket, Jupiter sent down Mercury to let him choose his ax out of three: a gold one, a silver one, and his own. He chose his own, was given the other two as well, and by selling them became rich. Others, hearing his story, bought axes if they had none and lost them in order to get rich. They were offered the choice, chose the gold, and had their heads chopped off—all this by Jupiter's order. The moral, indicated from the outset and stressed several times later (pp. 525, 526, 534, 536), is this: "So wish for moderation [médiocrité]; it will come to you, and all the more duly, if in the meantime you are tilling and working" (p. 537).

The two ideals—being content with what is ours, and cheerful disregard of things beyond our control—constitute the message of the Prologue. This is not the exuberant optimism of the first two books, but an exhortation to be untroubled and joyful if we can. This quest of resolute cheer sets the tone of the last three books.

The sixty-seven chapters of the *Fourth Book* comprise twenty episodes, eight of which fill much of it. In general, the 1548 material—most of the first twenty-five chapters—is relatively unpolemical, the remaining two-thirds equally Evangelical and more outspokenly Gallican.

In skeletal outline, listed by chapters, the book appears as follows: the Evangelical departure (1); the arrival at Medamothi [Nowhere], the fantastic purchases, the exchange of letters and messages with Gargantua (2–4); Dindenault the sheep merchant, how he taunted Panurge, and how Panurge got him drowned (5–8); Ennasin, the Island of Alliances (9); the Island of Cheli [Peace], ruled by King Saint Panigon (10–11); Procuration, the land of the Chiquanous (process-servers), who make their living by being beaten, and Panurge's story of how the Lord of Basché managed to have them beaten with impunity (12–16); the islands of Thohu and Bohu, and the strange death of the giant Bringuenarilles, who swallowed windmills (17); the tempest, and Panurge's helpless and superstitious cowardice (18–24). Next the travelers come to the island of the Macræons [the Long-Lived], with the stories of the deaths of Langey and of Pan (25–28); pass the Island of Tapinois, ruled by Quaresmeprenant [Lent-Observer], a gloomy giant of feeble brain who reminds Pantagruel of the children of Antiphysie [Antinature], who include Calvin and Dupuyherbault (29–32); have victorious encounters with the whale (33–34) and with Quaresmeprenant's enemies the Chitterlings (35–42); and reach the island of Ruach [Wind or Spirit] (43–44). In 45–47 they visit the home of the Papefigues [Pope-Figgers] who "make the sign of the fig" to the Pope—a desolate island where a little devil is fooled by an ingenious native woman; in 48–54, the Island of the Papimanes [Papimaniacs], who worship the Pope as God on earth and wax ecstatic over the divine Decretals, which support the Roman curia with French money and consign all heretics to hell on earth and below. In 55–56 they hear, see, and touch the frozen and unfrozen words; in 57–62 they visit the island and manor of Messere Gaster [Stomach], the one great source of human invention and artifice, and his court, where Pantagruel abominates Gaster's worshipers. The concluding chapters bring the travelers to the island of Chaneph [Hypocrisy] (63); to a calm spell at sea where they compete to "haulser le temps" [raise the weather; i.e., pass the time] (64–65); and finally to the island of Ganabin [Robbers] where, prompted by Pantagruel's Socratic daemon, they do not land, and to the abrupt conclusion off Ganabin where the ships fire their cannon and Panurge beshits his breeches but laughs it off glibly with a final invitation to drink (66–67).

Of the twenty episodes, eight fill almost two-thirds of the book: Dindenault (four chapters), the Chiquanous (five), the tempest (seven), Quaresmeprenant (four), the Chitterlings (eight), the Papefigues (three), the Papimanes (seven), and Messere Gaster (six).

For all the scholarship of the last seventy, and especially the last twenty, years, the over-all plan and sense of the *Fourth Book* are still elusive. The traditional view, of Abel Lefranc and his collaborators, related it mainly to the geographical explorations of the time. For later scholars this has not sufficed. Saulnier's view of it in *Le Dessein de Rabelais* as the quest of a conscience for true answers amid the ambushes of the world seems appealing but still stretches the text, which has little to say or suggest about the conscience of Panurge. Most useful, in my judgment, are a series of insights mainly by Saulnier, Marichal, and especially Screech about individual episodes which find, behind much of the fantasy, a covert Evangelism and a Gallicanism that inform the books and fit the historical Rabelais. There may be still more to be found, but at least there is clearly this; it is enough to explain why Rabelais wrote the book, and is far more satisfying than the explorational view.

Harder to discern is any pattern that knits more than a few episodes together. Six of them pair off well—tempest-Macraeons, Quaresmeprenant-Chitterlings, Papefigues-Papimanes—but how does one pair lead to the next, why do the others come in the order they do, and why is the conclusion so abrupt? The book still appears rather episodic, lacking the obvious structure of the first two and the last, and the subtler structure of the *Third*. It is of course an Evangelical and Gallican voyage in quest of an answer; but some episodes seem to have little to do with either the quest or the answer.

Whereas *Pantagruel* is devoted mainly to comedy and adventure; *Gargantua* to comedy, adventure, and ideas; and the *Third Book* to ideas and comedy—with some satire also present, and religion important, in all three—the *Fourth Book* includes, besides comedy and ideas (especially religious), a great deal of satire and fantasy. The dominance of these elements distinguishes the last two books from the first three.

Often combined with other elements, fantasy abounds in the *Fourth Book*. Already in Medamothi (2–4), besides the account of the homing pigeon, we read that the travelers purchase pictures of Plato's Ideas, Epicurus' Atoms, Echo, the rape of Philomela by Tereus (not realistically portrayed), five unicorns, and that marvelous beast the "tarande." In Ennasin they find a race resembling the "red-painted Poitevins," but with noses like the ace of clubs (9). Cheli offers too much feasting and civilities, and Frère Jean, as a good monk, resorts to the affluent kitchens (10–11). On Thohu and Bohu the travelers learn that the giant Bringuenarilles, for lack of his usual windmills, has swallowed all the pots, pans, and caldrons, but has choked to death on a piece of fresh butter eaten at the mouth of a hot oven by his doctors' prescriptions (17).

The laments and disturbances of earth, sea, and sky at the death of a daemon or a hero constitute a more serious kind of fantasy (26, 612). Chapters 33-34 tell of the monstrous whale who attacked and drenched all the ships with his spouting, apparently immune to shots from the ships' guns, but easily killed by Pantagruel's accurate javelins and darts. Fantasy abounds in the encounter with the bellicose Chitterlings, their horrendous slaughter by Frère Jean and by Pantagruel's aptly named cooks, and the intervention of their god, the brilliantly colored flying pig, casting down quantities of mustard and crying "Mardigras!" (35-42). It permeates the story of Ruach, whose inhabitants live on wind (43-44), and reappears in the frozen words (55-56). There are fantastic elements in the Gaster episode (57-62), especially the way bullets and cannon balls may be stopped in mid-flight and sent back to the one who fired them.

The fantasy of the *Fourth Book* is continued in the *Fifth*.

In the *Fourth Book* comedy is almost always mixed with other elements and usually subordinated to them. It is prominent in the Prologue with Priapus and Couillatris, and in the rich "slice-of-life" bargaining between Panurge and Dindenault (5-7). A hard-boiled sort appears in the drowning of Dindenault (8), the account of the Chiquanous (12-16), and the murderous trick played by François Villon on Friar Estienne Tappecoue (13). It abounds in the tempest, where Panurge's superstitious blubbering is opposed to Frère Jean's blasphemous but useful activity (18-24), and in the encounter with the Chitterlings (35-42). Beyond that I do not find much: the refrain "Et tout pour la trippe" [And all for tripes] of the first chapter on Messere Gaster (57); the time off Chaneph and the problem of "haulser le temps" (63-65); the trick played on Panurge off Ganabin, and the ready response of his bowels (66-67).

Less prominent than in the earlier books, especially the first two, comedy is most striking in those chapters that first appeared in the partial edition of 1548; in 1552 Rabelais seems to have less heart for it, even as Pantagruel is more removed. He is no longer an observer of Panurge's deadly trick on Dindenault (6-8); and at the start of 16 (p. 584)—again only in 1552—he rebukes Panurge for his cruel story of Villon and Tappecoue and of the Chiquanous: " 'That story,' said

Pantagruel, 'would seem joyous were it not that we must continually have the fear of God before our eyes.'" In the last two books, and even in the *Third*, pure comedy seems more of an effort than in the happier days of *Pantagruel* and *Gargantua*.

In the *Fourth Book* satire replaces some of the comedy. It is prominent in six principal episodes and many minor ones. Ennasin caricatures the more or less Platonic alliances popular at the time (9). The Chiquanous episode satirizes legal procedure and harassment by summonses (12–16). In anatomizing Quaresmeprenant (29–32), Xenomanes compares his brain in size, color, substance, and vigor to the left testicle of a male mite; and the rest of his anatomy is proportionate. Quaresmeprenant's activities consist of seeking things where obviously they cannot be. No wonder he reminds Pantagruel of Antiphysie and her progeny.

Although the chapters on the Chitterlings feature fantasy, comedy, and ideas (mainly religious), there is satire of their combined weakness and bellicosity; although it is they who attack Pantagruel's party, they could hardly be more feeble. The story of Ruach satirizes those who seek to live by spirit alone.

Satire abounds in the episode of the Papimaniacs. The travelers are greeted on sight with the cry "'Have you seen him, travelers? have you seen him?'" (48, 667). On the next page we learn that "him" is the "God on earth," the Pope. After elaborate preparations and the opening of forty-six locks, they are allowed to see a picture of the Pope and kiss the other end of a stick that touches it (50, 673–74). Most of the account of Papimania is the satiric presentation of its bishop Homenaz, his readiness to exterminate heretics, and his worship of the divine Decretals, which give the Papacy its power and its riches, most of these last extracted from France.

In the story of Messere Gaster (57–62) there is clear satire, not of him—he knows he is no god—but of his worshipers, the Gastrolâtres and Engastrimythes, whom Pantagruel detests (58, 697–99). Both groups represent doctors of the Sorbonne, and their god is their belly; but the Engastrimythes are not only gluttons but hypocrites as well.[5] In all this there is much parody also, but mainly satire of monks and theologians.

Finally, Ganabin is a satiric picture of the robbers and cutthroats whom Rabelais represents as the persecutors and heresy-hunters of Paris (66–67).

Religious ideas, mostly Evangelical and Gallican, are prominent in a dozen episodes and especially in six of the main ones.

The departure (1, 540–41) is markedly Evangelical, with its lay sermon, prayer in the vernacular (understood by all), and singing of Psalm 114 (in Marot's translation, condemned by the Sorbonne), which for the Evangelicals symbolized their plight in France.

Apart from Pantagruel's letter to Gargantua (4, 549–50) and his rebuke to Panurge for not showing a proper fear of God in his stories of the Chiquanous and Villon (16, 584), there is little more until we approach the tempest (18, 591). Then the travelers meet nine ships loaded with monks of many orders (thirteen named), "who were going to the Council of Chesil to examine the articles of faith against the new heretics." Panurge is delighted to see them, and throws money and thirst-provoking victuals into their ships. Pantagruel, however, remains pensive and melancholy. Although the tempest is not clearly blamed on the monks—Frère Jean blames it on Panurge (20, 597), and the Macrobe and Pantagruel on the death of a hero or daemon (26, 612–13)—they remain suspect. And the Council of Trent is treated not only as the Council of Fools [Chesil], but later, by Xenomanes (35, 636), as the "national council of fools" because of its domination by Italians.

We have noted the threefold pattern that Rabelais creates in the tempest in the 1552 edition (19, 594): Pantagruel praying, then working; Frère Jean and the others working; Panurge weeping and blubbering. It is a little reminiscent of Plato with his three functions of the soul and his classes of citizens in the *Republic*; but here Pantagruel's distinction is not his rationality but his piety. As in his prayer before doing battle with Loup Garou (29, 290–91), we see his author's view that in danger man must both pray and act in his own behalf.

The whole story of the tempest has a religious and moral message, in which again Panurge is at the bottom, Frère Jean a bit above, and Pantagruel at the top (18–24). Panurge constantly warns Frère Jean that his blasphemy is sinful; meanwhile he himself does nothing to help; and he vows, if he lives, to erect "a fine big little chapel or two" to the saints—"Sainct Michel d'Aure, sainct Nicolas"—on whom he so superstitiously calls (19, 596). Once the danger is past, however (24, 609), he explains that he meant an alembic to distill perfumes [chapelle d'eau rose]. Nowhere else, not even off Ganabin, does he show up as badly as here.

Throughout the tempest Frère Jean blasphemes, works, and taunts Panurge with his cowardly uselessness. Pantagruel, however (from 1552 on), not only works as usefully as Frère Jean, but three times invokes God's help (twice in prayer), and once asks that God's will, not his own, be done.

In chapter 27 the discussion of the death of heroes and daemons leads Pantagruel to a statement that goes back through Aquinas to Aristotle: " 'I believe,' said Pantagruel, 'that all intellective souls are exempt from the scissors of Atropos. All are immortal, those of angels, daemons, and humans' " (27, 617).[6]

In the following chapter Pantagruel, drawing on Plutarch, tells of the death of Pan and the supernatural command to the Egyptian pilot Thamous to announce it, then says that he interprets it to mean the death of Christ, our All. His piety and emotion are striking. Then Rabelais (or Alcofribas) concludes by proclaiming that Pantagruel's tears were the size of ostrich eggs.[7] The twist is very Rabelaisian. The comic undercuts the pathetic but does not destroy it; both the giant comedy and the religious emotion remain.

In chapters 29–32 Quaresmeprenant is not seen but anatomized and discussed at length. He is primarily superstitious, stupid, and sad, "abounding in pardons, indulgences, and stations, a worthy man, a good Catholic and very devout. He weeps three quarters of the day" (29, 620). Xenomanes compares his brain with a mite's testicle (30, 621). He is the mortal enemy of the Chitterlings. His anatomy (30–32), mainly ingenious and fantastic, ends with a series of pointless activities looking for things where they cannot be: "He bathed on the top of high steeples, dried himself in the ponds and rivers. He fished in the air and caught big crawfish. He hunted in the depths of the sea and there found ibexes, wild goats, and chamois" (32, 627).

Frère Jean wants to send him a challenge; but Pantagruel says that this "strange and monstrous figure of a man, if I am to call him a man" (32, 627), reminds him of Amodunt [Immoderate] and Discordance, children of Antiphysie [Antinature]. Their heads were spherical, their ears as big as asses' ears, their eyes protuberant; and they walked on their heads in a sort of cartwheel. Antiphysie, the adversary of Physis [Nature], persuaded many fools that her children were models of natural beauty, then went on to have more of them:

Depuys elle engendra les Matagotz, Cagotz et Papelars, les maniacles Pistoletz, les Démoniacles Calvins, imposteurs de Genève, les enraigéz Putherbes, Briffaulx, Caphars, Chattemites, Canibales et aultres monstres difformes et contrefaicts en despit de Nature. (32, 629)

[Later she engendered the Bigot monkeys, Hypocrites, and falsely pious, the maniacal Postels,* the demoniacal Calvins, impostors of Geneva, the rabid Putherbes,† the gluttonous monks, hypocritical monks, other hypocrites, cannibals, and other monsters deformed and misshapen in despite of Nature.]

The episode represents the observance of Lent as gloomy, monstrous, and unnatural. Enforcement of this was stiffened by the Council of Trent in 1547 over the opposition of France and the Empire.[8] Rabelais's attack is quite as Gallican as it is Evangelical.

The Chitterlings [Andouilles] of 35–42 are the age-old enemies of Quaresmeprenant, who would have exterminated them but for their protector Mardigras (29, 621), and are more or less identified with the Swiss (38, 643; cf. 35, 635) and hence possibly with the Calvinists. They too are hostile to the travelers, but ineffectively so.

The Papefigues (45–47), now "poor, unhappy, and subject to the Papimaniacs" (45, 660), represent not Calvinists or Lutherans but the Waldensians [Vaudois] of southern France, massacred in large numbers by Montmorency's army in 1545. In a chapel the travelers find a man hidden up to his nose in a basin of holy water, and learn of his difficulties with a little devil who claimed his field and the right to choose the part of the crop he wanted, above or under ground. The devil is not a good farmer: when the Papefigue plants wheat, he chooses what is underground; when he plants turnips, he chooses what is above. Infuriated at his humiliation when he tries to sell his "crops," the devil threatens the Papefigue with a scratching match until one of them quits. The Papefigue, terrified, hides in the holy water; his ingenious wife takes over, and routs the devil by showing him her vagina, that "enormous dissolution of continuity in all dimensions" (47, 667), and telling him that her "wound" was caused by a mere scratch from her husband.

Earlier the *diablotin* had given a left-handed compliment to the Evangelicals in telling of "Sir Lucifer's" eating habits:

"And he used to have lunch on students. But alas, I don't know by what misfortune, for some years they have added the Holy Bible to their studies; for this reason we can no longer draw a single one to the Devil. And I think that unless the hypocritical monks help us, taking their Saint Paul out of their

---

* The "Pistoletz" presumably represent Guillaume Postel (1510–81). See A. J. Krailsheimer, "Rabelais et Postel," *BHR* 13: 187–90, 1951; also Screech, "The Death of Pan," pp. 38–39.
† Gabriel Dupuyherbault (Putherbeus), who had violently attacked Rabelais in his *Theotimus* (1549).

hands by threats, injuries, force, violence, and burnings, we will not have them to nibble on down here any more." (46, 664)

From there the travelers journey pleasantly to the island of the Papimaniacs, where they are warmly welcomed as having seen Him, God on earth,[9] the Pope, by all the people, including their host Homenaz, bishop of Papimania (48, 667).[10] Homenaz has two objects of worship: the Pope and the sacred Decretals, which were papal epistles written mainly in the thirteenth century and compiled in 1500.[11] The travelers are allowed to see the holy book of the Decretals and to kiss a stick that touches an ill-painted portrait of a pope. Panurge protests that the pope should be dressed for war, for it is thus that he has usually seen them; and Homenaz explains:

"That was against the rebels, heretics, desperate Protestants, not obedient to the sanctity of this good God on earth. To him that is not only permitted and allowed, but commanded by the holy Decretals; and he must promptly put Emperors, Kings, Dukes, Princes, Republics to fire and sword, the moment they transgress one iota of his commands; despoil them of their goods; dispossess them of their kingdoms, proscribe them, anathematize them, and not only slaughter their bodies and those of their children and other relatives, but also damn their souls in the depths of the fieriest caldron there is in Hell." (50, 675)

Three full chapters (51–53) about Papimania are devoted to Homenaz's ecstatic praise—reminiscent of Panurge on debts—of the Decretals, and to explanations of how some people were harmed by contact with them for lack of reverence, and how they draw gold subtly from France to Rome. In his frenzy of delight he burps, farts, laughs, foams at the mouth, sweats, weeps, and beats his chest (53, 686–87). Once again we see his murderous hatred of the heretics who refuse to acknowledge the Decretals:

"Encores ces diables hæréticques ne les veulent apprendre et sçavoir. Bruslez, tenaillez, cizaillez, noyez, pendez, empallez, espaultrez, démembrez, exentérez, découppez, fricassez, grislez, transonnez, crucifiez, bouillez, escarbouillez, escartelez, débezillez, dehinguandez, carbonnadez ces meschans hæréticques décrétalifuges, décrétalicides, pires que homicides, pires que parricides, décrétalictones du diable." (53, 684–85)

["Still these heretical devils will not learn and know them. Burn, torture with pincers, cut with shears, drown, hang, impale, deshoulder, dismember, disembowel, cut to bits, fricassee, grill, break in pieces, crucify, boil, squash, quarter, put in pieces, cut off legs, roast these wicked heretics, decretalifuges, decretalicides, worse than homicides, worse than parricides, decretalictones* of the Devil."]

* Murderers of the Decretals.

Throughout the episode Panurge, Frère Jean, and Epistémon show derision, and Epistémon disgust when he says he must relieve his bowels (51, 678). Pantagruel is mainly aloof, though once—for the only time in all Rabelais—he rebukes Frère Jean severely for telling a disgustingly irreverent story. His last words in the episode are these: "Car oncques ne veiz Christians meilleurs que sont ces bons Papimanes" (54, 688) ["For never did I see better Christians than these good Papimaniacs"]; and he leaves them gifts on his departure. In context, however, these words must be ironic, like those used of Quaresmeprenant earlier. There is no other suggestion of ambiguity in Rabelais's damning caricature of Homenaz and the Papimaniacs.

From Papimania the travelers move to the confines of the glacial sea (55-56), and Pantagruel, high above the rest, hears in the air the "frozen words": not only words but sounds, of a battle fought (the pilot says) the previous winter between the Arimaspians and the Nephelibates [Walkers on Clouds]. Pantagruel throws several handfuls on the deck, where they are visible and produce their sounds on thawing out. The travelers cannot understand them, for their language is barbaric (56, 692). Panurge—at first terrified, then calmer—wishes he could hear among them the word of the Divine Bottle (56, 694).

In Saulnier's interpretation,[12] the Arimaspians represent the German Protestant princes, the Nephelibates the (Catholic) subjects of the Emperor; or more generally, the innovators and traditionalists in religion. The Protestant princes are wrong to try to conquer by force of arms, but then the Arimaspians have only one eye. The message of the episode for Saulnier is *hésuchisme*, or covert Evangelism. In the time of the Chambre Ardente and heretic-burning, words must remain frozen until they may again be safely uttered and heard. Behind this, a more general sense is possible: that words may pass for some time ununderstood as if frozen, then thaw out and yield their meaning at some future time. Implicit in Saulnier's *hésuchisme*, this notion goes beyond it to adumbrate Stendhal's 1830 prediction of readers who would understand him in 1880.

Next the travelers reach the earthly island paradise of "Messere Gaster, first master of arts in the world" (57, 694-95). Gaster [Stomach] is an imperious master, whose slightest command all men and beasts obey. Pantagruel, as we have noted, detests his two classes of worshipers, the Gastrolâtres and the Engastrimythes, but not Gaster himself, the inventor of all human crafts: those of the smith, of agriculture, medicine, fire, cooking, clocks to cook by, transport by land and sea, rain control, arms (defensive and offensive), even to that of stopping cannon balls (by a magnet) and sending them back at those who fired them—all these and many others, too.

In his excellent discussion of this episode, Robert Marichal[13] shows Rabelais's debt to Lemaire de Belges's *Concorde des deux langages* for the site, and his parody of Lemaire's Honneur in the person of Gaster, also his similar parody of Ficino's Amor[14] in his commentary on Plato's *Symposium*. More to the point, he argues, the Gastrolâtres, being "coquillons" [doctors], are, whether monks or not, the doctors of the Sorbonne. The Engastrimythes, though different, are actually a hypocritical type of Gastrolâtre, whom Rabelais calls "diviners, enchanters, and abusers of the simple populace" (58, 698). True of both groups is Saint Paul's saying in Philippians 3:19 that their "God is their belly" (58, 699). The stomach itself he does not condemn; it is not a god (and knows it), but simply an implacable master, source of all human invention. Pantagruel's abomination is reserved for the humans who worship it.

Finally there is Ganabin, the island of robbers that the friends pass without stopping, since Pantagruel has an inner warning, like that of Socrates' daemon, not to land (66). In Saulnier's persuasive interpretation,[15] the robbers represent the "justice" that persecutes the innovators. Panurge locates them in "la Conciergie" (the prison called "La Conciergerie du Châtelet"), and says that they would eat the travelers alive. After Pantagruel decides not to land and Panurge goes below decks to hide, Frère Jean proposes to fire the cannon to frighten Panurge and "to salute the Muses of this Mount Antiparnassus" [de cestuy mons Antiparnasse] (66, 725). This allusion to the Montparnasse section of Paris points to the many Ganabin, or forces of oppression, located there.

The Ganabin episode, followed by Panurge's terror and defecation, ends the *Fourth Book* appropriately by covertly denouncing those who persecute the religious innovators. Gallican in many of its parts, the book ends as it begins, on a strongly Evangelical note.

Most of the ideas in the *Fourth Book* are related to religion. The others are often dealt with only in passing or for the sake of comedy; the exceptions are the Prologue and the Gaster episode.

In the Prologue we have already noted the definition of Pantagruelism (p. 523) as a cheerful Stoical disregard for things beyond our control, and the stress on "médiocrité" (525–26, 534, 536–37), meaning moderation and acceptance of our allotted place in life.

In the Isle des Alliances, or Ennasin (9), the travelers meet a strange people, all allied to one another, looking like red Poitevins except for noses like the ace of clubs. The greetings between numberless allies reveal them crudely but comically as sexual partners. In Cheli [Peace] (10–11), the king, St. Panigon, wants the queen, her daughters, and the ladies of the court all to kiss Pantagruel and his company; this is done to all except Frère Jean, who has fled to Cheli's well-stocked kitchens. Pantagruel and his company are urged to spend the night; he demurs, and is given leave to go only after everyone has drunk twenty-five or thirty times. The same two chapters offer Frère Jean's protests against ceremonial kissing and a discussion of why monks are so often found in kitchens. Again Marichal is an excellent guide. In the alliances of Ennasin, he points out, Rabelais shows the sexual underside of the supposedly Platonic alliances then popular in France, especially among the Italian courtiers; and in the excessive politeness and consumption of food and drink at Cheli, says Marichal, he shows another aspect of the modish Italianism that had spread in France since the marriage of Catherine de' Medici in 1533 to the future Henry II. Rabelais, an early Platonist, reacted after 1540 against a mundane neo-Platonism that he associated with Italianate snobbery.[16]

In the farcical story of the Chiquanous (12–16) there are a few obvious ideas: that the law allows the greedy to sue decent people unjustly, so that these often take out their outrage on the summons-servers and are punished for it. Hence the lunatic logic by which the Chiquanous beg to be beaten to make their living.

The account of the frozen words (55–56) offers one nonreligious idea important to the literary enterprise: that the word (presumably, whether spoken or written), even if unheard in its own time, may have its day to thaw out and be understood.

The Gaster story expounds an earthy theory of human and animal inventiveness: "Tout pour la trippe!" [And all for tripes!], all an obedient response to the commands of the almighty stomach. Here Rabelais fills out exuberantly a theme dear to his heart: that we are comic body as well as (possibly) sublime spirit; that we do not (as on Ruach) live on wind; and that the quest of nourishment, to sustain life and for its own enjoyment, is perhaps the most basic drive of men and animals. Thus the nonreligious ideas of the *Fourth Book* are two: a gaily Stoical acceptance of what is beyond our control, and a recognition that man is an earthy creature whose body is as important as his soul—a fact that he will do well to acknowledge.

The *Fourth Book*, as we have seen, is closely related to the *Third* and the *Fifth* in both chronology (1546–53) and theme (the quest of an answer for Panurge), yet is very different from the *Third* in its story of travel, in its focus on the creatures and characters encountered, and in the greater importance of fantasy and ideas, mainly religious. If the book itself is more combative, the tone set in the Prologue is more resigned. The main characters are less freely alive, more set in patterns that become increasingly rigid between the partial edition of 1548 and the complete one of 1552—patterns toward which they had been moving from the *Third Book* on. Panurge is more than ever the coward and superstitious heresy-sniffer; Frère Jean is more courageous, often even rash (and a bit of a braggart in the *Fifth Book*), and blasphemous; Pantagruel is more pious and remote, but also the kindly ideal king. Here, as in the *Third* and *Fifth Books*, the carnivalesque element is less marked than in *Books One* and *Two*; the Chitterling account in certain aspects, parts of those of Papimania and Messere Gaster, and the banquet off Chaneph (64) are exceptions.

Besides the travel, the main difference from the *Third Book* is in the importance of fantasy, satire, and religious ideas. The joyous Stoicism, the acceptance of the lot God has given us, are familiar already but more explicit here. Rabelais's Evangelism is as marked here as anywhere except in *Gargantua*. The anti-Roman Gallicanism, appropriate to the time when the book was written, is a striking new feature of this book.

The *Fourth Book* follows naturally from the *Third*, and leads directly to the *Fifth*. Already in the Prologue to the *Third*, Rabelais had announced a fourth book, but said nothing about a fifth. When did he decide that one more book, the *Fourth*, would not suffice for what he still had to say? Obviously before he published the *Fourth*, for that does not take us to the word of the Divine Bottle. And why? Presumably he had too much to say and show before he let the travelers reach their goal. Why does he say nothing about the fifth book that he needs to complete his story? These are all questions that cannot, I think, be answered in the present state of Rabelais studies, but that need to be, and that relate to the problem of the authenticity of the *Fifth Book*. To this we turn our attention next.

The *Fifth Book*
(1562–1564)

The posthumous *Fifth Book* poses serious problems of texts and authenticity. A partial version of it was published in 1562, nine years after Rabelais's death, the year of the tolerant Edict of January and the outbreak of the religious civil wars. Entitled *L'Isle sonante* [The Ringing Island] from its principal episode, it comprised chapters 1–15 of the complete book plus a sixteenth, the account of the Apedeftes [Ignoramuses], which appears in neither of the other two texts.

In 1564 appeared *Le Cinquiesme et Dernier Livre des faicts et dicts heroïques du bon Pantagruel* [The Fifth and Last Book of the Heroic Deeds and Sayings of the Good Pantagruel]. This edition, whose title is patterned on that of the *Third* and *Fourth Books*, includes a Prologue and forty-seven chapters, of which the first fifteen follow those of *L'Isle sonante*.

The third text is a manuscript in the Bibliothèque Nationale in Paris, put in writing in the late sixteenth century by someone other than the author or editor. Much like the 1564 edition in the main, it differs by omitting the two chapters on the chess pageant and all but the first part of the Prologue, and by adding one chapter on the supper of the Lady Lanterns.

From a close study of these texts, Jacques Boulenger concluded that the manuscript was copied after the *Isle sonante* but before the 1564 edition, and that therefore the *Isle sonante* is the basic text for chapters 1–16, and the manuscript for the rest, though its many errors must often be corrected by the 1564 edition. His views are incorporated in the Pléiade text. In another excellent scholarly reader's version (Garnier, 1962, 2 vols.), Pierre Jourda uses the 1564 edition as his basic text, while two leading English translations, by Urquhart–Le Motteux and J. M. Cohen, handle the matter each in its own way. One unhappy result is that chapter numbers vary from one text to another. The Pléiade numbering is used in this book; a collation with the other texts follows:

EDITION	Boulenger	Jourda	Urquhart–Le Motteux	Cohen
CHAPTERS	1–15	1–15	1–15	1–15
	16	16 (MS)	16	16
	17–33	16(1564)–32	17–33	17–33
	33 bis	32 bis	–	–
	34–41	33–40	34–41	34–41
	42–42 bis	41–42	42	42–43
	43–47	43–47	43–47	44–48

Between the texts and editions the difference is not great.

To me the text of the manuscript, although often very defective in detail, is generally preferable to that of the 1564 edition. I find the Jourda edition of the 1564 text more useful than the Boulenger edition based on the manuscript, but less concise and convenient; also, its chapter numberings are less accepted. Both editions are good; I have chosen to follow the Pléiade.

The authenticity of the *Fifth Book* is still a question and may always be so. It has been studied from many angles with varying results. Some ignore the book because of its doubtfulness;[1] others warily accept it. Evidence on both sides—and in between—abounds.[2]

Much suggests that the *Fifth Book* is not completely authentic. The differences in texts give pause. The complete Prologue, the Apedeftes, the chess pageant, the supper of the Lady Lanterns—each of these appears in one text alone: two of them in the same text, and one in each of the other two texts. How are we to explain this discrepancy, if one of the texts is genuine?

The book's publication dates make it suspect. Why did it take nine years after Rabelais's death to publish any of it, eleven to publish it all? Why did the antiestablishment first part (ch. 1–16) come out just at the outbreak of the religious civil wars?

The text in detail offers one apparent reference to a work published in 1557, four years after Rabelais's death,* and abounds in repetitions

* Scaliger's *Exercitationes adversus Cardanum:* see V: 19, 801.

from earlier books of Rabelais.[3] In the four books that we know were his, however, Rabelais rarely copies or repeats himself.

The book is hardly Evangelical at all, as are the earlier ones, especially *Gargantua*; it is mainly Gallican, like the *Fourth Book* but more so. As such it may be seen either as capping Rabelais's movement in this direction, or as moving even farther from his position in *Books One* and *Two*.

Many readers find the main characters in the *Fifth Book* flat compared to what they were earlier. Pantagruel becomes rather shadowy, Panurge more jocular about his cowardice and heresy-sniffing, Frère Jean boastful and aggressive. (These differences, however, might point in any direction.)

The episode of the Furred Cats (11–15) shows none of the legal learning displayed by the creator of Judge Bridoye or even of Baisecul and Humevesne. Although his purpose is indeed different, the fact is surprising.

Many readers, of whom I am one, find several chapters uninspired and even a bit boring: 19–25 on Entelechy and Quintessence, and 30–41 on the land of Satin, Lanternois, and aspects of the temple of Bacbuc. To be sure, Rabelais had shown before, as in his account of Thelème (1:55–56), a fondness for sumptuous detail, but had never indulged this so fully.

Seven chapters are highly imitative. Francesco Colonna's popular *Poliphili Hypnerotomachia* [The Strife of Love in a Dreame] of 1499 is the source of most of chapters 24–25 and much of 38 and 41–42, while 39 and 40 are heavily indebted to Lucian's *Bacchus* (or *Dionysos*). Now Rabelais knew Lucian well, admired him, and often used him, and he had often borrowed from Colonna before; but for him these borrowings are extraordinarily heavy.[4]

The first fifteen chapters, whose comic verve and presence in all three texts makes them the likeliest to be genuine Rabelais, seem to some readers too vindictive for that, more so than anything in the earlier books. To me the tone of the Ringing Island differs from that of Papimania only in degree, not in kind; but the Furred Cats form the ugliest picture in all five books. Could Rabelais have changed that much in the last year and a half of his life?*

More important, could even he, for all his facility, have written the entire book in the time he had? If, as seems likely, he wrote it only

---

* Assuming that these parts were by Rabelais and not written, as of course they may possibly have been, before the *Fourth Book* was published.

after submitting the *Fourth Book* to the press, he had only a year and a half to live. Even if he started earlier—writing parts of it before deciding where to place them—this would presumably not have been before 1548 (the partial edition of the *Fourth Book*); and he must have spent much time completing the *Fourth Book* and seeing it through the press (1551–52). Where was the time to write the entire *Fifth Book*?

Finally, the only explicit testimony about authorship by a man of such an age that he might have known, denies that the author was Rabelais. Antoine du Verdier, born in 1544 and writing in 1604, deplores the books published under Rabelais's name "which are not by him, like the *Isle sonante*, written by a student from Valence, and others."[5] In the same year Dr. Louis Guyon wrote, also of the *Isle sonante*, that it was not by Rabelais, but "was composed long after his death; I was in Paris when it was written, and I know very well who was the author, who was not a doctor."[6]

There is a strong case, however, for partial authenticity. Few of the preceding arguments rule it out, and many support it.

A minor one is the reference (33 bis, 854)[7] to the lady friend of Pierre Amy or Lamy, Rabelais's friend at Fontenay-le-Comte. The narrator says he had known her; they choose her to guide them to the island of the Divine Bottle. This makes it sound like Rabelais writing; but of course the detail may have been put in to simulate authenticity.

The author shows great erudition and knowledge of regions that Rabelais knew well, notably Touraine and the Chinonais. Studies of aspects of his erudition, including music,[8] seem to lead to the same conclusion: that on this basis, Rabelais might have written the book.

A stronger argument is this. Rabelais announced the plan to consult the Divine Bottle already in the *Third Book* (47, 492), published in 1546 and given to the printer late in 1545. He seems then already to have had a conclusion in mind for the entire work, but to have anticipated only one more book—four in all, not five.[9] I think we may assume that the *Fourth Book*—easily his longest—"got out of hand"; that this journey through strange islands so stimulated Rabelais's imagination that a *Fifth Book* proved necessary to complete the journey and his story.

However this may be, when the *Fourth Book* ends off Ganabin we are not yet even near the Divine Bottle or its word, which Rabelais had announced in the *Third*. He had promised his readers more; he may have already written or at least sketched some of what lay ahead; he probably knew how he meant the work to end; he had always been able to work fast; as it turned out, he still had about a year and a half (about which we know virtually nothing) to write it. In these circumstances, I find it hard to believe that at his death he could have left nothing whatever of a *Fifth Book*.

One final argument for at least partial authenticity. If the *Fifth Book* was entirely composed by someone else, who could it have been? Of course there has been much conjecture. The signature of the concluding epigram, NATURE QUITE,* looks like an anagram and has suggested such names as Jean Quentin or Quintin and Dr. Turquet. Also, the Protestant Hellenist and storyteller Henri Estienne has been proposed; but no nominations have been found acceptable.[10] In short, despite much learned speculation, there seems general agreement that only Rabelais could have written many parts of the book.

What emerges from all these arguments, objective and subjective, is a vague consensus[11] that the *Fifth Book* is at least partly by Rabelais. The usual main criteria (my own included) seem to be ultimately subjective: does this page or that chapter seem to be genuine Rabelais or not? My own view is that chapters 1–16—those of the *Isle sonante* (the Ringing Island, Furred Cats, and Apedeftes)—and 26–29 (the Isle des Odes and the Frères Fredons) are entirely, or almost entirely, Rabelais's own; that the conclusion (42 bis–47: the oracle of the Bottle and its interpretation) is largely by him, though possibly completed by another hand from his notes. Thus I would accept twenty-six chapters as authentic or largely so.

The seven derivative chapters, 24–25 (the chess pageant) and 38–42 (description of the temple of Bacbuc), as well as the Prologue, seem to me unlikely to be his work.

The remaining sixteen chapters—17–23, 30–37 including 33 bis:

---

* The epigram (p. 891) runs as follows:

> Rabelais est-il mort? Voicy encore un livre.
> Non, sa meilleure part a repris ses esprits
> Pour nous faire présent de l'un de ses escrits
> Qui le rend entre tous immortel et fait vivre.
>   NATURE QUITE
>
> [Is Rabelais dead? Here's one more book, *Book Five*.
> No; spirit has returned to his best part
> To give us one more product of his art
> Which brings him back immortal and alive.]

Quinte Essence, Satin, Lanternois, and entry into the temple of the Bottle—seem to me the most questionable: possibly Rabelais's but, I think, more probably not. Naturally I shall give most attention to those parts I think likeliest to be genuine.

To the rule that all Rabelais's Prologues deserve careful attention, this one is the exception. It appears entire in the 1564 edition, in very truncated form in the manuscript, and not at all in the *Isle sonante*. Entire, it fills eight pages in Jourda's edition (277–84), of which the first two plus (277–79) give the truncated version reproduced in the Pléiade edition by Boulenger (749–50). The theme is the proverb "le monde n'est plus fat" [the world's no longer foolish]. At times the author seems to suggest that this is because of religious reform, apparently because Rabelais's books, once condemned, are now widely accepted. Following the manifesto of the young Pléiade poets, Joachim du Bellay's *Deffence et Illustration de la langue françoyse* (1549), Rabelais praises those authors who—like himself—have written in French rather than Latin, and concludes by urging all good drinkers to buy his books.

Borrowings abound from the Prologue to the *Third Book* and the Old Prologue to the *Fourth:* from the *Third Book* such phrases as "prosopopée," "à chacun n'est octroyé hanter et habiter Corinthe," "servir les massons," "rappetasseurs de vieilles ferrailles latines," and "vous suppliant au nom et reverence" (Jourda, ed., pp. 281–84); from the *Fourth* two offers (like Timon's in the Old Prologue) of a tree from which his critics are welcome to hang themselves, and the comparison of these critics with men who spit on meat to spoil it for others (pp. 280–81, 283).

This Prologue cannot bear comparison with the first four. The author is clearly a diligent student of Rabelais, but clearly not Rabelais himself.

The account of the *Isle sonante* (ch. 1–8), like that of Papimania, is a satire of Rome. Here the clergy have become birds who sing to the din of the eternal bells, and Rabelais exposes their idle gluttony and the parents whom poverty drives to put their unwanted children into religious orders. Whereas in Papimania Homenaz worshiped everything, the guide here, Editus, is no fool; but he too relishes the conspicuous consumption that abounds in the Ringing Island. Pantagruel seems more critical, and takes no joy in the prospect of four days of guzzling (6, 762). The threats against all who reject the sway of Rome are similar. There is more sheer comedy in Papimania, more satire here, but to my mind no sharp contrast between the two.

The travelers stay four days within earshot of the Ringing Island with a little hermit who makes them fast (ch. 1); then they cross to the island and are welcomed by Editus [Sacristan], who explains about the humanoid birds who live there—Clersgaux, Monesgaux, Prestregaulx, Abbegaulx, Evesquegaulx, Cardingaulx, and Papegault*—and the females from Clergesse to Papegesse (ch. 2). However, a number of Cagotz [Bigots] have arrived lately and made a mess. Editus tells how, without copulation, Monesgaux and Prestregaulx are born of Clersgaulx, and so on; how they all sing whenever the bells over their cages are rung, and how the unwanted children from the lands of Joursanspain [Breadlessdays] and Tropdiceulx [Too Many of Them], after a sketchy tonsure and ordination, leave their inhospitable families and fly to the Ringing Island as Clersgaulx to live on the fat of the land. A few, to be sure, have recently left; but that leaves all the more food and drink for the rest. In 5 he deals with the military orders ("Gourmandeurs" instead of "Commandeurs") and urges the company to four days of diligent eating and drinking. He tells in 6 how all their provisions come from "the other world" (except lately some northern countries, meaning England and Germany) and will never fail, and that he and his compatriots have the best of this world and the one to come. In 7 Panurge, who finds sex lacking, tells the story of the well-fed charger and the sex-starved donkey. In chapter 8 Editus at last shows them Papegault, whom Panurge takes for a hoopoe ("une duppe," which already implies a dupe); and warns of the frightful dangers when Panurge wants to strike an old Evesquegault. With that we leave the Ringing Island.

A few passages deserve quotation. Here is Editus on the children who become Clersgaulx: "Ordinarily they are hunchbacked, one-eyed, lame, one-armed, gouty, deformed, and bewitched, a useless burden to the earth. . . . I marvel . . . how the mothers over there bear them nine months in their loins, seeing that in their house they cannot bear or endure them for nine years, or even most often for seven" (4, 758–59). Later he returns to the subject:

"A greater number comes to us from Breadlessdays, which is excessively long. For the Asaphsars† who inhabit that country, when they are in danger of suffering ill-counseling hunger, through not having enough to feed them-

---

* Translated by Le Motteux as "Clerk-hawks," etc.; by J. M. Cohen as "Clerijays," etc., up to "Popinjay."
† From the Hebrew *oussaph*, assembled people.

selves and either not knowing how, or not being willing, to work at some honest craft or trade, or to give faithful service to some worthy family; also those who have not been able to enjoy their loves, who have not succeeded in their enterprises and are desperate; likewise those who have wickedly committed some criminal act and are sought out to be put ignominiously to death—all come flying here. Here they have their life laid out for them; here they remain, as fat as dormice, they who before were as thin as magpies; here they have perfect security, immunity, and sanctuary."

Twice in chapter 8 Editus warns Panurge of the power of the Pope to do harm. The first time is when Panurge insists that the Pope has a crest [une duppe]: "If he once hears you blaspheming thus, you are lost, my good folks. Do you see a basin there in his cage? Out of that will come thunder, lightning, devils, and tempests, by which in a moment you will be sunk a hundred feet beneath the earth" (p. 769). Later, when they hear and watch the pretty Abbegesse singing to the snoring old Evesquegault, Panurge tries in vain to stir him and finally picks up a stone to hit him with. Here Editus cries out:

"Worthy man, strike, cut, kill, and murder all the kings and princes in the world, by treason, poison, or any other way, whenever you will; pluck down the angels from their nests in heaven; for all this you shall have pardon from the Papegault. These sacred birds do not touch, insofar as you love life, profit, and property, not only yours but those of your relatives and friends, alive and dead; even those to be born after them would suffer misfortune." (p. 771)

On this ominous note the account of the Ringing Island ends. More strongly than even in Papimania, the threat of the militant Papacy, to kings as well as subjects, by foul means as well as fair, has been made clear.

Leaving the Ringing Island, the travelers stop at the Isle des Ferremens [Iron Tools], where tools and weapons may be shaken from the trees they grow on (ch. 9), and then at the Isle de Cassade [Cheating], where sharping at dice is the rule (ch. 10). From there they come to the Guichet [Wicket], ruled by Grippeminault, Archduke of the Chats Fourréz [Furred Cats]. Pantagruel wisely decides not to land; the others do, and are imprisoned and harshly questioned by Grippeminault (11–15).

The Furred Cats are the judges, described as "horrible and frightful," and as eaters of little children (11, 775). Their hair grows inward, and nothing escapes their long claws. They all wear game pouches for the *épices*, the gifts that the judges of Rabelais's time expected and received. Before the travelers enter their den, they are warned by a courageous poorhouse beggar (776–77) that the Furred Cats are the source of most of the evil in the world, and by their machinations will soon possess all Europe:

"Among them rules the sixth essence, by which they seize everything, devour everything, and beshit everything. They hang, burn, quarter, behead, murder, imprison, undermine and ruin everything without distinction between good and evil. For among them vice is called virtue; wickedness is surnamed goodness; treason takes the name of loyalty; theft is said to be liberality. Plunder is their motto, and, performed by them, is found good by all men (except only the heretics); and they do it all with sovereign and unbreakable authority."

Panurge wants to leave, but they are locked in. To get out, they must pass before the monster Grippeminault, who "had hands full of blood, claws like a harpy's, a muzzle like a crow's beak, the teeth of a four-year-old boar, eyes like the throat of hell" (11, 778). The presiding image—of "Justice"—is an old woman wearing glasses and holding a sickle-sheath and a scale in which one dish, full of gold, far outweighs the empty other one. Grippeminault's constant refrain is "Or sà!"—normally "Well, now!" but also, in this context, "Money here!" He admits that the laws are like cobwebs, which catch gnats and butterflies but not big gadflies. The narrator, unable to solve his riddle, proclaims his innocence, only to learn from Grippeminault that that is no ground for escaping their tortures. Panurge solves the riddle but still pays the Furred Cats to set him and his comrades free (ch. 13). After two chapters (14–15) on how the Furred Cats live on corruption and how Frère Jean (alone of the group) wants to return and plunder them, they go back to Pantagruel and after some difficulty sail away.

The picture of the Furred Cats is one of ugliness almost unrelieved by humor, which Thomas M. Greene has called "Rabelais's darkest and fiercest image of cruelty."[12] Even as he avoids Ganabin at the end of the *Fourth Book*, Pantagruel does not disembark here. The cowed narrator can only protest his innocence—in vain; Epistémon, if indeed he is present, is silent; Frère Jean can only mutter between his teeth; Panurge shows resourcefulness by solving the riddle, but still pays to get them out. The reason for Pantagruel's absence seems clear: he is by definition as nearly all-powerful as a natural being can be; and Rabelais wants to show that against the power, the riddles, and the greed of the judges ordinary mortals have no recourse—except of course to pay through the nose.

The Apedeftes of chapter 16—the judges and counselors of the tax courts—are less terrifying, since they destroy only property, not life and limb, and do not threaten the travelers, who merely observe them. The governing image of these courts is a gigantic wine press into which go not only vines and vineyards but also parks, forests, and châteaus. Out of these the tenders of the press, whose fingernails are two feet long to let nothing escape, squeeze "potable gold." Why, asks Panurge, are these crafty exploiters called ignorant? Because, replies their guide Gagnebeaucoup [Get Plenty], they may not be clerics, ignorance must prevail, and the only reason they give for anything is that "their Lordships have said it, their Lordships will it, their Lordships have ordained it" (16, 793).

Leaving the Apedeftes, the travelers pass Outre—meaning "on" or "beyond" (a familiar expression) or else a "leather wine bottle"—whose inhabitants are inflated like full leather bottles and die by bursting, as does one, after inviting his friends to a feast, while the visitors are there. Chapter 18 tells how their ship is stranded on a sandbank (whereupon Panurge again renounces marriage), and then pulled free by a ship returning from Quintessence. In 19 they arrive at Entelechy, the kingdom of Quintessence, and Pantagruel makes one of his rare appearances as a giant. The next two chapters tell how the Queen, by appropriate songs, cures the incurables without even touching them, while her officers by various simple devices cure the other invalids. We learn of the occupations—some magical, some futile, some proverbial—of the officers, and the Queen retains the travelers among her Abstractors (of Quintessence). At their supper the Queen does not really eat, but only swallows premasticated food. Chapters 24–25 tell of the three chess games performed as a pageant by human chessmen on a vast "board" of tapestry. Although the gold side moves first (at least in the first game), the silver wins twice, then the gold once; in the first game the author nods once, as three gold Custodes (rooks) are taken (818–19).

Sailing from Entelechy, in two days they arrive (ch. 26) at the "Isle des Odes,* en laquelle les chemins cheminent" [Island of Odes, in which the Roads Go Places], and find roads that indeed, like rivers, carry travelers to their destination, fulfilling the promise of the question "Where does this road go?" The play on such fancies is worthy of Rabelais's comic ingenuity.

Chapters 27–29 deal with the Frères Fredons [Semiquaver Friars][13] in a most Rabelaisian way. With codpieces aft as well as fore, round

* Cf. classical Greek ὁδός and modern Greek odos, road.

shoes, hoods turned back to front, and the backs of their heads shaven and made up like faces, they keep their faces hidden and move either forward or backward, lunch on yawns, and claim to despise fortune. As we learn in chapter 27, their meals are alternately sumptuous and meager, and their official occupations, as they wait for the Judgment Day, are useless and ridiculous.

A long dialogue in chapter 28–117 responses on either side, as Panurge questions a Frère Fredon and gets nothing but monosyllabic answers—tells us more about their unofficial occupations: their twenty girl friends, how they feed them, and mainly how they copulate with them—on the average, six times each day and ten each night. In chapter 29 Pantagruel and Epistémon note that March is their busiest time, August their idlest; Epistémon points to Lenten foods as a source of lust as well as illness. Panurge playfully asks the friar if Epistémon is not a heretic, and he answers in monosyllables that he is, and should be burned like the rest.

The idea of monosyllabic responses was not new with Rabelais; not long before, the brilliant storyteller Bonaventure des Périers, in his *Nouvelles Récréations et Joyeux Devis* [Novel Pastimes and Merry Tales], no. 58, had introduced a series of ten of them.[14] In Rabelais all the answers are clear, to the point, and comic. Let a short example suffice, as Panurge asks the friar about the girls:

"P. Les yeulx, quelz?	F. Noirs.
P. Les tétins?	F. Ronds.
P. Le minois?	F. Coinct.*
P. Les sourcils?	F. Molz.
P. Leurs attraictz?	F. Meurs.
P. Leur regard?	F. Franc.
P. Les piedz, quels?	F. Platz.
P. Les talons?	F. Courtz." (p. 831)

[P. Their eyes, what color?	F. Dark.
P. Their breasts?	F. Round.
P. Their expression?	F. Nice.
P. Their eyebrows?	F. Soft.
P. Their charms?	F. Ripe.
P. Their glance?	F. Free.
P. Their feet?	F. Flat.
P. Their heels?	F. Short.]†

I think only Rabelais could have written these chapters; and the themes are favorites of his.

* As in Jourda; not "Court" [Short], as in Boulenger.
† A stock joke of the time: the better to help them fall on their backs.

Chapters 30–31 bring the travelers to the land of Satin, where they see many wonders (reminiscent of Medamothi, IV: 2), and also Ouyr-Dire [Hearsay] (recalling Messere Gaster, IV: 57 ff.), who keeps a school for witnesses. In 32–33 they arrive in Lanternois [Lanternland]; 33 bis gives a long Rabelaisian list of the foods served to the Lady Lanterns for supper, and tells how the travelers chose Pierre Amy's (or Lamy's) woman friend as the Lantern to guide them to the Divine Bottle. In 34, arriving at the island of the Bottle, they fill their shoes with vine leaves to symbolize their control over wine before passing under an arch of flagons, glasses, and thirst-provoking foods, so that Bacbuc, priestess of the Bottle, will receive them. In 35–36 they go underground into the temple of the Bottle, down the fated 108 steps;[15] Panurge, terrified by the darkness, once more offers not to marry; Frère Jean boasts of his own fearlessness and predicts that Panurge will be a cuckold. In 37 the great brass doors open as if by magic, and two inscriptions are revealed:

Ducunt volentem fata, nolentem trahunt.

[The fates lead him who will, drag him who will not.]

ΠΡΟΣ ΤΕΛΟΣ ΑΥΤΩΝ ΠΑΝΤΑ ΚΙΝΕΙΤΑΙ.

[All things move to their own end.]

Chapters 38, 41, and 42, which lean heavily on Colonna's *Strife of Love in a Dreame*, give sumptuous descriptions of the paving of the temple, the lamp that lights it, and the marvelous fountain at its center. Following Lucian's *Bacchus*, 39 and 40 tell of the magnificent mosaic in the vault, representing the battle won by Bacchus against the Indians. These five chapters seem too derivative to be by Rabelais.

With chapter 42 bis the conclusion begins to unfold. Bacbuc has the travelers drink from the fountain; they pronounce it excellent water. She then tells them they have not recognized its taste, and has them eat tongue, ham, sausages, and caviar to freshen their throats and then try it again while imagining the wine they want to taste. Panurge declares it to be Beaune, Frère Jean Graves, Pantagruel Mirevaux.

Next (43), Bacbuc summons Panurge to hear the word of the Bottle. Telling him to listen with only one ear, she prepares him suitably, then takes him into a small adjoining chapel, also with a fountain, in the middle of which is the Divine Bottle. After more ritual and a prayer sung to the Bottle (44), she tosses something into the fountain that makes the water boil; a strong buzzing follows, and then the word TRINCH. She congratulates Panurge on a swift and happy answer. He at first thinks the Bottle has merely cracked, not spoken, and remarks that he has learned nothing.

Then she brings Panurge back into the main temple, has him swallow some wine from what appears to be a book (with the message "Do not read, but swallow, this gloss") (45–46). Panurge is still slow to understand. She tells him that TRINCH is a universal word and explains: "Et icy mainctenons que non rire, ains boyre est le propre de l'homme" (45, 883) ["And here we maintain that not laughing, but drinking, is the proper role of man"]. But the command to drink also needs explanation, and she gives it:

". . . je ne dis boyre simplement et absoluement, car aussi bien beuvent les bestes; je dis boyre vin bon et fraiz. Notez, amys, que de vin divin on devient. . . . Vos Académicques l'afferment, rendans l'étymologie de vin, et disent en grec οἶνος estre comme *vis*, force, puissance, pour ce qu'il emplist l'âme de toute vérité, tout savoir et toute philosophie. Si avez noté ce qu'est en lettres ionicques escript dessus la porte du temple, vous avez peu entendre que en vin est vérité cachée. La dive Bouteille vous y envoye, soyés vous-mesmes interprètes de vostre entreprise." (45, 883)

[". . . I do not mean simply and absolutely drinking, for the animals also drink. I mean drinking good cool wine. Note, my friends, that by wine one becomes divine. . . . Your Academics affirm this in giving the etymology of *wine*, and say that in Greek οἶνος is like *vis* (power, strength), because it fills the soul with all truth, all knowledge, and all philosophy. If you noted what is written in Ionic letters over the door to the temple, you were able to understand that the truth is hidden in wine. The Divine Bottle sends you to it; you yourselves be the interpreters of your undertaking."]

Pantagruel applauds the advice, since it echoes his own, urges Panurge to TRINCH, and asks what his heart cries out in Bacchic frenzy. Panurge replies, in twenty-three verses of rhyme, that this oracle is infallible, and that he will marry and copulate to his heart's content. Frère Jean pronounces Panurge crazy (ch. 46); but Pantagruel (also in verse) says that Panurge's frenzy is poetic, Bacchic, and not to be mocked. Frère Jean protests that they must all be drunk and wishes Gargantua could see them; but then even he breaks into four tidy little verses. Panurge proclaims that truth lies in wine and urges Frère Jean to consult the oracle about marriage for himself. Frère Jean protests that he wants no part of marriage. Panurge, again in verse, tells Frère Jean that while he, Panurge, is saved, Frère Jean will be damned, and imagines him copulating with Proserpina. Here Frère Jean calls a halt to rhyming and suggests that they settle their score with Bacbuc, and thus the chapter ends.

In a long farewell speech that fills most of the final chapter (47), Bacbuc tells the travelers that her world takes pleasure not in receiving but in giving, and that there is no score to settle as long as they are content; but she asks them to leave their names and addresses, and they do. She urges them to proclaim to their world (above ground) the wonders of her underground world, source of vast riches and powers. For their voyage home and through life she wishes them "the guidance of God and company of man" (p. 889). (About here the 1564 edition ends; we now follow the text of the manuscript.)

With God's guidance and the company of some bright Lantern, Bacbuc goes on, your philosophers may learn many secrets, for Time is the father of Truth.

She gives the travelers three leather bottles full of magical waters that will ensure a safe voyage home, tells them they will find their ships stocked and ready to go, sends her greetings and a letter to Gargantua, and bids them Godspeed. Over lovely country they make their way to the waiting ships; and the book ends.

Comedy for its own sake, "pure" comedy unmixed (or almost unmixed) with fantasy or satire, is even scarcer in the *Fifth Book* than the *Fourth*. The story of the charger and the donkey (ch. 7), the bursting wine bottle at Outre (17), some activities of the officers of Quintessence (22), some aspects of the traveling roads (26), the monosyllabic answers of the Frère Fredon (28–29—though much of this is satire)—and the exchange in rhyme between Panurge and Frère Jean (46): these are about all the comedy. Indeed laughter seems no longer the proper function of man. If Rabelais is the author of much of the book, this suggests a continued darkening of his final vision of life. What comes to comfort the reader at the end is not so much the comic as the lofty and serene.

As in the *Fourth Book*, perhaps because of the nature of the subject, fantasy is more luxuriant here than in the first three books. Only a little of it is mainly comic: the island of the Iron Tools (9), that of Outre (17), and to some extent the idea of ladies as lanterns (32–33 bis). Most of it—especially in those parts which I consider most suspect—is a fantasy of riches and splendor: most of Entelechy, the land of Quintessence (19–25), the marvels of Satin (30–31), and the description of the wondrous temple of the Bottle (35–42). Most of the *Isle sonante* part (1–16) is satirical fantasy: the humanoid birds that compose the religious orders; the simple grotesqueness of the single-minded—and effective—Apedeftes; the horrible grotesqueness of the equally single-minded—and effective—Furred Cats—these episodes bear a serious message about the corruption of respected and enormously powerful institutions. The Furred Cats also show us that Rabelais, more and more in his last days, could use fantasy, when he chose, to portray monstrous ugliness. As the comic decreases in his last work, the wickedly ugly increases. Even fantasy from time to time takes on the dark color of his final mood.

In the *Fifth Book* satire is found mainly in the accounts of the *Isle sonante* and the Frères Fredons (1–16, 27–29). Beyond that I see only bits, again in the earlier chapters: of gluttony in Outre (17), of futile pursuits among the officers of Quintessence (ch. 22). The Ringing Island (ch. 1–8) satirizes the subhumanness of the bird-clergy, their robot responses to the bells, their laziness (the snoring Evesquegault), and above all their gluttony and their readiness for vicious reprisal if attacked or even criticized. The callous cruelty and greed of judges, their indifference to anything but money, is satirized in the Furred Cats, while the greed—less cruel but equally unscrupulous—of the tax courts is the target in the Apedeftes. With the Frères Fredons the objects of satire seem to be duplicity (facing two ways) and one-track minds (monosyllabic answers), and clearly include laziness (rising at noon; their occupations), boredom (breakfasting on yawns), readiness to condemn heretics, gluttony in season, blind acceptance of Lent for fasting and busiest copulation, and of course unbridled lechery in the account of their strenuous sex lives.

In the satire of corrupt and oppressive institutions of Church and State, Rabelais has been said to be struggling for the welfare of the little man, of the people.[16] I do not find this true. The travelers are, to be sure, not grandees; but as trusty companions of a rich and powerful prince, they are otherwise idle and well-to-do—enough so to undertake the voyage they do just to satisfy Panurge's craving for another answer to his marital problem. The depredations of the Apedeftes, which include reducing to potable gold "manors, parks, forests," do not seem likely to affect the poor (16, 792). Although Rabelais seems clearly to like such a "little man" as Couillatris (IV, Prologue), his ambiguous account of those welcome to Theleme still suggests that for him nice people are found more often among nobles than among commoners; and his ideal men are clearly King Gargantua and Prince Pantagruel. In short, he seems to accept the social hierarchy much as he finds it.[17] It is not the institutions of power and authority that he satirizes, it is their abuse.

Except for the episode of the Frères Fredons, the satire is concentrated in the first third of the book, which is easily the most polemical. Adding this to what we have already observed, I find an interesting movement in the last three books.[18] The *Third Book* (1546) seems rather unpolemical, as does the first part (ch. 1–28) of the *Fourth*, most of which appeared in 1548. For the rest of the *Fourth Book* (ch. 29–67), beginning with Quaresmeprenant, the tone is less comic and more satiric as Rabelais strikes out at enemies and abuses. This continues for the first third of the *Fifth Book* (ch. 1–16), only to give way to peaceful restraint. Thus a comparatively quiet period around 1545–48 is followed by a more belligerent one. In his final years, was Rabelais by turns angered by renewed criticism and censure, and heartened to fight back by the protection of Chastillon and the support of Henry II? This is how it appears to me.

Of course if the conclusion of the *Fifth Book* is Rabelais's own and was composed last, we must postulate a final serene appeasement before death closed his career. Perhaps we should do just that.

The conclusion seems to me so superb and appropriate that I believe Rabelais must be at least the principal author. As Montaigne once wrote of a similar matter, "I would be unhappy to be dislodged from this belief."[19] Let me begin my reasons with two rather tangential points.

Bacbuc in the final chapter stresses the value of God's guidance and human companionship, and hopes that with these aids philosophers will find Time to be the father of Truth. The second point recalls the optimism about human progress of the last two chapters of the *Third Book* (51–52), where hemp has given man such power that even the Olympian gods fear him as a rival.

The first point is double. The importance of human companionship is never explicitly argued but seems implicit throughout Rabelais, especially in Panurge's fear that without creditors or a wife he will be left unfriended and alone (III: 9, 359, etc.). All the principals rejoice in the company of their fellows; there are hardly any loners in Rabelais. Even Pantagruel, who seems self-sufficient, clearly enjoys the society of his friends, and is ready to marry when his father suggests it. The need for God's guidance is clear in the *Third Book* in the advice of Pantagruel and Hippothadée to Panurge about his marriage, and perhaps clearest in the case of Picrochole in *Gargantua*. At the very end Bacbuc invokes a benign, rather intellectual God as governing the world; and so Rabelais appears to view Him—whenever the question arises—throughout the five books.

Panurge, as instructed, listens to the oracle of the Bottle with only one ear. If this is meant to symbolize equal attention (with the other ear) to knowing his own mind, this again would recall the advice he receives from Pantagruel and Hippothadée.

The notion of controlling drinking, symbolized by treading on the vine leaves worn in the shoes (34, 857), may of course not be Rabelais's own (I find that chapter as a whole suspect, though this idea might be his), but would fit him better than one might suppose. The invitations to drink and stress on the joys of drinking in the Prologues by the voice of Alcofribas should not drown out the Pantagruelistic reply found in the chapters on Gargantua's education, where a moderate sobriety is the rule.

One aspect of the conclusion seems a reversal: the reactions of Panurge and Frère Jean when Panurge has had his answer after they and Pantagruel have drunk of the fountain. Panurge is slow to understand (44–45, 882–883) but at last (p. 884) breaks into a Bacchic frenzy. Frère Jean calls him crazy; and only when Pantagruel rebukes him and joins Panurge in verse does Frère Jean follow suit. In all this and what follows—his rejection of marriage and Panurge's prediction that he will be damned—Frère Jean seems less sympathetic than Panurge and in a sense sacrificed to him. (To some extent this is prepared by his frequent boasting earlier in this book, as in chapter 15.) This is quite a change from the *Third* and *Fourth Books*. Does it mean that ultimately, in Rabelais's eyes, the celibate, self-centered monk finds less favor than—for all his sins and vices—the more outgoing Panurge? It might just be. Such a reversal would seem to me less likely for a recaster or pasticher (how would he dare?) than for Rabelais himself, who had already changed Frère Jean a little, and Pantagruel and Panurge very much, especially in moving from the first two books to the *Third*.

This is not the only reversal. Almost twenty years earlier, in the liminary dizain to *Gargantua*, Rabelais had written: "Pour ce que rire est le propre de l'homme" (p. 2) [Because laughter is the proper role of man]. Now in the *Fifth Book* the matter comes up twice. Someone—I should think a pasticher or recaster—repeated this idea when he wrote of the "propre humain, qui est rire" (25, 821) [proper role of man, which is laughter]. But in chapter 45 Bacbuc proclaims: "Et icy mainctenons que non rire, ains boyre est le propre de l'homme" (p. 883) ["And here we maintain that not laughing, but drinking, is the proper role of man"], and goes on to explain what kind of drinking she means.

This reversal too seems to me, for the same reason, more probably the work of Rabelais himself than of a pasticher or continuator. I find it likelier that such a man wrote the meek paraphrase (ch. 25) of Rabelais's earlier verse. Such a change, implausible for someone else, seems to me perfectly plausible for Rabelais. His work suggests that in his final years the purely comic, even if occasionally possible, is no longer solace enough for the evils of the world. As comedy recedes more and more from his work, he turns elsewhere for comfort.

And where is that elsewhere? "TRINCH" and "Boyre est le propre de l'homme." We seem to have come full circle, back to the exhortations to drink in the first Prologues. But as we have seen, these two quotations lead to long glosses that are clearly important. According to chapter 42 bis, what the three travelers drink is not wine but water, which, after they are suitably prepared, tastes to them like wine—but a different wine to each. The Bottle is an oracle (by definition cryptic, perhaps symbolic); its mysteries are stressed. Bacbuc's long gloss tells us that the proper role of man is not to drink simply and absolutely, as even animals do, but to become divine (cf. III: 51–52) and gain power (from the play on *vis*) by filling our souls with "all truth, all knowledge, and all philosophy." We may object that this is "only" Bacbuc speaking; but Bacbuc makes very good sense, and no one challenges a word she speaks.

Thus the message of "TRINCH" is not simply "Drink your fill of wine" (even of cool fresh wine), but drink in philosophy, knowledge, truth; reach out, as Rabelais had urged in his chapters on education in the first two books, for all the wonders to be learned in the world. Reach out to them, embrace them, drink them in. With God's guidance and human company, you may well become "an abyss of knowledge."

This stands unchallenged. Rabelais has not given up his thirst for learning. Well and good. But where does that leave Panurge, or any other mere mortal with a simple (or not so simple) human problem? Must he suddenly become a philosopher, a researcher, another Pantagruel?

Hardly. In the same speech just quoted, Bacbuc's final words are the key: "You yourselves be the interpreters of your undertaking." Just as Pantagruel, Panurge, and Frère Jean each tasted a different wine in the water of the fountain, so each, after these words, is prompted by his Bacchic frenzy to a different rhymed message. "TRINCH" does not so much solve a problem as point in a direction; its interpretation is left to each hearer.

This seems to take us back to the *Third Book;* in many ways these chapters are the conclusion of Panurge's quest. "Aren't you assured of your will?" Pantagruel had asked him, and Hippothadée had urged: "First you must counsel yourself." These announce the final advice: Be your own interpreter.

But this time there is a difference: now for the first time Panurge accepts, ecstatically; for the first time he hears the voice of his own will, his own θέλημα.[20] To be sure, what he looks for in marriage is still simply the chance to copulate like mad in safety. But still he does reach out—to companionship, to marriage, perhaps Rabelais means to life—in some ways in which Frère Jean does not; and Rabelais (if it is he) seems to give him his parting blessing. Reach out, he seems to say, to all life offers, for all its tribulations; to do that is to be human. Drink of it deeply, accept its challenge and intoxication; you will be happier by doing so than by refusing it.

And perhaps—again if it is he—he is adding: for all its trials I have found it, on balance, happy. Drink deep, and you may find it happier than I did. Perhaps.

Comedy and
the Carnivalesque

In speaking of Rabelaisian comedy, I have been content up till now to distinguish between comedy of fantasy, marked by the exotic and unreal; that of satire, marked by serious ideas; and what I have called "pure" comedy, which seems intended simply to make us laugh. These demarcations, however, do not distinguish the nature of comedy in Rabelais from that, for example, of Molière or Voltaire.

Despite their congeniality and affinities, the comedy of these three is very different: Voltaire's almost always polite, witty, satirical, often understated; Molière's very wide in its range, from slapstick to "high comedy," usually based on character, extending from the witty Voltairian to the earthy Rabelaisian; Rabelais's seldom witty and always exuberant and earthy.

The best key to Rabelaisian comedy, in my opinion, is the one provided by Mikhail Bakhtin in *Rabelais and His World*.[1] Bakhtin was of course not the first to recognize Rabelais's fondness for popular-festive materials—almost all who studied him had noted it; but he was the first to offer an analysis of it and a wealth of illustrations. Despite some weaknesses—repetition in the late chapters; ignoring the serious Pantagruelistic voice in favor of that of Alcofribas; bias in favor of the popular-festive-grotesque and against the bourgeois-classical—Bakhtin's is a seminal book.

I find it hard to say precisely what Bakhtin's main categories are, since his Introduction suggests one grouping, his chapter headings another. They seem to be these: that Rabelais draws mainly on, and expresses supremely well, the unofficial, popular culture of the feast day and the market place, which turns official values and mores upside down, favors the grotesque over the classical, the "open body" over the closed, and sees in man primarily the "material bodily lower stratum." In short, his major cultural source is the carnivalesque.

The culture of the feast day makes everyone equal and often turns kings into fools; we may think of Epistémon's visit to hell (II: 30) or the fates of kings Anarche and Picrochole. Unfettered rejoicing in abundant food and drink pervades Rabelais, especially the first two books. The culture of the feast day reveled in comic shows and parodies—Rabelais is full of these—and for almost every story told there is not just one listener, but an audience, which helps to make them all dramatic. The language of the market place abounds in imaginative curses, oaths, and popular blazons. In Rabelais the curses and oaths are everywhere. For the blazons, see any of the long lists, such as Gargantua's games (I: 22); the *couillons* [testicles], flourishing and decrepit, blazoned by Panurge and Frère Jean (III: 26 and 28); and the blazon of Triboullet by Pantagruel and Panurge (III: 38). The "grotesque open body" (as against the "closed classical") means that part which in a sense is open to the world, mainly the "material bodily lower stratum," but not solely: nose, ears, and mouth as well as nipples, anus, genitalia. Of these, all but ears and nipples are prominent in Rabelais. The correspondence of these parts with Rabelaisian obscenity is obvious: noses, and the reason why Frère Jean's is sturdy and well-formed (I: 40), which also brings in breasts; the almost ever-present mouth, hungry and thirsty; the genital humor, especially the horrific dimensions of woman's "wound," the vagina (II: 15; IV, 47; etc.); and the fact that Rabelais's obscenity—always gay* but never titillating—is as concerned with elimination as with generation.

Rabelais's humor, whether or not involved with fantasy or satire or both, is almost always carnivalesque and grotesque. Whatever else it is, it is not witty; it is coarse, earthy, and exuberant. The only example of wit I can think of is in *Book One* (1, 8), when Rabelais describes the ancient book of Gargantua's genealogy as "plus, mais non mieulx sentent que roses" [smelling more, but not better, than roses]. Wit calls for a smile, usually at some human foible; Rabelais's humor calls

* Need I say that I am using the word "gay," as does Iswolsky, in its legitimate sense, and not to mean "homosexual"? However, Iswolsky makes something "gay" out of almost anything that in the most polite society one does not mention freely: the pox, urinating, etc. Whether or not these are all truly "gay" is for the reader to decide.

for a belly laugh at some distorted lower-stratum aspect of the human condition: the enormous size of vaginas and their availability on the market; the dimensions of appetite for eating and drinking; the millions that a giant (or his mare) can drown in his (or her) urine; and the like. Wit tends to avoid the preposterous; Rabelaisian comedy revels in it.

Rabelaisian humor is earthy, by which I mean obscene without being pornographic or titillating; and this earthiness is part of what Bakhtin means by grotesque and carnivalesque. Rabelais is constantly "dirty"; yet he would be the despair of any "porno artist." References to sexual play are lacking; those to copulation are almost always grotesque. More of this in the next chapter.

The exuberance that marks Rabelais is normally opposed to wit and obviously related, even by etymology, to the carnivalesque. In his book there are always food and drink—and words—aplenty. No one ever counts calories—or how many bottles, barrels, or carcasses of meat there are left, or how much there is in them. Likewise with words. Both before and after Rabelais—perhaps especially since Pascal wrote in the 1650s that he lacked the time to make one of his *Provincial Letters* shorter—we have known that shorter is better, that every word cut is a gain in spareness and probably in clarity. No one seems to have told Rabelais this, and we his readers are the gainers. He can tell a crisp story when he chooses to; but why use two words, he seems as a rule to ask, when sixteen or sixty are available? Very few writers have had such an appetite for words or indulged it so felicitously. Once again, this appetite is characteristic of the carnivalesque.

Let us see how Bakhtin's main themes are illustrated in Rabelais's text. He draws most of his examples from the most "popular" parts of the work, *Books One* and *Two* and the first four Prologues. (He barely touches on the *Fifth Book* because of its doubtful authenticity.) In virtually all the episodes he treats, he finds an abundance of popular-festive themes. Here are some of the examples, most of them Bakhtin's, that I find especially striking.

The sheer number of banqueting scenes is remarkable. Invitations to drink and celebrations of drinking are everywhere, from the opening Prologue to the "TRINCH" of the Divine Bottle. Festive eating is almost as prominent. In *Pantagruel*, feasts follow the Baisecul-Humevesne trial (14, 226–27), the debate in signs with Thaumaste (20, 259), the burning of the 660 horsemen of Anarche (27), and Epistémon's visit to hell

(30); and Anarche's army gets itself stone drunk (28, 285–86). In *Gargantua* there is the great feast at his birth (4, 15 ff.), a chapter (5) devoted to the talk of the topers, his cry at birth "A boyre!" and his gigantic consumption of food and drink (6–7, 23–25). The Picrocho-line war starts over a few cakes (ch. 25), and a feast marks Gargantua's arrival to help his father in the war (37, 39, 40). Even in the *Third Book* the three expert consultants give their advice at a Sunday dinner (29, 434; 30–36). In the *Fourth Book* Papimania is a scene of feasting, as is the Ringing Island in the *Fifth*; the Chitterlings are put to rout mainly by cooks; feasting solves the problems off Chaneph (64, 718–21); and the Gaster episode, which assigns all human inventiveness to the stomach, contains what Bakhtin calls (p. 280) "the longest list of foods of all world literature" (59–60, 700–07).

Bakhtin stresses the role of the king in the carnival: treated as clown, parodized, abused, sometimes even killed, dismembered, and re-placed by the new king (pp. 197, 212, 217, and *passim*). Among his examples are, in *Pantagruel*, the treatment of kings (all reduced to menial status) in Epistémon's visit to his carnivalesque hell (ch. 30), and Anarche, who is made a crier of green sauce and married to an old whore who beats him (ch. 31). In *Gargantua* he finds a king-as-clown type in Janotus de Bragmardo, chosen spokesman for the powerful (or once-powerful) Sorbonne, who plays the clown to everyone's delight (17–20). King Picrochole is not only beaten but ridiculed. When his horse stumbled as they fled, he killed him in his anger, tried to take a donkey in his place from a nearby mill, and was beaten and stripped by the millers. Replaced on his throne by his son and lost from the sight of all, he is said to be now an underpaid porter in Lyons (49–50). Even Panurge's behavior in the *Third Book*, his fear of cuckoldry and re-fusal to risk it, Bakhtin sees (p. 242) as a desire to be the eternal old king—which is of course impossible—and not beaten and robbed by his wife and replaced by the new king-lover who will make him a cuckold. And in the *Fourth Book* (16, 585), even the behavior of the beaten Chiquanous, "happy as a king or two" after his drubbing by Frère Jean, is represented by Bakhtin (pp. 196–97) as another instance of the beaten king, the king as clown.

Parody, which Bakhtin finds abundant in the carnival, sometimes but not always at the king's expense, abounds in Rabelais. In *Pantagruel* we note the language of the Limousin student (6), the titles of the books of St.-Victor (7), the Baisecul-Humevesne lawsuit (10–13), and the resurrection of Epistémon (30). For Bakhtin (pp. 229–30), the 600,014 dogs who follow Panurge's unfortunate lady of Paris to piss on her and try to mount her (22, 266–67) are a parody of the Corpus Christi procession. In *Gargantua* there is much parody of words of the Gospel, as in the "Sitio" ["I thirst"] spoken by Christ on the cross (John 19:28) in the talk of the topers (5,20); the more elaborate "Ad formam nasi cognoscitur ad te levavi" (40, 120) [By the shape of the nose is known "I raised to thee"] (presumably an allusion to the penis), echoing Psalms 123:1; and when Gargantua drowns 260,418 Parisians in his urine, "not counting the women and little children" (17, 54), parodying the stories of the loaves and fishes. There is parody of the medieval doctrine of faith as what cannot be understood, in Gargantua's birth through his mother's ear (6, 23–24). The whole episode of Janotus and the bells is a parody (17–20). In the *Third Book* there is Bridoye and his use of dice. There is less of it in the last two books.

Bakhtin finds in Rabelais two or three examples of the dismembered body (usually that of the king), a frequent phenomenon in the folklore of the carnival. In *Gargantua* Frère Jean des Entommeures [Friar John of the Hashes] twice makes mincemeat of his adversaries: in his slaughter of 13,622 members of Picrochole's army who attack the abbey of Seuillé and its vineyard (27, 85–87), and the later slaughter of those other enemies who had held him captive (44, 127–29). The other example is the Chiquanous—and Basché's "wedding guest" hosts who beat them (IV: 14–16)—and the episode that Panurge also narrates just before, in which François Villon, denied a modest favor for his passion play by Friar Estienne Tappecoue, gets his own "devils" to frighten Tappecoue's mare until she causes her rider to be literally torn to shreds (13).

Another category of Bakhtin's is oaths and praise and abuse. Both are found almost everywhere in Rabelais: the oaths especially in the mouth of Frère Jean, and most profusely (in the original version) in those of the Parisians whom Gargantua bepissed on his arrival in their town (I: 17, 54). Praise and abuse are especially evident in the Prologues, notably in that of *Pantagruel* (praise of the book, abuse of those who might not believe every word of it) and in that of the *Third Book* (praise of the Pantagruelistic drinkers, abuse of the never-laughing censors who damn Rabelais's book).

Another major category of Bakhtin's is the market place, found mainly in the Prologues—especially the first three books', and the Old Prologue to the *Fourth*—where Rabelais's address to the reader is the old French *cri*, the spiel of the hawker trying to sell his wares. The usual address, to good people, drinkers, the gouty, and the pox-ridden, promotes a convivial gaiety, and even the diseases attributed to his hearers are "gay" in the sense that they arise from excessive or imprudent enjoyment of food, drink, and sex.

The other major themes in Bakhtin relate to the grotesque body and its material lower stratum. The grotesque body itself he finds (p. 341) featured in the treatment of the giants, especially early in *Books One* and *Two* when the giants are young, lusty, and uncouth. Elsewhere too it is often prominent: in *Pantagruel* particularly, in the curses that conclude the Prologue, in the account of Pantagruel's genealogy in chapter 1, and in Panurge's plans for building the walls of Paris (15). One of its features, the gaping mouth—seen in "Geoffroy à la grand dent" [Geoffrey of the Big Tooth] (5, 187); in the gaping jaws of Loup Garou (29, 291); and of course in the world that the narrator finds in Pantagruel's mouth (ch. 32)—is for Bakhtin the "hero" of *Pantagruel*.[2] I confess I cannot follow him this far.

The other main aspects of the grotesque body are urine and excrement—for Bakhtin, the elements that in a sense join the body to the sea and the earth respectively. Urine is especially prominent in what he reads as examples of grotesque debasement by besmirching (as in dung-slinging as the origin of mud-slinging), and notably in three horrific drownings in floods of urine: Anarche's army in Pantagruel's (II: 28, 287), the Parisians in Gargantua's (I: 17, 54), and Picrochole's army in that of Gargantua's mare (I: 36, 107). Excrement is probably featured most in Gargantua's discovery of the perfect ass-wipe (I: 13, 42–46; Bakhtin, pp. 371–77), the research project that proved to Grandgousier that his son was ready for a good education, and in many details of which (face-wipers used as ass-wipers) Bakhtin finds the face in effect replaced by the buttocks. The grotesque body may be simply anal: Pantagruel's fart and fizzle make the earth tremble for nine leagues around and engender a whole nation of dwarf men and women, more than 53,000 of each (II: 27, 282); and when Panurge brings Epistémon back to life (II: 30, 295; Bakhtin, p. 382), the final sign of his resuscitation (after breathing, opening his eyes, yawning, and sneezing) is that he "fist un gros pet de mesnage" [let a big household fart].

Genitalia are of course features of the "grotesque body," often enormous in Rabelais: the testicles and penis especially in the genealogy of Pantagruel (II: 1, 173), and the vagina notably in Gargantua's lament for Badebec (II: 3, 181), in Panurge's story (II: 15, 234–36) of the lion, the fox, and the old woman, and in the account of the naïve little devil and the Papefigue wife (IV: 47, 666).

Finally, the body that is so grotesquely celebrated in folklore and in

Rabelais has, for Bakhtin, a sort of immortality, not individual but social. This is why there is nothing tragic about death in Rabelais (Bakhtin, pp. 404–07); for the race always lives on, and that is what matters. Even in serious parts like the letter from Gargantua to Pantagruel (II: 8, 202–03), this theme is clear; Bakhtin (p. 324) finds it prominent in the *Third Book*, especially at the end of chapter 4 (on the duty and debt of marriage) and again (p. 425) in chapter 26, with Panurge's notion of dying only with the testicles empty, thus "leaving man for man." In Bakhtin's view (p. 39; cf. pp. 91–94), this sense that death is not to be feared makes Rabelais's "the most fearless book in world literature."

This chapter, devoted largely to Bakhtin's Rabelais, has sought to show not only the elasticity but the appropriateness of his categories. His "carnivalesque," or "popular-festive," clearly diminishes after *Books One* and *Two*, the "giant" books; Rabelais seems less enamored of it the further he goes; it is only one part of the essential Rabelais. However, it is a very large part, the one that most of us generally recognize as Rabelaisian, and without which, I suspect, no one but a few scholars would be reading and studying Rabelais today.

Obscenity

I take my definition of "obscene" from Webster's Unabridged Dictionary, 2nd edition: "Offensive to chastity of mind or to modesty; expressing or presenting to the mind or view something that delicacy, purity, and decency forbid to be exposed; lewd; indecent. . . ." Any application of such a definition obviously depends on time, place, and individual reader; "delicacy, purity, and decency" are far less forbidding today than twenty, fifty, or a hundred years ago; but most readers of Rabelais, even in emancipated times like his own and ours, have found him obscene. All his obscenity is comic; almost all his comedy is obscene.

As the last chapter showed, his comic obscenity is generally carnivalesque. To say this, however, is not (with Bakhtin, p. 224) to explain it as a different but widely accepted norm. As Grève has shown,[1] many contemporaries of Rabelais, without necessarily being shocked, considered him obscene. Carnivalesque obscenity is normally gay and relatively free from the erotic.* Together with the medical, which is rarely metaphysical about the human body, this is the tradition on which Rabelais draws and from which he springs. Thus once again Bakhtin is a valuable guide. Some critics, in trying to explain the impression of natural innocence that emanates from Rabelais's obscenity, and perhaps in reaction against the charge that it was cynical, have declared it naïve. Bakhtin, rightly I think, rejects both notions,[2] since

---

* I am using "erotic" not in Rollo May's sense of daimonic as against merely sexual, but in the familiar sense (recognized in Webster II) of that which relates to "sexual love" or "sexual desire" or both. For me it includes the pornographic and titillating, but need not be either.

both are extreme. "Naïve" is probably the closer of the two to the truth, but only in its older, etymological sense of natural. Naturalness is certainly one of the chief characteristics of Rabelais's obscenity; his "dirt" is that of a dirt road.

But while he is obscene, he is never pornographic, titillating, or even really erotic unless in an unusually broad sense of the term. From the first he has been compared with Aristophanes,[3] and not without reason: they share a similar exuberance, gaiety, love of words, and carnival quality. However, sexual desire, almost always grotesque in Rabelais, is portrayed—even if comically—much more realistically and erotically in Aristophanes, as in the scene in *Lysistrata* where Myrrhine, to get him to vote for peace, teases her conspicuously desirous husband Cinesias until he is ready to explode—and then runs off. In all Rabelais there is nothing remotely comparable. For all their many affinities, a similar contrast appears between Rabelais and Joyce. There is nothing in Rabelais like Molly Bloom's soliloquy at the end of *Ulysses*. Rabelais never, for example, shows erotic foreplay, or afterplay, or any conversation leading to sexual intercourse; and whenever he deals with the act itself, the grotesque always wins out over the titillating or even the realistic.

To show this, let us examine briefly Rabelais's handling of the erotic, first in episodes and then in words and expressions.

In *Pantagruel*, as we have seen, Gargantua laments the death of his wife Badebec in childbirth in serious and lofty terms, then lapses into the comically obscene (3,181). The Limousin schoolboy refers explicitly to the whoring in which he and his comrades indulge, but does so matter-of-factly in ridiculous Latinized French (6, 191). Equally matter-of-fact are the few erotic titles in the Library of St.-Victor (7, 198, etc.). The female genitalia with which—partly because of their cheapness—Panurge proposes to build the walls of Paris, are wholly disembodied and grotesque (15, 233). In the same chapter the old woman's "wound," kept free from flies by the fox at the lion's behest, is perfumed by her fizzling and anything but erotic (pp. 234–36). No more erotic is Panurge's boast of having laid 417 women in Paris since his arrival nine days before, which gives nothing but the statistic, or his story of the man carrying two little girls aged two or three and saying he thinks the one in front is probably a virgin, but he has no idea about the other. Again Rabelais gives no details about the copulation that Panurge arranges, for money, between ugly old women and poor men (17, 245–46).

Panurge's wooing of the lady of Paris (21–22), to be sure, is an attempted seduction, the only one in Rabelais; but it too is pretty matter-of-fact. In various ways he urges her directly to have intercourse with him, saying that she will enjoy it, but he does so in comically grotesque terms; he once tries to embrace her; on every occasion she sends him about his business. Nor is his revenge by means of the dogs calculated to arouse desire. His story of why the leagues are shortest in and near Paris and longer the further away one goes (23, 268) is erotic in substance but not in effect, as is his boast that he will lay all the 150,000 beautiful whores in Anarche's army (26, 278).

In *Gargantua*, sexually explicit episodes are rarer. Rabelais tells how Grandgousier and Gargamelle "often played the two-backed beast, joyously rubbing their bacon together," but carries it no further (3, 13). When Gargantua was between three and five, we learn that he loved to feel his nurses above and below, before and behind, and that they enjoyed playing with his penis and "burst out laughing when it raised its ears" (11, 38–39); here the tone is childishly playful. Once the gigantic grotesque is left behind, there remain only two slightly erotic disquisitions by Frère Jean: why a young lady's thighs are always cool (39, 115–16), and how the pilgrims are sure to find their wives pregnant on their return home, since "even the shadow of an abbey's bell tower is fertile" (45, 132).

The *Third Book* is richer in erotic material, as befits its subject. There is a passing allusion in the Prologue (p. 322) to the readiness of the ancient Corinthian women for the battle of love. Worthy of note is Rabelais's supplication—"on nom et révérence des quatre fesses qui vous engendrèrent, et de la vivificque cheville qui pour lors les coupploit" (p. 328) [in the name and reverence of the four buttocks that engendered you, and of the life-giving peg which for that time coupled them]—for here at last is a direct account of the sexual act. But the misrepresentation of how that act works is comic; the impersonality is complete; no emotion or desire is involved—or aroused; and the picture showing nothing but four buttocks coupled by a peg is, to my mind at least, grotesque.

Panurge's account (4, 346) of how the body prepares for generation is simply clinical, and his remarks about Frère Enguainnant [Friar Sheathing] and the exhaustion of newlywed men (6, 350) are hardly titillating. In many places (such as 7, 353) he tells of his itch to marry and copulate endlessly; but these are mere expressions, as are his verses on the wife whose husband left his codpiece unarmed (8, 357). When the Sibyl of Panzoust bids the visitors good-by by showing them her nether parts, there is of course comment on "the Sibyl's hole" (17, 389), but nothing else. More to the point is Panurge's account (19, 396) of the mute Roman lady who took an innocent inquiry from a young man as a request for sexual relations and eagerly granted it; but the only details concern the supposed request. Much the same is true of his next story (19, 396–97), of how Soeur Fessue [Sister Buttocky] was impregnated by Frère Royddimet [Friar Put-it-in-stiff], and when the fact became obvious, explained her plight and her problem to her abbess: she could not break the convent's law of silence by crying out; she signaled all she could—with her buttocks—but no one came to her aid; she confessed to the friar before he left, and he imposed the penance of telling no one. Even here the erotic yields to the comic: the story of the seduction (or rape) is told only in the nun's naïve answers to her abbess; and when it is done, Pantagruel is emphatically not amused.

After noting in passing Panurge's statement that Her Trippa's wife was enjoyed by the court lackeys (25, 416–17) while he was telling the king about transcendent celestial matters, we pass to Frère Jean's story of Hans Carvel's ring (28, 432–33). An able older man married to a sexy young wife, Carvel tried to persuade her to control her urges. One night in a dream he told his troubles to the Devil, who put a ring on his finger and told him that if he kept it on he would never be a cuckold. He agreed, awoke, and found he had his finger in what Rabelais likes to call his wife's what's-its-name. Frère Jean goes on to tell how the wife drew back as if to say, "Yes, no, that's not what you should put there." The main narration is of the dream, and the method advised to avoid cuckoldry is surely comic and grotesque.

Besides the blazoning of the testicles by Panurge and Frère Jean (ch. 26 and 28), which is hardly pornographic, there remains only Rondibilis, with his account of how carnal concupiscence may be checked (31), and how—and especially why—cuckoldry naturally follows marriage (ch. 32). Eloquent as he is about how a woman is possessed by an insatiably sexual animal inside her, the uterus, he still gives a strictly clinical account of the phenomenon. After him I see nothing worth mentioning in this vein in the *Third Book*.

In the Prologue to the *Fourth Book* Rabelais makes much of two aspects of Priapus (528–33): his most prominent feature and his play on the word "coingnée" [ax; screwed]; yet the verses he quotes are far more comic than erotic. When Panurge, in Medamothi (2, 543), buys a copy of Philomela's picture of her rape by Tereus, Rabelais explains that it does not represent "un homme couplé sus une fille. Cela est trop sot et trop lourd" [a man coupled on top of a woman. That is too stupid and too heavy-handed]. Panurge's exasperated question to Dindenault (5, 553)—what would you do with my prick if it remained inside your wife after I had screwed her?—leads to the typically Rabelaisian and hardly titillating conclusion: "Would you pull it out with your teeth?" Chapter 9, on Ennasin, the Island of Alliances, is full of frank suggestions of copulation between the partners; but these are all either grotesque or simply comic. The woman playing the bride in the ceremony staged for the Chiquanous (15, 583) complains that she has been sexually molested by him, but describes his misdeed in a grotesque newly coined word of fourteen syllables, "trepignemampenillo-rifrizonoufressuré." (And again, this story is told by Panurge, to the mild but clear disapproval of Pantagruel: 16, 584.) In Papimania Frère Jean asks for two or three cartloads of the girls who served them (54, 688–89) to use in the obvious way; but once again, his mode of expression is comic and a bit grotesque.

The erotic is even harder to find in the *Fifth Book*. In the story of the charger and the donkey (ch. 7), the latter is eager to copulate, but even *his* eagerness remains just that. The only other episode worth noting in this domain is that of the Frères Fredons; chapter 28 is devoted mainly to the friars' monosyllabic answers telling of their girls and how often they lay them. Monosyllabism, however, is hard to ally with the pornographic.

I hope this survey of the passages and episodes in Rabelais that might be considered erotic has shown that they are not very many—compare any contemporary novel—or very striking. Rabelais delights in the obscene but avoids the pornographic, and normally skirts the potentially erotic as he seeks the grotesque or the purely comic.

As for terms and expressions, these may be tested for eroticism briefly—but, I think, satisfactorily—with the help of an excellent article that analyzes the verbs Rabelais uses to express the act of copulation. In "An Aspect of Obscenity in Rabelais,"[4] Raymond C. La Charité finds thirty-six expressions so used, of which fifteen are Rabelais's own fabrications. (In contrast, the fifteenth-century *Cent Nouvelles nouvelles*, full of erotic activity, offer only fourteen in all.)

They range in length from simple words like "bouter" [put, place, drive] to more complex forms like "faire la beste à deux dos," already found in *Cent Nouvelles nouvelles*, no. 20, and picked up by Shakespeare in *Othello* (I, i) as "making the beast with two backs"; or the more cryptic "jouer des manequins à basses marches"; or to such Rabelaisian creations as "bubujaller," "fanfrelucher," "fretinfretailler," "gimbretiletolleter," "rataconniculer," and "sacsacbezevezinemasser." Rabelais's images for copulation are drawn mainly from trades, instruments, devices, gymnastics, animal life, and most of all human anatomy.

To my mind, La Charité's findings reveal a Rabelais far more concerned with the comic and the grotesque than with the erotic, let alone the pornographic or titillating. Moreover, if we drew a line between strong glorification of the sexual act, as in a D. H. Lawrence, and strong denigration, as in a Jonathan Swift, Rabelais, I suspect, would be less close to Lawrence than one might suppose, and perhaps closer to Swift.

We know that he had his three illegitimate children, probably by two different women, perhaps even by three. We know nothing of how he felt about the women or the act; we can only draw inferences from his life and his book. To me the book suggests that his feelings were very mixed: a considerable desire for the act and for a partner in it, and a considerable feeling—perhaps partly monastic, partly medical, partly carnivalesque—that the act is not to be idealized or beautified, but rather seen and treated as comic, grotesque, perhaps even debasing.

Obscenity normally aims not only to amuse but to shock. Sometimes the purpose of the shock is didactic: to remind us that humans are flesh and blood as well as mind and spirit, buttocks and genitals as well as eyes and brain; or, as Montaigne puts it (whose obscenity is in this sense normally didactic), that we are just as much beast as angel, and often—if not always—more so.

I think there is such a didactic element in much of Rabelais's obscenity, not as clear as in Montaigne, in whom it almost balances the comic, but still clear at times. One example we have noted in another context. When Badebec has died giving birth to Pantagruel, Gargantua laments her (II: 3, 181; quoted above, p. viii) at first in lofty words as "my darling, my love . . ." But then he goes on to say "my little cunt" (and corrects the "little" by specific, and horrific, dimensions), "my tender thing, my codpiece, my shoe, my slipper"—all erotic terms in

the usage of the time. I take this to mean that Gargantua loved Badebec in many ways, not the least of which was as a sexual partner, and
that Rabelais wants to remind us that this is an important part of
marriage and of what a bereaved spouse will miss. It remains of course
comic and obscene; but it is also a reminder of our human condition.[5]

Perhaps the best way to show Rabelais's innocence of pornography
is to compare his treatments of gigantic procreation with that of his
main source. Here is his account of how Pantagruel was begotten (II:
2, 177): "Gargantua, en son eage de quatre cens quatre-vingtz quarante
et quatre ans, engendra son filz Pantagruel de sa femme, nommée Badebec, fille du roy des Amaurotes en Utopie, laquelle mourut du mal
d'enfant." [Gargantua, at the age of four hundred and fourscore and
forty-four years, begat his son Pantagruel by his wife, named Badebec,
daughter of the king of the Amaurotes in Utopia, and she died in
childbirth.] The making of Gargantua, as we have noted, is only a
little livelier:

> En son cage virile [Grandgousier] espousa Gargamelle, fille du roy des
> Parpaillos, belle gouge et de bonne troigne, et faisoient eux deux souvent
> ensemble la beste à deux doz, joyeusement se frotans leur lard, tant qu'elle
> engroissa d'un beau filz et le porta jusques à l'unzieome moys. (I: 3, 13)

> [In the age of manhood [Grandgousier] married Gargamelle, daughter
> of the king of the Parpaillons, a good-looking wench with a nice mug, and
> together the two of them often played the two-backed beast, joyfully rub-
> bing their bacon against each other, so much so that she grew big with a
> handsome son and carried him to the eleventh month.]

Here now is his model in the *Grandes et inestimables cronicques*.[6]
To help King Arthur, Merlin has magically created, on the highest
mountain in the Orient, first Grant-Gosier, then Galemelle. When
they have named each other, he sends them down from the mountain
to find and bring him the mare that he has created for them.

> Adonc par le commandement de Merlin Grant-Gosier et Galemelle
> descendirent au bas de la montagne pour aller querir la grant jument.
> Grant-Gosier, qui fut le premier au bas de la montagne, regardoit venir
> Galemelle, et prenoit plaisir à regarder l'entre-deux de ses chausses (car ilz
> estoyent tous nudz). Adonc que Galemelle fut descendue, il luy demanda
> quelle chausse elle avoit là. Adonc luy respond en eslargissant ses cuysses
> qu'elle avoit cette playe de nature. Grant-Gosier regardant la playe large
> et rouge comme le feu Sainct-Anthoine, le membre luy dressa, lequel il
> avoit gros comme le ventre d'une cacque de haranc, et long à l'advenant. Il
> dist à Galemelle que il estoit barbier, et que de son membre feroit esprou-
> vette pour savoir se la playe estoit parfonde; à laquelle playe il ne trouva

nul fons. Toutesfoys, si bien leur agréa le jeu que ilz engendrèrent Gargantua; puis menèrent la grant jument à Merlin.

[Then by Merlin's command Grant-Gosier and Galemelle went down to the foot of the mountain to go and find the big mare. Grant-Gosier, who was the first at the foot of the mountain, watched Galemelle come down, and took pleasure in looking at the gap between her hose (for they were both naked). Then when Galemelle was down, he asked her what hose she had on there. Then she answered him, spreading her thighs, that she had that wound by nature. As Grant-Gosier looked at the wound, broad, and red like St. Anthony's fire, his member came erect, which was as big as the center of a herring barrel, and long in proportion. He said to Galemelle that he was a barber [i.e., a surgeon's assistant], and that of his member he would make a probe to find out if the wound was deep; to which wound he found no bottom. However, they enjoyed the sport so much that they engendered Gargantua; then they took the big mare to Merlin.]

The passages speak for themselves. Compared to the author of the *Grandes Cronicques*—the most logical term of comparison—for eroticism, titillation, or pornography, Rabelais seems like a prude.

In short, I think that Rabelais's obscenity belongs clearly to the carnivalesque tradition (even in its "didactic" aspect) but is not completely defined by it. Although it qualifies as obscene by offending "delicacy" and the like, it seeks the grotesque and the "purely" comic, avoids the erotic in the usual sense of the term, and rejects the pornographic entirely. I do not find the same tone in any other author I have read. Carnivalesque it surely is, but it is also surely Rabelais's very own.[7]

Satire and Fantasy

I have already noted the presence of both these elements in the *Fourth* and *Fifth Books,* and that of satire in *Pantagruel.* Here I would like to offer an overview and a few generalizations.

I am not speaking of satire in the Menippean sense used by Northrop Frye and Dorothy Coleman, but rather to mean a comic representation—usually exaggerated—of some human vice or folly with the aim of exposing, discrediting, and perhaps amending it. In *Modern English Usage* H. W. Fowler distinguishes satire from other forms of humor by its motive or aim (amendment), its province (morals and manners), its method or means (accentuation), and its audience (the self-satisfied).* Satire often verges on caricature (when comic deformation is prominent and ridicule is a major aim), and on parody (when the factor of imitation stands out). Rabelais's satire, rarely ironic or sarcastic, is often caricatural or parodic.

Fantasy I find harder to define. Fowler quotes the Oxford English Dictionary as finding its "predominant sense" in "caprice, whim, fanciful invention." To these I would add, from Webster, a "chimerical or fantastical notion." What seems to me the truest fantasy in Rabelais is that which is marked by irreality or unreality.

Obviously satire and fantasy are quite different things; but they so often go hand in hand in Rabelais that they may be dealt with together.

---

* For Fowler, sarcasm seeks to inflict pain, by inversion, in the province of faults and foibles, for an audience of victim and bystander; irony seeks exclusiveness, by mystification, in the province of statement of facts, addressing an inner circle.

Almost from the first, and especially since the eighteenth century, some readers have seen Rabelais as primarily a satirist, notably those who read his book as a *roman à clef* exposing the inequities of his society. This view is no longer accepted, and the center of his humor is found elsewhere. I find satire frequent only in the *Fourth Book* and the first third of the *Fifth*.

In *Pantagruel* there is little satire, most of which is parodic: the catalogue of the Library of St.-Victor (7); the setting for the Baisecul-Humevesne trial, showing how a lawsuit should, and should not, be conducted (10); and some aspects (such as profound thought without words) of the debate in signs with Thaumaste (18–20). I see little else.

Gargantua is not much richer. There is satire of the allegories read by some into Homer (Prologue, p. 5); of the prevalent theories of the symbolic meaning of colors (9, 31); of the bad old education, from texts and methods to study habits (14 and 21–22). The episode of Janotus de Bragmardo (18–20) seems to me mainly caricature and parody; but his response to his Sorbonne colleagues (20, 61) is satirical as well as indignant. The other satirical bits deal with war: its ridiculously petty causes (25–26), the aggressor king Picrochole (26, 28, 32–33, 47), and to some extent his fate (49). And that is about it.

The times may explain the scarcity of satire in these first two books, for when Rabelais wrote them he seemed confident that the ideas he championed would triumph. Satire is the weapon of an underdog or of someone who regards himself as such; the top dog has other weapons, including ridicule. In *Books One* and *Two* Rabelais seems to have seen himself as being on top. Janotus could be ridiculed; Quaresmeprenant and Homenaz require stronger weapons.

In the *Third Book*, however, satire is still rare—I think because Rabelais is trying, to some extent at least, to avoid dangerous polemics. I see mainly irony and parody in Panurge's opening praise of debts (2–4), and possible irony and parody (again, of the rhetorical eulogy) in the closing chapters on Pantagruelion (49–52). Chapter 48 on marriage without parental consent is indignant but hardly satiric. In the account of Judge Bridoye (ch. 39–44) there is satire of legal foibles—the endless citation of Latin authorities, the use of the *alea judiciorum*, and of course the refrain "comme vous aultres, Messieurs"—but it is overshadowed by the purely comic and bounded by the serious suggestion of Christian folly. The account of Her Trippa (25) is mainly caricature and parody, with perhaps some satiric aim of exposing his faith in his "mancies." The main elements of satire in the *Third Book* are directed at Panurge: his heresy-sniffing (22, 405; etc.), his frantic desire to have things all his own way in marriage, and his consequent inability to make up his mind whether to marry or not.

The *Fourth Book* is the richest in satire, most of which we have noted in our chapter 6. There is ironic satire in the portrait of the sneering, boastful sheep merchant Dindenault (5–7), and more in the highly sexual alliances of Ennasin Island (9). Satire as well as caricature marks the treatment of the summons-serving Chiquanous (12–16), and the detailed anatomization of the giant Lent-observer Quaresme-prenant(29–32). Fantasy marks the account of the Chitterlings (35–42), but I find in it also satire of their weakness and bellicosity combined, as there clearly is in chapters 43–44 on the people of Ruach and how they live on wind alone. Those who would deny believers access to the Bible are satirized in the lament of the little devil in Papefigue land over the students no longer available for Lucifer's lunch (46, 664). Satire is the essence of Papimania (48–54), as already noted—mainly that of worship of the Pope and of the unscrupulous greed and cruelty of the Roman curia. Already noted also is the satire of the Gastrolâtres and the Engastrimythes in the account of Messere Gaster (57–62); and it is present as well in the treatment of Ganabin (66), home of the robbers who persecute the Evangelicals.

In the *Fifth Book* satire abounds in the Ringing Island (1–8) with its lazy, gluttonous, robotlike birds who represent the clergy, and is at its ugliest in the portrayal of the greedy and ruthless Furred Cats of the law, who live on corruptions (11–15), and of the stupid and greedy Apedeftes of the tax courts (16), who squeeze potable gold out of everything. The account of the Frères Fredons (27–29) is extremely satirical: of their facing two ways, breakfasting on yawns, and above all copulating—diligently but apparently mechanically—especially during Lent.

Satire in Rabelais is most prominent in the *Fourth Book* and the first third of the *Fifth*. Unnecessary in the first two, scanted probably for reasons of caution in the *Third*, it emerges in the last two as the best way for an admitted but unresigned underdog to get back at powerful and oppressive enemies. Understandably, much of it in the last two books is less gay than grim: parts at least of Papimania, the Ringing Island, the Furred Cats, and the Apedeftes are striking examples.

Fantasy is also most abundant in the last two books. In the first two, to be sure, there is a sort of fantasy in the giantism. However, this is a given, which we accept as such from the beginning; and the giants are often portrayed as though of normal size. Virtually the only fantasy that I see in *Gargantua* is such episodes as Gargantua combing cannon balls out of his hair and Grandgousier thinking they are lice (I: 37, 109–10), and Gargantua eating (without harm to them) six pilgrims in a salad (I: 38, 111–13).[1] *Pantagruel* includes similar episodes of giantism, as for instance the world in Pantagruel's mouth and the mining of his bowels in 32–33, and others that touch on fantasy: Panurge's use of many languages, including several of Rabelais's invention (9); the fantastic nonsense of Baisecul and Humevesne (11–13); many details of Panurge's escape from the Turks (14); his plans for building the walls of Paris (15); his debate with Thaumaste (18–20); his (and others') exploits in the war (25, etc.); Loup Garou with his three hundred giants and magic mace (29); and Epistémon's visit to hell and restoration to life (30). Yet most of these episodes tell of remarkable things performed by humans, but lack the preternatural element found in the later books. They do not require quite the same suspension of disbelief as do Quaresmeprenant, the Chitterlings, Messere Gaster, the humanoid birds of the Ringing Island, or the Furred Cats.

The *Third Book* is almost completely devoid of fantasy. Rabelais skirts it in four episodes: the weird Sibyl of Panzoust (17); the dying poet Raminagrobis, supernaturally endowed with the gift of divination but not really using it in the consultation (21); the quasi-magician Her Trippa (25); and the Pantagruelion with its miraculous powers (49–52). Yet none of these seems quite to belong to the world of fantasy.

In the *Fourth Book* we have the fantastic objects purchased at Medamothi [Nowhere] (2–4); the inhabitants of the Island of Alliances (9) with their noses shaped like the ace of clubs; in Thohu and Bohu (17), the giant Bringuenarilles, who swallowed pots and pans for lack of windmills, but choked on a pat of butter; the supernatural disturbances (tempests and the like) upon the death of heroes (26); the account of the whale (perhaps realistic for its time) and of Pantagruel's superhuman prowess in hurling darts (33–34); and the animate, indeed humanoid Chitterlings with their tutelary god, the Idea (or form) of Mardigras, a flying pig spouting mustard (35–42). There is fantasy in the wind-eating inhabitants of Ruach (43–44), in the account of the Frozen Words (55–56), and in the story of Messere Gaster (57–62), inspirer of all human inventions, including even that of a "boomerang" cannon ball.

In the *Fifth Book*, especially in parts whose authenticity seems most suspect, there is a different sort of fantasy of sumptuous detail, reminiscent of the Abbey of Theleme but going beyond it: Entelechy (19–25), the land of Satin (30–31), and especially the temple of the Divine Bottle and its approaches (35–42)—the great doors opening apparently by magic, the mosaic of the vault portraying Bacchus' victory over the Indians, the wonderful lamp, and the details of the temple itself and of the oracular fountain. Primarily comic is the fantasy of the Isle des Ferremens (9), where metal tools may be shaken off the trees; of Outre, whose "people" are like bursting leather wine bottles (17); and of the lady Lanterns of Lanternois (32–33 bis), especially in view of the erotic connotations of "lanterner" [copulate]. Satiric and often dark, as so often in the last two books, is the fantasy of the Ringing Island (1–8), with the clerics as birds; of the terrifying Furred Cats of the law (11–15), with their long claws whose clutches nothing escapes; and of the ignorant Apedeftes with their giant wine press (16).

In short, there is a sort of fantasy of giantism that recurs often in *Books One* and *Two;* a good deal of another sort, human and not very fantastical, in *Pantagruel,* especially relating to Panurge; and a little of another, that of sumptuous detail, in the account of the Abbey of Theleme. This is about all for the first three books. The fantasy of the preternatural is largely confined to the last two books, especially the last two-thirds of the *Fourth* and the first third of the *Fifth,* in which it abounds.

As we now have seen, satire and fantasy are used increasingly, and become linked and often somber, in the last two books. In the first three, neither one seems to be an important weapon in Rabelais's arsenal: partly, no doubt, because of his chosen subject matter, but mainly, I think, because of the times and his relation to them. In the hopeful days of the first two books they must have seemed unneeded, and in the tentative days of the *Third Book,* uncalled for; nor are they prominent in the first third (the 1548 part) of the *Fourth Book.* It is mainly in the years 1552–53, the last two of Rabelais's life—again, assuming the *Fifth Book* is in part at least by Rabelais—that they emerge: fantasy no doubt as a sort of escape from the ugly world of reality, satire as the recourse of the underdog who is partly oppressed, and partly just appalled, by the abuse of enormous power. They offer Rabelais some solace, and a way to have his say, in a bad time. In spite of the support of Odet de Chastillon, I think that the last few years of his life were such a time for Rabelais.

Storytelling

Storytelling is one of Rabelais's greatest gifts. All his readers have recognized this; many have noted it without analyzing it, or have dealt thoroughly with aspects tangential to it; but only one writer I know of has found the tools for a real analysis.

Among the most useful treatments of tangential questions I would list six: Bakhtin's book on the carnivalesque;[1] La Charité's article on the unity of *Pantagruel*, with its demonstration of recurrent patterns such as inflation followed by deflation; Floyd Gray's perceptive articles on the persona in the Prologues to *Book One* and the *Third Book*; Gérard Defaux's study in *ER* XI of Alcofribas Nasier as character and narrator; François Rigolot's chapter on the language of the storyteller (*Les Langages de Rabelais*, ch. 4); and Dorothy Gabe Coleman's *Rabelais: A Critical Study in Prose Fiction*, with its attention to the persona, to style (paratactic and hypotactic, etc.), and to the genre (Menippean satire or comic romance) to which Rabelais's book belongs. None of the six, however, offers much on narrative as such.

The most useful book in this area is Abraham C. Keller's *The Telling of Tales in Rabelais: Aspects of His Narrative Art* (Frankfurt am Main: Klostermann, 1963). He has seen many questions to ask about narrative, asked them, and found many interesting answers. Much more remains to be done in this area, but he has made an excellent start.

Keller has given his main attention to the stories and anecdotes that are not part of Rabelais's main plot but that are told for their own sake. With appropriate reservations but a sure hand, he has divided these into the more fully developed "stories" and the briefer, less circumstantial "anecdotes." He has counted each type in each book—including the *Fifth*, but without accepting its authenticity—and examined them in various ways, including their close or loose relationship to the main plot. He has much to offer on oral quality, spontaneity, pace, build-up, the "live" audience, specific preparation, delay (and its purposes and techniques), the "topping" of stories, and the story within a story. Keller is clearly himself a storyteller who has given much thought to the aims and techniques of the art. When he writes of Rabelais's crafty delays in the stories of Couillatris and Dindenault as examples of oral rather than literary storytelling (p. 14; cf. pp. 9–17, *passim*), and concludes that "like every good storyteller, Rabelais has in both cases made a short story long" (p. 18), we know we are in good hands.

Keller's principal findings are these. Except in the *Fifth Book*, Rabelais tells more stories and anecdotes the further he goes. Keller's counts for the five books, arranged in chronological order (pp. 29–30, 35–37), are the following: stories—II, 6; I, 3; III, 7; IV, 8; V, 1; anecdotes—II, 2; I, 2; III, 12; IV, 26, V, 1. Moreover, in the first two books all but one or two stories "form part of the sustained narrative" (p. 28), whereas later almost all are "extras." The anecdotes too are generally more closely linked with the main narrative in *Books One* and *Two* than in the next two. (Because the separable narratives in the *Fifth Book* are so rare and because of its doubtful authenticity—on which Keller's findings cast further doubt—he leaves it out of consideration and concentrates on the first four, mainly on the first two in contrast with the *Third* and the *Fourth*.) He finds the subordinate narratives of the *Third* and *Fourth Books* more adroitly prepared and built up than those of *One* and *Two*, showing a marked progress in the storyteller's art. Of the *Fourth Book* he writes: "It is by this time only that Rabelais was a master at reproducing the storytelling atmosphere" (p. 19); and of the *Third* and the *Fourth*, that in moving to them from *One* and *Two* we rise to "regions of subtler intellect and higher art" (p. 27).

Already in these last statements we have moved a long way from mere findings toward conclusions, as we have in Keller's near-identification of Rabelais *as creator* with Panurge (pp. 58–60). Among actual conclusions I would place his sense that the later books are the best and his subordination of Pantagruelism to what he calls "Rabelaisianism": the wilder, more comic, less lofty spirit that inspires many of the stories and is incarnated in Panurge. For him this represents Rabelais's "unconscious attitudes"; in contrast, Pantagruelism "is literature, not life"; the art of Maistre François is Rabelaisianism, his Pantagruelism mere propaganda (pp. 76–77).

I cannot follow Keller in all his conclusions. It seems to me more assumed than demonstrated that each of Rabelais's first four books is better than the one before; that the product of the writer's subconscious or unconscious is superior to that of his conscious (Keller himself has shown Rabelais's conscious artistry in telling tales); that the stories represent "life" as against mere "literature" (Keller has shown their literary artistry); that Rabelais's serious messages are only propaganda, and the stories alone true art. The fact that the separable narratives (stories and anecdotes) multiply rapidly and separate from the main plot after the first two books may reflect mainly the fact that only the first two books have a strong story line.

For many of his readers (of whom I am one), Rabelais's greatest achievement lies less in his skill as a teller of separable tales—or even in his extraordinary comic inventiveness—than in his unique blend of the narrative, the comic, and the serious and lofty; less in either his "Rabelaisianism" or Pantagruelism alone than in the way he mixes both. Many excellent readers of Rabelais prefer *Pantagruel* or *Gargantua* to any of the later books. Rabelais's contemporary, Bonaventure des Périers, was also a superb teller of comic tales. If Rabelais had sensed, as Keller seems close to arguing, that his own greatest gift was as a teller of separable tales, it seems that logically he should have moved from writing his "novel" to composing tales like Des Périers and many others. Instead he did more, and wrote the *Third* and *Fourth Books*—and perhaps at least parts of the *Fifth*.

Keller's near-identification of Rabelais as creator with Panurge seems dubious to me. The further Rabelais goes—until the end of the *Fifth Book*, with which Keller does not deal—the more Panurge becomes a coward and a superstitious heresy-sniffer. I can imagine Rabelais portraying an alter ego of his own as a coward, but not as a heresy-sniffer, for that would clash with his own strongest commitments.

Finally the very term "Rabelaisianism," as used to designate the opposite of Pantagruelism, seems to me loaded; for it implies that Pantagruelism is not truly Rabelaisian. I agree with Keller that the importance of Pantagruelism may have been overstressed by Rabelais scholars; but to dismiss it as mere propaganda and (at least by implication) as un-Rabelaisian seems to me a serious mistake.

Keller's major findings, however, remain solid and important. They show Rabelais as an artful storyteller working more in an oral than a literary tradition, increasingly eager to spin yarns for their own sake and not merely to advance the main story, increasingly adept at preparing them, filling them out, and prolonging them by such devices as interruption (Couillatris) and suspenseful stalling (Dindenault). The further he goes, the more he creates the effect of a live audience, and with this, more topping of stories one by another, more stories within stories, and altogether a more natural storytelling situation. A master of pace, he is swift or leisurely in turn as he senses the demands of the circumstances and of the reader. As he moves away (in the *Third* and *Fourth Books*) from a ready-made plot and a strong story line, the separable stories more and more become "extras" brought in simply "à propos" and take a major place in the book; and he himself becomes not so much the narrator (through a persona, to be sure) of a single unified story as the maestro whose virtuosity sets his many characters spinning separable stories and anecdotes to the live and appreciative audience of one another. Whether this change makes Rabelais a greater artist or merely constitutes a resourceful compensation is, to my mind, open to question; but it seems to me unquestionably a significant change that Keller has taught us to see.

Most of the other work that touches on Rabelais as narrator—the studies by Coleman, Defaux, Gray, and Rigolot—deals mainly with his narrative persona. Agreement now seems general that his narrator—whether labeled Alcofribas or not, whether in the Prologues or in the text itself—is a true persona, not to be mistaken for the author, and whose interposition is one of Rabelais's many games with his reader. I think we shall, and should, see more studies of this question. To me the Rabelaisian narrative persona appears almost as arbitrarily variable as the size of the giants. I simply do not believe that the carnivalesque hucksters of the Prologues are all the same, and that there is not a progression in subtlety and erudition from the speaker of the Prologue of *Book Two* to that (or those) of *Book One, Book Three,* or *Book Four.* Nor can I believe that this persona (if it is one; at least that of the *First,* the *Third,* and the *Fourth Book*) is the same person as the naïve Alcofribas who explores—and shits in—the vast land in Pantagruel's mouth. In short, now that we have several good studies of Rabelais's *persona,* I hope to see more of his *personae;* for I think these are many and need to be explored.

In conclusion I would like to make one point of my own. Of all the comic storytellers I know, perhaps of all storytellers, Rabelais is the one whose stories suffer most in retelling. Surely all his admirers know the phenomenon: a glazing of the listener's eyes and the reaction, spoken or silent: "Well! I don't see what's so funny or so great about *that!*" This—at least in my experience—is not true of a story by Herodotus or Aristophanes, Swift or Voltaire, or again Des Périers. If the reader has not done so already, he or she might try retelling some of Rabelais's best stories—the lion, the fox, and the old woman (II: 15); Panurge and the lady of Paris (II: 21–22); Janotus de Bragmardo (I: 18–20); Diogenes and his tub (III: Prologue); Couillatris and his ax (IV: Prologue); Dindenault and his sheep (IV: 5–8); or the horse and the ass (V: 7)—and watch them fall like the proverbial lead balloon. This, I think, is a fact; it shows that Rabelais can take mediocre materials and make of them delightful works of art.

More studies comparing passages of his narrative with their sources would show better just what he does with his materials. Further analysis of his narrative style and techniques, which would follow up Keller's excellent start, is one of the great needs in Rabelais scholarship today.

The Exuberant Style

For all that has been written about Rabelais's style by all who have studied him, we still need a book about it. I have found the studies of Spitzer, Auerbach, Gray, Coleman, and Rigolot most helpful.[1] But Spitzer, for all his learning, remains somewhat subjective and romantic; Auerbach is mostly concerned with themes, Gray and Coleman with personne, Rigolot with language.

The aspects of Rabelais's style that strike me most are its oral quality, its variety, and its exuberance.

As numberless critics have noted, Rabelais's style is preeminently oral. For all his humanist enthusiasm for the printing press, in the main he harks back to the spoken style that was still strong in his time. Not only does he love actual dialogue; his speech in his narrative persona is often a dialogue with his reader; and he seeks dialogue more the further he goes. One phrase will illustrate this. In *Book Two*, chapter 4, the child Pantagruel is chained up, after devouring a cow and a bear, and left all alone when Gargantua gives a big banquet. Here are the successive versions of what follows (4, 185):

> (1532) Voicy qu'il fist. Il essaya . . .
>
> [Here is what he did. He tried . . .]
>
> (1534) Que fist-il? Il essaya . . .
>
> [What did he do? He tried . . .]
>
> (1542) Que fist-il?/ Qu'il fist, mes bonnes gens? Escoutez./ Il
>   essaya . . .

[What did he do?/ What he did, my good folk? Listen./ He tried . . .]

The Prologues, of course, are the prime examples of the oral style. In each one, through his persona, Rabelais addresses his readers, draws them into his confidence, and talks to them throughout. Except for the end of the Old Prologue to the *Fourth Book*, each Prologue begins and ends with an address. *Pantagruel* opens with "Most illustrious and most chivalrous champions," and closes with frightful imprecations "in case you do not firmly believe all I shall tell you in this present *Chronicle!*" *Gargantua* begins: "Most illustrious drinkers, and you, most precious pockified blades (for to you, not to others, my writings are dedicated)"; and ends: "Remember to drink to me in your turn, and I will pledge you in a moment." The Prologue of the *Third Book* proceeds from "Good folk, most illustrious drinkers, and you most precious pockified blades," to the concluding imprecations against the readers that Rabelais does not want. The Old Prologue to the *Fourth Book*, to be sure, after opening with the usual address to illustrious topers and the precious pox-ridden, closes, following Timon of Athens, with a promise to Rabelais's calumniators, whom he does not address. But the definitive Prologue to the *Fourth Book*, probably the last one that Rabelais wrote, begins with an address to "Good folks" and ends with an invitation to cough and drink in good health and listen to the latest news of Pantagruel.

The text itself abounds in examples, some of which unfortunately resist translation, or are too long to quote and translate here, or both. Such is Panurge's story of the lion, the fox, and the old woman (II: 15, 234–36) in *Pantagruel*; the scene between Picrochole and his advisers (I: 33) and Frère Jean's soliloquy (I: 39, 116–17, already quoted here in part) in *Gargantua*; and in the *Third Book*, Panurge's eulogy of debts (III: 2–4, 335–46), Pantagruel's echoing replies to Panurge's tergiversations about marriage (III: 9, 358–60), the exchange between Frère Jean and Panurge (III: 26–28), and Panurge's dialogue with the theologian Hippothadée. Much the same is true in the *Fourth Book* of Panurge's dialogues with Dindenault (5–8) and with Frère Jean during the tempest (19–22), and of Homenaz's virtual soliloquy in Papimania (49–54); and in the *Fifth Book*, of Panurge's dialogue with the Frères Fredons (28–29).

Perhaps two samples of Rabelais's oral style, both from *Gargantua*, may suffice. The first is from the talk of the topers:

"—Je ne boy que à mes heures, comme la mulle du pape.
—Je ne boy que en mon bréviaire, comme un beau père guardian.
—Qui feut premier, soif ou beuverye?
—Soif, car qui eust beu sans soif durant le temps de innocence?
—Beuverye, car *privatio presupponit habitum.* Je suis clerc.
   Fæcundi calices quem non fecere disertum?
—Nous aultres innocens ne beuvons que trop sans soif." (5, 16–17)

["I drink only at my hours, like the Pope's mule."
"I drink only from my breviary (flask), like a good Father Superior."
"Which came first, thirst or drinking?"
"Thirst, for in the time of innocence who would have drunk without
   thirst?"
"Drinking, for *privatio presupponit habitum.** I'm a cleric.
Fæcundi calices quem non fecere disertum?"†
"We innocents drink only too much without thirst."]

The second is from the scene between Grandgousier, Gargantua,
Frère Jean, and the pilgrims, after Grandgousier has warned the pilgrims against the impostor priests who preach worship of the saints:

Luy disans ces parolles, entra le moyne tout délibéré, et leurs demanda:
   "Dont este-vous, vous aultres pauvres hayres?
—De Sainct Genou, dirent-ilz.
—Et comment (dist le moyne) se porte l'abbé Tranchelion, le bon
   beuveur? Et les moynes, quelle chère font-ilz? Le cor Dieu! ilz
   biscotent voz femmes, cependent que estes en romivage!
—Hin, hen! (dist Lasdaller) je n'ay pas peur de la mienne, car qui la
   verra de jour ne se rompera jà le col pour l'aller visiter la nuict.
—C'est (dict le moyne) bien rentré de picques! Elle pourroit estre
   aussi layde que Proserpine, elle aura, par Dieu, la saccade puis-
   qu'il y a moynes autour, car un bon ouvrier mect indifférente-
   ment toutes pièces en oeuvre. Que j'aye la vérolle en cas que
   ne les trouviez engroissées à vostre retour, car seulement l'ombre
   du clochier d'une abbaye est féconde.
—C'est (dist Gargantua) comme l'eau du Nile en Egypte si vous
   croyez Strabo; et Pline, *lib. vij* chap. *iij,* advise que c'est de la
   miche, des habitz et des corps."
Lors dist Grandgousier:
   "Allez-vous-en, pauvres gens, au nom de Dieu le créateur, lequel vous
   soit en guide perpétuelle, et dorénavant ne soyez faciles à ces
   ocieux‡ et inutilles voyages." (45, 131–32)

[As he spoke these words, in came the monk all resolute, and asked them:
   "Where are you from, you poor wretches?"

* Privation presupposes habit.
† Who has not been made eloquent by his cups?
‡ The Pléiade text incorrectly reads "odieux" [odious].

131

"From Saint-Genou," they said.

"And how," said the monk, "is that good toper Abbot Tranchelion? And what cheer are the monks making? God's body, they're screwing your wives while you're out on your pilgrimage!"

"Heh, heh!" said Wearybones, "I'm not afraid for mine, for anyone who sees her by day won't ever break his neck to go visit her by night."

"You've hit it just fine!" said the monk. "She could be as ugly as Proserpina, by God, she'll get the works as long as there are monks around, for a good workman makes use of every piece of material indiscriminately. May I get the pox in case you don't find them big with child on your return, for even the shadow of an abbey bell tower is fertile."

"It's like the water of the Nile in Egypt," said Gargantua, "if you believe Strabo; and Pliny, *book vii*, chap. *iii*, says it can come from crumbs, clothes, and bodies."

Then said Grandgousier:

"Go your way, you poor folk, in the name of God the Creator; may He ever be your guide; and henceforth don't be easy marks for these idle and useless trips."]

The oral quality of both passages speaks for itself. Rabelais had an extraordinary ear for the human voice; his whole book should be read aloud even when read alone; only then does it have its proper life. His knowledge of the stage is everywhere apparent, and much of his book is well appropriated to the stage.

Especially striking in these two passages is the variety of the dialogue. In the talk of the topers readers have distinguished many voices; even in the short passage quoted we hear at least three or four. In the passage involving the pilgrims every voice is clearly distinguished in form and in content: the good-natured but cynical voice of Frère Jean; the humble and submissive voice of the pilgrims; the disabused snicker of Lasdaller [Wearybones], obviously enjoying his vacation from marriage; the learned tones of Gargantua, who in his father's presence contents himself with an erudite gloss; and the wise, benign solemnity of Grandgousier. Except that Gargantua is capable of speaking like his father, each speaker is identifiable not only by what he says but by how he says it.

This is one of Rabelais's triumphs: that generally—not always as brilliantly as here,[2] but most of the time—he gives each speaker a style of his own. He would have been a great comic dramatist; presumably he had too much of his own to say to elect that genre. But his many and varied voices are voices that we recognize as true.

In *Les Langages de Rabelais* François Rigolot distinguishes five Rabelaisian voices: those of the presenter (in the Prologues), of the giants and men, of the humanist, of the storyteller, and of the *topiqueur*, the eloquent arguer. The elements of Rabelais's style that strike me most are: (1) the grotesque and carnivalesque, (2) the erudite (and *topiqueur*), (3) the quintessential, (4) the lofty, and (5) the mixture of the lofty and the grotesque. I have already quoted for other reasons many of my favorite examples of these; but many others remain.

In dealing with comedy and the carnivalesque, I have been allusive and avoided quoting at length. The Prologues are among the best illustrations, with their oral form, their cheerful greetings to topers and victims of "gay" diseases (gout, pox), their joyous praise of friends and grotesque abuse of enemies. In the text itself examples also abound. Let me merely point to the inspired grotesque inventiveness of the "esmouche" sequence (II: 15, 235) in Panurge's story of the fox whisking away the flies from the "wound" of the old woman, who fainted at the sight of the naïve but well-meaning lion.

Grotesque billingsgate abounds in the Dindenault episode (IV: 5–8) as the sheep merchant insults the (for once, and for a purpose) patient Panurge, calling him a cuckold and city slicker out to trick a simple man like himself. Let one example suffice (6, 554):

"Halas! halas! mon amy, nostre voisin, comment vous sçavez bien trupher des paouvres gens! Vrayement vous estez un gentil chalant! O le vaillant achapteur de moutons! Vraybis! vous portez le minoys non mie d'un achapteur de moutons, mais bien d'un couppeur de bourses. Deu Colas, faillon! qu'il feroit bon porter bourse pleine auprès de vous en la tripperie sur le dégel! Han, han, qui ne vous congnoistroyt, vous feriez bien des vostres! Mais voyez, hau, bonnes gens, comment il taille de l'historiographe!"

["Alas! alas! my friend and our neighbor, how well you know how to take poor folk in! Really, you're a nice customer! Oh, what a valiant sheep buyer! Honest to God, you don't look like a sheep buyer, but a cut-purse. Lord, pal, it would be nice to be near you with a full purse at a tripe-house when it thaws! Ho, ho, you'd take in anyone who didn't know you! But just look, good folk, haw, haw, how he puts on airs like a history writer!"]

Grotesque, carnivalesque parody is illustrated by the inspired harangue of Janotus de Bragmardo of the Sorbonne when he comes to ask Gargantua to return the bells. Again a short sample should suffice (I: 19, 57):

"Si vous nous les rendez à ma requeste, je y guaigneray six pans de saulcicces et une bonne paire de chausses que me feront grant bien à mes jambes, ou ilz ne me tiendront pas promesse. Ho! par Dieu, *Domine*, une pair de chausses est bon, *et vir sapiens non abhorrebit eam.* Ha! ha! il n'a pas pair de chausses qui veult, je le sçay bien quant est de moy! Advisez, *Domine*: il y a dix huyt jours que je suis à matagraboliser ceste belle harangue: *Reddite que sunt Cesaris Cesari, et que sunt Dei Deo. Ibi jacet lepus.*"

["If you give them back to us at my request, I shall earn six strings of sausages and a good pair of breeches which will do my legs much good, or else they won't keep their promise. Oh, by God, *Domine*, a pair of breeches is good, *et vir sapiens non abhorrebit eam.** Ha, ha, not everyone who wants has a pair of breeches, I know that full well from my own case! Consider, *Domine*: I have been eighteen days matagrabolizing this fine speech. *Reddite que sunt Cesaris Cesari, et que sunt Die Deo. Ibi jacet lepus.*"†]

Moreover, Janotus' Latin degenerates rapidly as he hits his stride later in his speech.

The grotesque and carnivalesque is probably the most important and original of Rabelais's styles; but it is one of many. Let us turn to some of the others.

The next three styles—erudite, quintessential, and lofty—have in common a serious appearance, hypotactic structure,[3] and concern for eloquence. However, Rabelais's erudite style is often parodic and unconsciously self-mocking, like the style of the *topiqueur*. The quintessential may be serious or self-mocking but is marked by long words and sublime subject matter. The lofty, although sometimes set off by the grotesque, is always serious. The different impacts of the three on the reader justify the distinction.

The best examples of the erudite and *topiqueur* are found in *Book One* and especially the *Third Book*. One is the learnedly clinical account in *Gargantua* (I: 27, 85–86) of Frère Jean's horrific slaughter of the Picrocholean troops who invaded the vineyard of his abbey. The *Third Book* abounds in illustrations, such as Judge Bridoye's tireless quoting of Latin legal precedents (39–42), and the indefatigable erudition about Pantagruelion. More readily detachable is the account by the discursive doctor, Rondibilis (31, 440), of the first of his five ways of restraining carnal lust, by wine:

"—J'entends (dist Rondibilis) par vin prins intempérament. Car par l'intempérance du vin advient au corps humain refroidissement de sang, résolution des nerfs, dissipation de semence générative, hébétation des sens, per-

* And the wise man will not shrink from them.
† Render therefore unto Caesar the things which be Caesar's, and unto God the things which be God's (Luke: 20:25). Here lies the hare (i.e., the point).

version des mouvemens, qui sont toutes impertinences à l'acte de génération. De faict, vous voyez painct Bacchus, dieu des yvroignes, sans barbe et en habit de femme, comme tout efféminé, comme eunuche et escouillé. Aultrement est du vin prins tempérément. L'antique proverbe nous le désigne, on quel est dict que Vénus se morfond sans la compaignie de Cérès et Bacchus. Et estoit l'opinion des anciens, scelon le récit de Diodore Sicilien, mesmement des Lampsaciens, comme atteste Pausanias, que messer Priapus feu filz de Bacchus et Vénus."

["I mean," said Rondibilis, "by wine taken intemperately. For from intemperance in wine there comes to the human body chillness of the blood, slackening of the muscles, dissipation of the generative seed, stupefaction of the senses, perversion of movements; which are all unsuitable to the act of generation. In fact you see Bacchus, god of the drunkards, portrayed beardless and in woman's dress, as wholly effeminate and as a gelded eunuch. It is otherwise with wine taken temperately. The ancient proverb points this out, in which it is said that Venus catches cold without the company of Ceres and of Bacchus. And it was the opinion of the ancients, according to Diodorus Siculus' story and especially that of the Lampsacenes, as Pausanias attests, that Messer Priapus was the son of Bacchus and Venus."]

Rondibilis likes to hear himself talk, and Rabelais likes to give him the chance. The exuberance of Rabelais's style appears in both this and the next passage.

For erudition in the *topiqueur* manner many parts of the Pantagruelion episode would do (III: 49–52), as would Homenaz's speech (IV: 49–53) in praise of the divine Decretals; but the obvious text is Panurge's praise of debts. In the following sample (III: 3, 339–40) Panurge replies to Pantagruel's mild reproaches for his debts:

". . . Dea! en ceste seule qualité je me réputois auguste, révérend et redoutable, que, sus l'opinion de tous philosophes (qui disent rien de rien n'estre faict), rien ne tenent ne matière première, estoys facteur et créateur.

"Avois crée quoy? Tant de beaulx et bons créditeurs. Créditeurs sont (je le maintiens jusques au feu exclusivement) créatures belles et bonnes. Qui rien ne preste, est créature laide et mauvaise, créature du grand villain diantre d'enfer.

"Et faict quoy? Debtes. O chose rare et antiquaire! Debtes, diz-je, excédentes le nombre des syllabes résultantes au couplement de toutes les consonantes avecques les vocales, jadis projecté et compté par le noble Xenocrates. A la numérosité des créditeurs si vous estimez la perfection des debteurs, vous ne errerez en arithmétique praticque."

[". . . Why, in that one quality I thought myself august, reverend, and redoubtable, in that in spite of the opinion of all philosophers (who say nothing is made out of nothing), I, having nothing nor any primal matter, was a maker and creator.

"I had created what? So many fine good creditors. Creditors (I maintain this up to the stake, exclusively) are fine good creatures. He who lends nothing is an ugly bad creature, a creature of the great repulsive Devil in hell.

"And made what? Debts. O rare and antiquarian thing! Debts, I say, exceeding the number of syllables resulting from the coupling of all the consonants with the vowels, a number once projected and counted by the noble Xenocrates.* If by the numerosity of creditors you estimate the perfection of debtors, you will make no mistake in practical arithmetic."]

Eloquence, erudition, and rhetoric in the service of a specious argument: these are the marks of Rabelais's *topiqueur* style.

If we include in it the love of sumptuous detail, the quintessential is a fairly common characteristic of Rabelais's style. I find touches of it when he explains the meaning of the colors white and blue in Gargantua's livery (I: 10), and more in his description of Theleme (I: 53 and 55–56) and the dress of its inhabitants. It is especially frequent in the *Fifth Book,* in the account (whose authenticity I doubt) of Quintessence, the description of the temple of the Divine Bottle (V: 34–45), and Bacbuc's concluding speech (V: 47). As an extreme example, perhaps not by Rabelais, let me quote in translation the start of Queen Quintessence's first speech to the travelers (V: 20, 804):

"The probity scintillating on the circumference of your persons gives me assured judgment of the virtue latent in the center of your minds; and seeing the mellifluous suavity of your eloquent reverences, I am easily persuaded that your hearts suffer no tempests, nor any sterility of liberal and lofty learning, but abound in many exotic and rare teachings, which it is easier at present, through the common usages of the unschooled vulgar, to wish for than to find."

Besides the elaborate hypotactic structure and the profusion of long abstract Latin derivatives, this passage is marked by Latinate inversions of word order which, for clarity, I have not shown in the translation. Such is Rabelais's—or someone's—quintessential style at its purest and most extreme.

By lofty style I mean the earnest, stately, at times moving style that Rabelais lends to his mature giants—or ex-giants. Generally erudite, it often skirts the quintessential, but it never parodies itself; it is serious, never ironic. No doubt it is less genially original than his carnivalesque

---

* The number, by Xenocrates' calculation, is 100,200,000.

style; but I find in it often a cadence, dignity, and resonance rarely achieved by Rabelais's contemporaries.

This style belongs mainly to the giants in their maturity. Except for an occasional bit by the narrator (III:· 2, etc.) and the speech by Epistémon (originally, and properly, by Pantagruel) explaining Bridoye's success as Christian folly (III: 44, 485–86), only twice are non-giants granted this eloquence: Ulrich Gallet in his harangue to Picrochole (I: 31), which at times comes close to self-parody, and Bacbuc in the concluding chapters (V: 42 ff. and especially 47). Notable examples from the mature giants are Grandgousier's address to the pilgrims (I: 45), Gargantua's to the vanquished (I: 50), Pantagruel's prayer before combat (II: 29), and almost any speech by Pantagruel anywhere in the last three books.

To illustrate this lofty vein I quote from the earliest example we have from Rabelais's pen, familiar, but deservedly so, as one of the great statements of the early French Renaissance thirst for learning: Gargantua's letter to Pantagruel (II: 8, 204–05):

"Mais, encores que mon feu père de bonne mémoire, Grandgousier, eust adonné tout son estude à ce que je proffitasse en toute perfection et sçavoir politique et que mon labeur et estude correspondît très bien, voire encores oultrepassast son désir, toutesfoys, comme tu peulx bien entendre, le temps n'estoit tant idoine ne commode ès lettres comme est de présent, et n'avoys copie de telz précepteurs comme tu as eu. Le temps estoit encores ténébreux et sentant l'infélicité et calamité des Gothz, qui avoient mis à destruction toute bonne litérature. Mais, par la bonté divine, la lumière et dignité a esté de mon eage rendue ès lettres, et y voy tel amendement que de présent à difficulté seroys-je reccu en la première classe des petitz grimaulx, qui en mon eage virile estoys (non à tord) réputé le plus sçavant dudict siècle. . . .

"Maintenant toutes disciplines sont restituées, les langues instaurées: grecque, sans laquelle c'est honte que une personne se die sçavant, hébraïcque, caldaïcque, latine; les impressions tant élégantes et correctes en usance, qui ont esté inventées de mon eage par inspiration divine, comme à contrefil l'artillerie par suggestion diabolicque. Tout le monde est plein de gens savans, de précepteurs très doctes, de librairies très amples, et m'est advis que, ny au temps de Platon, ny de Cicéron, ny de Papinian, n'estoit telle commodité d'estude qu'on y veoit maintenant, et ne se fauldra plus doresnavant trouver en place ny en compaignie, qui ne sera bien expoly en l'officine de Minerve."

["But although my late father of happy memory, Grandgousier, had devoted all his endeavors to having me profit in all perfection and political knowledge, and although my labor and study corresponded very well to, yes, even surpassed, his desire, nevertheless, as you can well understand, the times were not so fit and favorable for letters as they are at present, and I had no abundance of such tutors as you have had. The times were still dark, and smacking of the infelicity and calamity of the Goths, who had brought all good literature to destruction. But, by the divine goodness, light and dignity have been restored to letters in my time; and I see such improvement that at present I would hardly be accepted in the lowest grade of little schoolboys, I who in my prime was reputed (and not wrongly) the most learned of that century. . . .

"Now all disciplines are restored, the study of languages revived: Greek, without which it is shameful for a man to call himself learned, Hebrew, Chaldean, Latin. That most elegant and accurate art of printing is in use, which was invented in my time by divine inspiration, as, on the contrary, was artillery by diabolical suggestion. The whole world is full of learned men, of very erudite tutors, of very ample libraries; and it is my opinion that neither in the time of Plato, of Cicero, nor of Papinian, were there such facilities for study as we see now; and henceforth no one must any longer appear in public or in company who is not well polished in the workshop of Minerva."]

The characteristics of Rabelais's lofty style are all apparent here: complex (yet clear) hypotactic structure; earnest, dignified tone; abundance of long, learned abstract words; skillful use of cadence; and compelling eloquence. It is a style that he handles as a master.

From the Introduction on I have stressed the mixture of the lofty and grotesque in Rabelais; enough now to point to some instances of it. Already noted are Gargantua's lament for Badebec after the birth of Pantagruel (II: 3, 181), and Pantagruel's moving account of the death of Jesus (symbolized by the death of Pan), followed by his tears as big as ostrich eggs (IV: 28, 618–19). Earlier in this chapter I quoted a different kind of mixture in which Frère Jean's earthy warnings to the pilgrims contrast with Grandgousier's lofty words of advice (I: 45, 131–32). Similar examples abound in which the earthiness of Panurge or Frère Jean forms a grotesque contrast with the exaltedness of one of the giants, as in the comment in verse and prose by Pantagruel and Panurge after the initial victory over the Dipsodes (II: 27). When young Gargantua discovers the perfect ass-wipe (I: 13), his speech— consistently obscene in the verse—varies from lofty to grotesque in the prose as he talks now of sumptuous fabrics and then of the use he put them to. His conclusion illustrates this contrast (13, 46):

"Mais, concluent, je dys et maintiens qu'il n'y a tel torchecul que d'un oyzon bien dumeté, pourveu qu'on luy tienne la teste entre les jambes. Et m'en croyez sus mon honneur. Car vous sentez au trou du cul une volupté mirificque tant par la doulceur d'icelluy dumet que par la chaleur tempérée de l'oizon, laquelle facilement est communicquée au boyau culier et aultres intestines, jusques à venir à la région du cueur et du cerveau. Et ne pensez que la béatitude des heroes et semi-dieux, qui sont par les Champs Elysiens, soit en leur asphodèle, ou ambrosie, ou nectar, comme disent ces vieilles ycy. Elle est (scelon mon opinion) en ce qu'ilz se torchent le cul d'un oyzon, et telle est l'opinion de Maistre Jehan d'Escosse."

["But, to conclude, I say and maintain that there is no ass-wipe like a well-downed gosling, provided you hold his head between your legs. And take my word for this, upon my honor. For you feel a mirific voluptuousness in your ass-hole, both from the softness of this down and from the temperate warmth of the gosling; and this is easily communicated to the rectal bowel and other intestines, until it comes to the regions of the heart and the brain. And do not think that the beatitude of the heroes and demigods who are in the Elysian Fields lies in their asphodel, or ambrosia, or nectar, as these old women say. It lies, according to my opinion, in that they wipe their ass with a gosling, and such is the opinion of Master Duns Scotus."]

In various forms, the mixture of the lofty and the grotesque is present throughout Rabelais's book.

Of all the characteristics of Rabelais's style, perhaps the most striking is exuberance. Every page reveals his passionate love of words, his "ivresse lexicographique" [lexicographical intoxication]. In this he is of his time, when words were assigned a virtually magical power. The expanding vocabulary of French was seen as corresponding to the expanding world known to Europeans. Within the next century, economy and clarity were to become watchwords, effusiveness anathema; but in Rabelais's day expansiveness and abundance were highly regarded. Today we assume—not without reason—that normally what can be said in four words can be said better in two. Rabelais seems always to assume the opposite and to take as his motto: the more the merrier.

The most obvious example of his exuberance is his lists, of which nine or ten appear as such in the five books: the genealogy of sixty ancestors of Pantagruel (II: 1); the list of 218 games played by Gargantua as a "student" (I: 22); the blazon of the "couillons" [testicles] by Panurge and Frère Jean in 169 and 170 epithets respectively (III: 26, 28); the blazon of Triboullet by Pantagruel and Panurge, 104 items each (III: 38); the anatomization of Quaresmeprenant, 178 items (IV: 30–32); the 162 cooks, all named, concealed in the "Trojan" sow with which the visitors counterattack the Chitterlings (IV: 40); the 254-line list of foods—sometimes two to a line—offered in sacrifice to Messere

Gaster (IV: 59–60); the 133 questions posed to the Frère Fredon and his monosyllabic replies to each (V: 28–29); and the 130 foods served to, and 180 dances danced by, the lady Lanterns (V: 33 bis).

But these are only the most striking examples of Rabelais's logophilia; similar examples abound even when not printed two columns to a page. In *Pantagruel* there are the 139 titles of books in the Library of St.-Victor (7); the thirteen languages (ten real, three invented by Rabelais) in which Panurge addresses Pantagruel before lapsing into French (9); the inspired nonsense of the Baisecul-Humevesne trial (11–13); the myriad tricks and devices of Panurge (16–17); the elaborate description of gestures, including thumbing the nose, in the debate in signs with Thaumaste (19); and the eloquent impromptu verses of triumph by which Pantagruel and Panurge celebrate the first victory against the Dipsodes (27). In *Gargantua* we find the talk of the topers (5), the activities of the giant as a child (11), and two clinical accounts of horrendous slaughters by Frère Jean (27 and 44).

The *Third Book* opens with two impressive lists in the Prologue: the activities of the Corinthians preparing to defend their city, and of Diogenes driving his barrel up and down Mount Cranion. Later one finds Pantagruel's echoing replies to the perplexed Panurge (9); the countless "mancies" by which Her Trippa predicts Panurge's cuckoldry (25); Rondibilis' enjoyment of his own eloquence on how to check male concupiscence, on women's sexual appetite, and on cuckoldry (31–33); the resourceful evasiveness of the Pyrrhonist Trouillogan (35–36); Bridoye's tireless quoting of Latin legal sources (39–42); and Rabelais's learned account of the virtues of the herb Pantagruelion (49–52).

The *Fourth Book* offers the marvelous things seen and bought in Medamothi (2–4); the untiring though often erratic boasting of Dindenault about the virtues of his sheep (6–7); Homenaz's ecstatic raving about the wonders of the Decretals (49–53); and the admirable inventions of Messere Gaster (57, 61–62). Less rich in verbal displays, the *Fifth Book* offers the varied activities of Queen Quintessence and her officers (21–22) and the Bacchic rhyming of Panurge, Pantagruel, and finally even Frère Jean (45–46).

One example should suffice to show Rabelais's love of lists: the sixty-four verbs in the imperfect tense (for repeated or continuous action) which tell how Diogenes drove his barrel out of the city of Corinth and up and down Mount Cranion (III: Prologue, 322–23). Stripping down for action, he rolled it out and with great vehemence

. . . le tournoit, viroit, brouilloit, garbouilloit, hersoit, versoit, renversoit, nattoit, grattoit, flattoit, barattoit, bastoit, boutoit, butoit, tabustoit, culle-butoit, trepoit, trempoit, tapoit, timpoit, estouppoit, destouppoit, détraquoit, triquotoit, tripotoit, chapotoit, croulloit, élançoit, chamailloit, bransloit, es-branloit, levoit, lavoit, clavoit, entrevoit, bracquoit, bricquoit, blocquoit, tra-cassoit, ramassoit, clabossoit, afestoit, affustoit, baffouoit, enclouoit, ama-douoit, goildronnoit, mittonnoit, tastonnoit, bimbelotoit, clabossoit, terrassoit, bistorioit, vreloppoit, chaluppoit, charmoit, armoit, gizarmoit, enharnachoit, empennachoit, caparassonnoit, le dévalloit de mont à val, et præcipitoit par le Cranie, puys de val en mont le rapportoit.

For this passage translation seems unnecessary. Most of the verbs signify some sort of striking or moving, or both. What is apparent is how one sound leads to another similar one (hersoit-versoit-renversoit; nattoit-grattoit-flattoit-barattoit-bastoit; etc.) in a joyous cascade of words. Once again, why be content with one word—or two, or three, or a dozen—when sixty-four are available? Here is Rabelais's "lexico-graphical intoxication" at work producing the exuberant abundance that is one of the hallmarks of his style.

To return to variety, that of Rabelais's style—or styles—is so great that I find it impossible to do it justice. A brief examination of a sample will at least illustrate aspects not mentioned thus far. The sample is again a familiar one, from the first text the reader encounters, the Prologue to *Gargantua* (I: 4–5):

Crochetastes-vous oncques bouteilles? Caisgne! Réduisez à mémoire la contenence qu'aviez. Mais veistes-vous oncques chien rencontrant quelque os médulare? C'est, comme dict Platon *lib. ij de Rep.*, la beste du monde plus philosophe. Si veu l'avez, vous avez peu noter de quelle dévotion il le guette, de quel soing il le guarde, de quel ferveur il le tient, de quelle pru-dence il l'entomne, de quelle affection il le brise et de quelle diligence il le sugce. Qui le induict à ce faire? Quel est l'espoir de son estude? Quel bien prétend-il? Rien plus qu'un peu de mouelle. Vray est que ce peu plus est délicieux que le beaucoup de toutes aultres, pour ce que la mouelle est ali-ment élabouré à perfection de nature comme dict *Galen, iij Facu. natural.* et *xj De usu parti.*

A l'exemple d'icelluy vous convient estre saiges pour fleurer, sentir et estimer ces beaulx livres de haulte gresse, légiers au prochaz et hardiz à la rencontre; puis, par curieuse leçon et méditation fréquente, rompre l'os et sugcer la sustantificque mouelle—c'est à dire ce que j'entends par ces sym-boles Pythagoricques avecques espoir certain d'estre faictz escors et preux à ladicte lecture: car en icelle bien aultre goust trouverez et doctrine plus absconce, laquelle vous révéla de très haultz sacremens et mystères hor-rificques, tant en ce que concerne nostre religion que aussi l'estat politicque et vie œconomicque.

[Did you ever pick open a bottle or two? Son of a bitch! Call to mind the expression you had. But did you ever see a dog coming across a marrow-bone? That is, as Plato says in Book 2 of the *Republic,* the most philosophical animal in the world. If seen him you have, you were able to note with what devotion he watches it, with what care he guards it, with what fervor he holds it, with what prudence he bites it, with what affection he breaks it, and with what diligence he sucks it. What induces him to do this? What is the hope of his labor? What good does he aim at? Nothing more than a little marrow. True it is that this little is more delicious than the muchness of all other foods, because marrow, as Galen says in his third book *On the Natural Faculties* and his eleventh *On the Parts of the Body and Their Uses,* is an aliment elaborated to the perfection of nature.

Following his example, it becomes you to be wise in order to sniff out, smell, and esteem these fine full-bodied books, to be light-footed in pursuit and bold in bringing to bay; then, by studious reading and frequent meditation, to break the bone and suck out the substantific marrow—that is, what I mean by these Pythagorean symbols—with assured hope of being made wise and valorous by the said reading; for in it you will find a very different taste and more abstruse teaching, which will reveal to you some very lofty sacraments and horrific mysteries, as regards both our religion and also our political state and domestic life.]

Here is a characteristic mixture of styles, dominated by the lofty, more or less Ciceronian, here used in a mock-serious way. As is typical of the Prologues, there is an immediate, direct address to the reader, leading to the five questions of the first paragraph and the long concluding moral of the second. Rabelais's love of series is especially apparent in the first paragraph, with its six repetitions of "de quel" or "de quelle," closely parallel and in the same syntactical construction. Then come three rather rhetorical questions about the dog's motive, promptly answered. The second paragraph is full of pairs: "légiers . . . et hardiz," "leçon et méditation" (a pairing with chiasmus), "rompre . . . et sugcer," "escors et preux," "goust . . . et doctrine," "sacremens et mystères," "religion . . . estat politicque et vie œconomicque." Besides the obvious effects of abundance and movement, these lend a marked cadence especially to the second paragraph.

The passage displays the author's learning in many erudite words, some of them creations of Rabelais's: "os médulare," "curieuse leçon et méditation fréquente," "sustantificque mouelle," "symboles Pythagoricques," "doctrine plus absconce," "vie œconomicque"; and of course in the references to Plato and Galen. Mingled with these are effects that are archaizing or popularizing or both: "Caisgne!" the word order of "Si veu l'avez," "livres de haulte gresse, légiers au prochaz et hardiz à la rencontre," "escors et preux." Almost precious in its abstraction (reminiscent of the poet Maurice Scève) is "ce peu plus est délicieux que le beaucoup de toutes aultres."

Altogether it is a rich and savory mixture, moving from the carnivalesque opening to the lofty and serious, then to the mock-serious: a sort of microcosm of the whole Prologue. Here as always, Rabelais loves to play games with (and on) his reader, and does it to perfection. As he does so, his exuberant and varied style is one of his trump cards.

Giantism

When most Western readers think of giants in literature, they think of Rabelais and Swift; when they think of Rabelais and Swift, they think of giants. More people read the early parts of masterpieces than the late. Whether or not this is as it should be, this seems to be how it is.

Serious literature is often unkind to giants: witness the Cyclopes in the *Odyssey* (and their traces in the *Aeneid*), Goliath of Gath, the Morholt in *Tristan and Yseult*, the stupid monsters in Dante's *Inferno*, and Loup Garou in *Pantagruel*. In folk literature they seem to be either monstrous ogres, as in *Jack-in-the-Beanstalk*, or else rather good-natured supermen, as in the *Chronicles of Gargantua*—which makes one wonder if these aren't just the two basic father figures. Rabelais offers us a few giants besides his heroes: the terrifying but ultimately somewhat comic Loup Garou (II: 29); the grotesque but benign Bringuenarilles (IV: 17), the eater of windmills who chokes on a pat of butter; and the monstrous "half giant" Quaresmeprenant (IV: 29–32), not so much menacing as stupidly lugubrious, who reminds Pantagruel of Antiphysie and her brood. Rabelais's main giants are of course Grandgousier, Gargantua, and Pantagruel. By their good nature they are all in a sense descendants of the giants of the *Chronicles*; but they break away from them by soon developing into ideal sages and losing their gigantic stature.

Swift in *Gulliver's Travels*, and after him Voltaire in *Micromégas*, were to pick up from Rabelais—in whom I think it is accidental—the notion that bigger is apt to be wiser. They systematize it, making smaller mean pettier, which does not necessarily follow in Rabelais. Among the Lilliputians Gulliver makes sense, but not among the giant

Brobdingnagians; in *Micromégas* the Saturnian makes sense to the silly earthlings, but is little better than an earthling to the Sirian. In both these writers, who both knew Rabelais's work, the sizes are always precisely measured, as they never are in Rabelais. In Swift and Voltaire the plausibility of system prevails.

Rabelais's casual giantism is perhaps best seen in contrast with Swift. Swift takes great care with his measurements: Gulliver is twelve times as tall as the Lilliputians, thus 1,728 times as bulky; and the Brobdingnagians are twelve times as tall as he. In Rabelais the principal giants are whatever size (from human scale up—never pygmy) the author wants at the time he wants it. Swift asks the reader for a gamesome and partial "willing suspension of disbelief"; Rabelais, on the face of it (*Pantagruel*, Prologue), asks for this complete, but does so with tongue firmly in cheek; he seems to expect it less for the giants as giants than as wonderful humans to be loved and admired. All attempts that I know of to explain the size of his giants in a rational way have failed; the only explanation is the whim of the author at the moment.

Let us see how Rabelais's "own" giants appear in his book. Grandgousier is never really shown as a giant himself, although he accepts a gigantic mare for his son Gargantua (I: 16, 51–52) and takes the cannon balls in his son's hair for lice (I: 37, 109). He is comical in the early chapters (I: 3, 4, 6); benign, but easily misled from the ass-wipe episode through the naïve first attempt to educate his giant son (13–15); wise when he corrects his mistake about education (15–16), with the good results that follow in his absence (21–24). When he writes to Gargantua for help against Picrochole (29), he appears as a pious Christian king of normal size, and remains so from then on, as in chapter 45, where his advice to the pilgrims is a model of Evangelical humanism. After that he acts in 46, is mentioned in 47, and then disappears.

With Gargantua and Pantagruel the picture is more complicated. Both are gigantic in their childhood and once or twice later in *Books One* and *Two*, rarely in the later books. Let us look at them in the order in which Rabelais wrote about them.

Pantagruel in *Book Two* (1532) is gigantic in chapters 1–5; again in the start of 7; perhaps again (by his stentorian voice) in 18 (pp. 252–253); and perhaps by implication in 25, where he offers to fight the whole Dipsode army (p. 274). He is gigantic again in 27–29, where his fart shakes the earth and he fights and conquers Loup Garou and his three hundred giants; in 32, where he covers his army with his tongue and the narrator finds a "new world" inside his mouth; and in 33, where he is constipated and men are sent down in copper capsules to mine the excrement out of his bowels. In short, in Rabelais's first, most derivative, and most "gigantic" book, the giant hero figures as a giant in only thirteen chapters out of thirty-four—a little more than one-third.

In *Book One*, in which Pantagruel of course does not appear, Gargantua's giantism is mentioned in the genealogy (I: 1); he is described as a giant child in 7–8, and noted as one in passing for the weight of his breviary (21), and—perhaps—in certain aspects of his physical education (23, 72–74). He is clearly gigantic only in 17, when he takes the bells of Notre-Dame and bepisses the Parisians, and in the war, wielding a tree trunk, combing cannon balls from his hair as if they were insects, and eating the six pilgrims in his salad (36–38). In other words, in five chapters out of fifty-eight his stature is noted in passing (but hardly more), and in four others it is featured. It is true that we are often reminded of his theoretical size; but nine chapters out of fifty-eight are not much in a book whose readers expected giant stories. Thus even as early as *Gargantua* Rabelais seems to tire a little of the gigantic as a principal source of exploits or of comedy. Frère Jean provides more of both of these than does his giant friend and master.

In the later books there are almost no giants. All traces of giantism have disappeared from the titles. In the *Third Book*, in the three chapters in which he appears, Gargantua is majestic but not gigantic; and Pantagruel, who is present almost throughout, never appears gigantic either. The nearest thing to it is when we learn (51, 506) that he was as tall at birth as the full-grown herb Pantagruelion, which, we are told earlier (50, 500), is usually five or six feet tall but sometimes as tall as a lance. This is all for the *Third Book*; giantism is almost completely abandoned.

In the *Fourth Book* there is a slight increase of it as Rabelais turns from talk to adventures; but there is not much change. During the tempest Pantagruel holds the mast firm (19, 594), and later he speaks of having done so (22, 604); from the queen of the Chitterlings he learns that her spies took him for that "half giant" Quaresmeprenant (42, 653); these examples are hardly striking. More to the point are his tears when he tells of the death of Jesus—as big as ostrich eggs (28, 619). He is recognized as a giant by one of the Papimanes (48, 669–70); his height lets him hear and catch some frozen words before the others do (55–56); and he does show the size and prowess of a giant in the encounter with the whale (33–34), though even here his size seems overshadowed by his wonderful accuracy with darts. This makes only nine "giant" chapters out of the *Fourth Book*'s sixty-seven.

In the entire *Fifth Book* I find only one moment when Pantagruel appears as a giant: when Queen Quintessence's captain, unable to reach his height to converse with him, exclaims that the queen could make them all as big as that if she wanted to (19, 802).

Altogether the giantism of the giants in the five books is rather scarce: evident only in 13 chapters of the 34 in *Book Two*, 9 of the 58 in *One*, 1 of the 52 in the *Third Book*, 9 of the 67 in the *Fourth*, and 1 of the 49 (of the Pléiade text) in the *Fifth:* a total of 33 chapters out of 260 in all (about 13%), and of 11 out of 168 (about 6.5%) in the last three books; and many of these offer only momentary allusions.

It may be objected that mere statistics cannot measure the presence of an idea, and that the popular notion of Rabelais proves the presence of the giant idea throughout the five books. But by contrast, in Parts I and II of *Gulliver's Travels* and throughout *Micromégas* the reader is conscious of the size of the giants (and pygmies) in every chapter and on almost every page. My statistics do not *prove* much, but they point in a direction. And the popular notion of Rabelais is based on a reading of the giant parts of the first two books only—at least, so it would appear.

In short, in my judgment Rabelais's reputation as a writer about giants is exaggerated; his treatment of his giants as giants is consistently inconsistent and diminishes fairly steadily from the first book he wrote to the last; there is very little giantism in the last three books. Since giant stories were his starting point and the expectation of his first readers, it is likely that he wrote of them less and less because he wearied of them the more he wrote.

Even when the giants appear as giants, their size is not consistent. When Gargantua uproots a big tree to use for a stave or a lance (I: 36, 106–07), a tree of perhaps a hundred feet is used for a stave or lance normally perhaps five to sixteen feet long; thus the scale would be from 1/6 to 1/20, hence the giant (taking five feet as an average man's height in Rabelais's time) thirty to a hundred feet tall. When Gargantua takes the bells of Notre-Dame to hang on the neck of his mare (I: 17), I take the scale to be from 1/50 to 1/100, making the giant 250 to 500 feet tall. When he eats the pilgrims in a salad but has his sore tooth hurt by a pilgrim's staff (I: 38, 112), it is as if a man ate a homunculus about a quarter or a half inch tall; if so, the scale would be about 1/125 or 1/250, and the giant 625 to 1,250 feet tall. As for Pantagruel, when the men are sent to mine the fecal matter out of his bowels (II: 33), I would estimate the scale at about 1/250, and thus his height at 1,250 feet. When the narrator finds the world in Pantagruel's mouth, however (II: 32)—a world containing mountains, forests, fields, and many large cities—I would estimate the scale between 1/1,000,000 and 1/2,000,000, and thus Pantagruel's height between 1,000 and 2,000 *miles*. (I leave it to the reader to estimate, from Gargantua's remarks on II: 3, 181, what must have been the size of Badebec.)

(All these calculations of mine are at worst an absurd waste of time and at best only conjectural approximations; but they show the enormous disparities in the size of Rabelais's giants even when they are giants—and incidentally show why illustrating Rabelais seems such an exercise in futility.)

More than once I have heard it argued that Rabelais's giants tend to become normal size once they are educated—that for Rabelais, in this respect at least, wiser is smaller. Such a trend, however, if it exists, is very faint and unreliable. (For example, it is the educated Pantagruel whose height once seems to be between one and two thousand miles.) I think one may make two statements: that Rabelais's giantism is rarely comic once the giants are educated; and that once he gets into education he relies less and less on giantism. Beyond this we can attribute the varying size of Rabelais's giants to one thing only: his aim, mood, and requirements at any particular moment.

Even if we agree, however, that Rabelais's giantism, in the sense of the size he makes his giants, is limited, erratic, and decreasing in its use, there remains the matter of his own giantism.

What makes a man choose giants as his heroes? No doubt motives may vary. However, I suspect that the usual primary urge is simply to be (or to imagine oneself as being) larger, stronger, and swifter than others—much the same urge as is satisfied in contemporary popular heroes such as Superman or Batman, in John Wayne of the Westerns, in the fantasies of Walter Mitty. It is basically a childlike urge, though found in some degree in most humans.[1]

With great power, giant stature is seen as bestowing great freedom: to a giant the sky, as we say, is the limit. The ordinary limitations on human power—frailty, fallibility, family obligations, shortage of money, subservient social or economic status or both—never affect Rabelais's giants, or, thanks to the giants, his ordinary-sized heroes. Plagued as he was with such problems and with persecution as well, Rabelais seems to have found compensation in the freedom and power of giant fantasy, even as in the great optimism about human nature manifested in Gargantua's speech to the vanquished (I: 50) and in the rule of Theleme (I: 57). Again in contrast with Rabelais on this score is the apparent giantism (or pygmyism) of Voltaire in *Micromégas*, or the balanced account of Swift, whose Gulliver is first gigantic, then tiny. Both these authors show a relativism with a disillusioned stress on the puniness of man; their contrast with Rabelais is great.

There is yet another giantism in Rabelais that I think all readers feel; one shared by the author, his persona the narrator, and most of the main characters—notably Gargantua and Pantagruel and their friends. With his gigantic love of life, "To be or not to be" is a question never raised or even, I think, dreamed of in Rabelais's philosophy. Characteristically gigantic throughout the book are the appetites: for food and drink, for sexual conquests (Frère Jean and especially Panurge), for learning, for words, for life itself. Food and drink are always abundant and consumed in abundance. Panurge boasts of hundreds of sexual conquests in Paris—417 in nine days (II: 15, 236)—and is only a little worried about how he can thus service 150,000 beautiful Dipsode camp followers (II: 26, 278). The insatiable appetite for learning is apparent in the chapters on education in both the first two books. There is even something gigantic about the wisdom of the mature giants, as well as about the gloomy stupidity of Quaresmeprenant, the imbecile ecstasy of Homenaz, and the corrupt power of the Furred Cats.

The boundless love of words is not confined to the author or narrator; Panurge shares his creator's intoxication, as do to a lesser extent Pantagruel, Frère Jean, Rondibilis, Bridoye, Homenaz, and others. Rabelais's exuberance has a gigantic quality that is everywhere manifest in his unquenchable cascades of words. Almost everything in the book is larger than life.

In short, despite the limitations of Rabelais's use of giants, there is a genuine giantism of Rabelais himself as author. He is perhaps more consistently gigantic than any of his characters. It may be for this reason, as much as for any other, that when we think of Rabelais we do indeed think of a giant.

Humanism and
Evangelism

Most readers find at least two worlds in Rabelais: the popular, grotesque, carnivalesque, and the learned, lofty, and Evangelical-human-
istic. From his youth, his medieval heritage, perhaps his subconscious,
he derives the former; the latter from his conscious maturity, from the
ideas and ideals of the early French Renaissance in which he lived.
Although the two worlds interweave and overlap, they still form a
marked contrast. Already I have touched on his humanism and Evangelism in passing; I should like to look at them more closely now.

By humanism I mean both the thirst for knowledge and the knowledge itself of ancient literature, culture, and philosophy, especially of
ancient Greece and Rome—a knowledge that involves a mastery of
their languages; and with that, a sense that this is the road not only to
learning and culture but also to wisdom and virtue.

By Evangelism I mean a Christian belief whose insistence on the
primacy of the Bible makes the believer his own authority, rather than
the Church as the accredited interpreter of an authorized text. Sixteenth-century Evangelism was thus close to Protestantism, differing
mainly in seeking only peaceful reform within the Church. The typical Evangelical sought to know the Bible in the original Hebrew and
Greek, rejected the authority of the Latin Vulgate, and favored its
translation into the vernacular, so that each believer might understand
what he read and heard. He rejected five of the Church's seven sacraments—all but baptism and communion—as not established by the
Bible itself. Together with ordination as a sacrament, he rejected a
separate and sanctified priesthood, and celibacy as a requirement for it;
together with matrimony as a sacrament, he rejected the view that
priests might arrange and perform marriages without the parents' con-

sent. He denounced the worship of saints and of the Virgin Mary, accepting only Jesus as mediator between God and man; images and pictures in churches, as disobeying the commandment against graven images; and many other things that Rabelais refers to as "constitutions humaines et inventions dépravées" (II: 29, 291) [human institutions and depraved inventions].

One of the most striking phenomena in French letters of the first third of the sixteenth century is the close alliance of humanism and Evangelism. Both currents rejected as wrongheaded most medieval theology, especially late scholasticism and monasticism, and sought to restore a more primitive, hence truer, Christianity. Their common denominator was the desire to return, beyond the "Gothic darkness" that they ascribed to the Middle Ages, to the original texts, now far more available through the printing press, of the Bible and of classical antiquity, and thus both to a truer sense of pagan antiquity and to a Christianity closer to that of Christ.

Most of the leading French writers of the 1520s and 1530s combined humanistic and Evangelical leanings. Erasmus was the great model to many, including Rabelais and the poet Clément Marot. Others who in different ways combined these two veins were the theologian Jacques Lefèvre d'Etaples, the Hellenist Guillaume Budé; the belletrist Jean Lemaire de Belges; the mystic and erudite versifier and storyteller, Queen Margaret of Navarre; the scholar and storyteller Bonaventure des Périers; and a host of lesser figures. The King himself, Francis I, was drawn in this direction for many years by his love of arts and letters, the influence of his sister Margaret of Navarre, and his dislike of the Sorbonne. His foundation of the College of the Royal Lecturers in 1530 was a great step forward for Evangelical humanism. The chief opponents of the movement, of the College, and of most of the writers just named, were the Sorbonne and its bellicose, arch-conservative syndic, Noël Béda. After the Affair of the Placards in 1534 the innovators lost the support of the King; militant, authoritarian Protestantism emerged in French form in Geneva with Calvin; and the force of Evangelism waned, while humanist erudition turned from Biblical learning to the enrichment of vernacular literature with Ronsard, Du Bellay, and the other poets of the Pléiade.

In Rabelais as in most writers of his day, humanism and Evangelism are interwoven, but still separable for purposes of inspection. Most marked in his first two books—which were written before the Affair of the Placards—they are apparent throughout all five.

———

The most striking statement of Rabelais's humanism is the letter from Gargantua to Pantagruel (II: 8). We have noted its educational ideas and examined part of it as an example of Rabelais's lofty style. Let us briefly review it as the document of an Evangelical humanist.

Perhaps its most striking characteristic is the encyclopedic. The only branch of knowledge not recommended is divining astrology, which is paired with Raymond Lully's *Ars brevis* as "abuses and vanities." Books and languages are emphasized strongly but not exclusively: Pantagruel is to learn the "facts of nature"—fish, birds, flora, metals, "let nothing be unknown to you"—and to be a true Renaissance polymath. His shall be anything but a smattering of ignorance: of the liberal arts, geometry, arithmetic, and music, he has been given the rudiments as a child; so, says his father, "poursuys la reste" (205) [pursue the rest]. Depth as well as breadth is needed to produce the "abyss of knowledge" (206) that Gargantua intends to see in the person of his son.

For such an enterprise (Gargantua goes on) this is a golden age. Gone are the days of Gothic darkness when good letters languished; now the divinely inspired art of printing makes the best texts easy to come by; learned tutors are available. (The College of the Royal Lecturers is clearly in Rabelais's mind.) Never has there been such a time for learning, never such a chance for the student to make it his own.

Rabelais's stress on ancient languages is heavy: on Greek most of all ("without which it is shameful that a person should call himself learned"), but also Latin, Hebrew, Chaldean. The student must learn even to write them fluently and purely, taking Plato as his model for Greek, Cicero for Latin. But—and here the Evangelical strain comes in—the great importance of the Greek and the Hebrew is the access they give to the New and Old Testaments in the original, and these the student is to study daily.

For all the emphasis on learning, Pantagruel's education is to be moral as well: "un abysme de science" he may be, but "science sans conscience n'est que ruine de l'âme" (206) [knowledge without conscience is but ruin of the soul]. For Rabelais as for many of his contemporaries (Lefèvre, Erasmus, Budé), good letters tend to produce good morals; but religious piety and prayer are also essential.

Gargantua's letter to Pantagruel is the work—typical in all but its great eloquence—of an Evangelical humanist of the early French Renaissance. Almost alone in *Pantagruel*, it is the clearest document of its kind in all Rabelais.

———

The humanist stress is less marked in the education of Gargantua (I: 14-15, 21-24), which gives more attention to the physical and the experiential, and asks not what to study but how to learn it all in a short time. It is apparent, however, in the rejection of mediocre texts and mere memorization, in the stress on the sound mind in the sound body, the digestion of what is learned, the enjoyment of the process, the "field trips" on rainy days, and the texts rehearsed in the country outings (24). If the emphasis now is more on a well-rounded prince, that prince is still to be an abyss of knowledge.

Elsewhere in *Gargantua* the humanistic vein abounds: in the discourse on the meaning of the colors blue and white (9-10); in the merry ridicule of the utterly unhumanistic Sorbonicole Janotus de Bragmardo, with his innocent greed and eloquent pig Latin (17-20); in the lament of Grandgousier over the war, his letter to Gargantua, and Ulrich Gallet's harangue to Picrochole (28-31); in the treatment of monks and pilgrims (40, 45); in Gargantua's speech to the vanquished (50); and perhaps most of all in the educated freedom of the Abbey of Theleme. The most Evangelical of Rabelais's five books, *Gargantua* is also the most humanistic.

The last three books may be considered together for their humanism, and in terms of characters more than of episodes. In the *Third Book*, the most learned of the five, even the narrator displays his erudition, notably in the Prologue, the first chapter, and the last four on the herb Pantagruelion. In the *Third* and *Fourth Books* alike Epistémon is consistently erudite (and often little more), always ready with an example from classical antiquity. Pantagruel, who adds Christian to pagan erudition and wisdom to learning, leads the travelers in this respect as in others and sets the lofty tone for the whole band. His remarks are always those of a supremely wise Evangelical humanist. Whether Panurge deserves the title of humanist is questionable at best;* but he is certainly eloquent and learned, from the praise of debts on.

The *Third Book*, with its many moral and philosophical problems, offers the most humanistic discourse. We hear it from the author in chapter 1, on colonization; a parody of it from Panurge in praise of debts (2-4); more of it from him and Pantagruel in the next four chapters on debts, newlywed men exempted from military service, and

---

* Gérard Defaux considers him the direct opposite: *Pantagruel et les sophistes* (The Hague: Nijhoff, 1973).

the uses and dignity of codpieces; from Pantagruel on marriage and Virgilian lots (10–12), on prediction by dreams (13, with Panurge joining in, 14–15), on the sibyl of Panzoust and other sibyls (16, 18), on the prophetic powers of mutes (19) and dying poets (21); from Epistémon in Panurge's consultation with him (24); from Pantagruel again as he plans the fourfold consultation of experts (29) and comments on Trouillogan's reply (35), and in the discussion of the wisdom of fools (37), of the Christian folly of Bridoye (43–44), and of the "wise" folly of Triboullet (45–46); to some extent from Gargantua as he inveighs against marriages without parental consent and the monks who perform them (48); and from the narrator again in the concluding chapters on Pantagruelion (49–52). Moreover, Bridoye's long near-soliloquy (39–42) is a kind of parody of a humanist's talk about law. Except in a few consultations when Pantagruel is silent or absent, the humanistic note is everywhere.

It is less dominant in the last two books, especially the last. We find it in the exchange of letters with Gargantua on Medamothi (IV: 3–4); in some of the comments on the island of Cheli (11); in the author's discussion of Bringuenarilles and his death (17); in certain parts dealing with the tempest and Panurge's fear (23–24); in the exchange between the Macrobe and Pantagruel on the Islands of the Macræons (25–28); in Pantagruel's story of Antiphysie and her descendants (32); in much of the encounter with the whale (33–34), and parts of that with the Chitterlings (35–39); in the episode of the Frozen Words (55–56); in much of the account of Messere Gaster (57–58, 60–62); in some of Pantagruel's comments as they wait for wind and for dinner (63–65); and in the ensuing happenings off Ganabin (66–67). The number of chapters marked by humanistic comment is still great, but there is less of it per chapter than in the *Third Book*; and more of it is mere erudition, less of it wisdom applied to moral problems.

In the *Fifth Book* there are occasional bits of humanistic comment in some early chapters (1–2, 4, 6, 9–11, 15), and allusions in the kingdom of Entelechy (19–25) and the Isle des Odes (26). Epistémon's discussion of Lent (29) is that of an Evangelical humanist. The wonders of the land of Satin are learnedly described (30–31), as are aspects of Lanternland (33–33 bis) and of much of the land of the Divine Bottle (35–47). The priestess Bacbuc speaks like a true humanist (45–47). We find similar touches in many chapters, but most of them are little more than learned allusions; the weight and mass of humanistic comment and wisdom are lesser than in the earlier books.

Despite this decrease, the total of this weight and mass in all five books is a constant reminder that Rabelais was not only a storyteller but a humanist.

The view of Rabelais as an Evangelical, now generally accepted, is relatively recent. It was Augustin Renaudet, in his 1916 French thesis on "Prereform and Humanism in Paris during the First Italian Wars (1494–1517)," who really opened up the study of sixteenth-century French Evangelism. However Abel Lefranc, in his 1922 preface to *Pantagruel*,[1] pronounced Rabelais an atheist; and his eminence gave weight to this view, although some, like Etienne Gilson and Jean Plattard, were not convinced. In 1942 Lucien Febvre, in *Le Problème de l'incroyance au seizième siècle. La Religion de Rabelais*, refuted Lefranc's arguments and revealed Rabelais as an Evangelical Christian and disciple of Erasmus, a view which, with some modifications, has prevailed. V. L. Saulnier, in an important book* and many articles, has found Rabelais's later books filled with *hésuchisme*, a kind of crypto-Evangelism by which the Evangelical, caught between two equally repugnant authoritarianisms—the conservative Catholic and the Calvinist tried still to profess his faith covertly in the only way that might keep him safe from the stake.

M. A. Screech, who like Febvre makes much use of Will G. Moore's important book *La Réforme allemande et la littérature française* (1930), has given us a deeper and more precise sense of Rabelais's Evangelism in many articles,[2] editions (*Gargantua*, in collaboration, and the *Third Book*),[3] and especially two books: *The Rabelaisian Marriage* (London: Arnold, 1958) and *L'Evangélisme de Rabelais. Aspects de la satire religieuse au XVIᵉ siècle*, ER II (1959).

Screech reveals Rabelais's theology as far more complex than had been seen before: Lutheran sympathies in the birth of Gargantua (I: 6); an anti-Lutheran vein in Pantagruel's prayer and the answering voice from heaven (II: 29), in the "faith formed by charity" of Gargantua's letter to Pantagruel (II: 8, 206), and in the full freedom of Theleme (I: 57, 159–60); but still a persistent respect for Luther and his doctrine (*L'Evangélisme*, p. 42 and *passim*). He shows how Rabelais opposes Calvinism in the tempest in the *Fourth Book* (1: 18–24), where man's only hope is in God (not in the Virgin or in saints), but where man too must work for his own safety; in the *Almanachs* and *Prognostications*, where again man must work although God pre-

* *Le Dessein de Rabelais* (Paris: SEDES, 1957).

destines and decides; and in the behavior of Couillatris in the Prologue to the *Fourth Book*. He brings out Rabelais's anti-Roman Gallicanism in his treatment of "the God on earth" of the Papimanes (IV: 48–54), and concludes that the Reform Rabelais favors is the English kind brought about by Henry VIII (*L'Evangélisme*, pp. 94–95). On some doctrinal points, Screech shows, Rabelais even sides with the Sorbonne conservatives against both major Protestant sects. Generally, however, he keeps his distance from all three main authoritarianisms: conservative Catholic, Lutheran, and Calvinist. Against the first he rejects monastic orders, worship of saints and the Virgin, and belief in merit by works; against Luther and Calvin, he insists that man must collaborate with God to bring about His will, and that he has some power to do so; and against Calvin, he condemns the use of force in matters of faith.

On most of these points Rabelais is close to Erasmus; but Screech has shown him to be an expert theologian, finding his own way among the warring factions of his time, with considerable knowledge of the vast religious literature of his own and earlier times, and thus mainly eclectic and independent.

Rabelais's Evangelism is rarely manifest in *Pantagruel*, extremely prominent in *Gargantua*, and evident but mainly covert in the last three books. In *Pantagruel* there is the challenge to the conservatives in the catalogue of St.-Victor (7) and in the letter from Gargantua to Pantagruel (8), with its stress on learning Hebrew and Greek so as to read the Old and New Testaments in the original. Probably Evangelical is the urge that led Rabelais, in 1534, to add to his term "sophists" (for the debaters of the Sorbonne) the nine terms that begin with "Sorbillans" and end with "Saniborsans" (18, 253, fn. 3). The main Evangelical passage is Pantagruel's prayer (29, 290–91) before his combat with Loup Garou and his three hundred other giants. There he tells God his belief that He has authorized defensive war where faith is not concerned—and such war only—and promises that if God grants him victory he will have His holy Gospel preached "purely, simply, and in its entirety," and will exile from around him all the abuses of the false prophets who "by human institutions and depraved inventions" have envenomed the whole world. A voice from heaven tells him to do so, and he will be victorious. Except for a few later additions to the concluding chapter 34, this is all.

Already we have noted the Evangelism of *Gargantua*: the condemnation of monks, in contrast with the praise of Frère Jean (40), of pilgrimages and the preachers who encourage them (45), and of the Sorbonne, arch-enemy of the Evangelicals, mainly through Janotus de Bragmardo (18–20). We also noted how Rabelais went out of his way to praise the good Evangelical preachers, and, at the cost of confusion, offered them asylum in his Abbey of Theleme (54). The concluding enigma (58), at least as read by Pantagruel if not by Frère Jean, is a warning to all Evangelicals of persecutions to come and an exhortation to persevere in their faith. The richest of the five books in religious statements, *Gargantua* is among other things a manifesto of humanistic Evangelism.

Although Screech, in his critical edition, brings out many daring passages in the *Third Book*, I find it on the whole rather cautious. Evangelical views are set forth throughout for our admiration by Pantagruel, and at times by Hippothadée (30) and by Gargantua (48) on clandestine marriages. There is occasional satire of the Sorbonne; of monks who will not let a believer die in peace, in the words of the dying poet Raminagrobis (21); and of heresy-sniffing in the person of Panurge (22–23, etc.). Altogether, the Evangelical tone is maintained but—at least in comparison to *Gargantua*—subdued.

The *Fourth Book* is occasionally outspoken, but usually more Gallican than Evangelical. Evangelical, however, is the departure of the fleet from the port of Thalasse (1, 540–41), with the "short and holy" lay sermon, full of scriptural passages, by Pantagruel, the prayer to God evidently in the vernacular (since all the citizens not only hear but understand it), and the singing of Psalm 114 ("When Israel went out of Egypt"), a favorite of the Evangelicals as symbolizing their plight, in Clément Marot's verse translation, which the Sorbonne had condemned.[4] In the 1552 revision of 1548 material we are struck by Pantagruel's piety during the tempest; and this is at times specifically Evangelical as well as generally Christian. In the later parts added in 1552 Panurge, who in 1548 had prayed to two saints (19, 596), now prays to the Virgin, too (18, 593), and then reneges on his vow (24, 609). There are Evangelical touches in Pantagruel's account of the death of Jesus (28); in the ridicule of Quaresmeprenant (29–32), and Rabelais's blast at the authoritarian extremists on either side, Putherbeus and Calvin (32); in Pantagruel's detestation of the Gastrolâtres and Engastrimythes (58), and in the account of Ganabin.[5] Most striking is the passage already quoted in which the little devil in the land of the Papefigues (46, 664) laments the fact that, since the students have added the Bible to their readings, Lucifer can no longer eat them for lunch unless the hypocrites force them to stop reading Saint Paul.

The whole part on Papimania (48–54), with its satire of the greed and cruelty of the Roman curia, is in no sense anti-Evangelical but still primarily Gallican. It is this fact, as Robert Marichal has shown,[6] which, being palatable to the Sorbonne, probably contributed to checking their censure of the book.

The *Fifth Book* is hardly Evangelical at all. The opening episode of the Ringing Island (1–8) might be called that, with its satire of the bells and the gluttonous clergy; but the obvious allusion to Rome makes it, like Papimania, mainly Gallican. Only the account of the lecherous Frères Fredons, followed by Epistémon's diatribe against Lent, seems truly Evangelical. Nothing in this book conflicts with Evangelism, but there is little that asserts it.

In short, Rabelais's Evangelism is clear but not very common in *Pantagruel*, clear and very common in *Gargantua*, and generally less aggressive thereafter: rarely polemical in the *Third Book*, more frequent but verging on Gallicanism in the *Fourth Book*, and less marked than his Gallicanism in the *Fifth Book*. Taken altogether, however, it remains the most important religious commitment of his entire work. Even when obliged to be mainly cryptic for fear of the stake, Rabelais still dared to speak. No wonder an excellent recent book about this "impenitent old Evangelical" is subtitled "A Study in Comic Courage."[7]

Rabelais is clearly a courageous, independent, and very learned Evangelical, to whom his view of Christian doctrine was all his life a matter of the utmost importance. His Evangelism and his humanism are the two convictions that give his entire work its intellectual tone and flavor.

Characters and Their
Interaction

Rabelais is not primarily a creator of characters. Most of his are hardly more than sketches; but those sketches are skillfully drawn. From the giants down to Janotus and Editus, in the main Rabelais allows them, as in a play, to portray themselves mostly by their own words and actions. Rather than telling us that Pantagruel (or Panurge) was this or that kind of man, and therefore did this or that, he tells us that Pantagruel (or Panurge) did this or that, and leaves us to figure out why. He fathered no Hamlet or Lear, no Don Quixote or Sancho, nor any of the Emma Bovarys or Becky Sharps of later years; but he did create several major characters—Gargantua, Pantagruel, Panurge, Frère Jean—and a score of minor ones who remain alive and memorable to this day.

It is the giants, of course, for whom the books are named and who are probably the best remembered. As we have noted, all three start as gigantically comic and soon become sage and benign.

Grandgousier has the smallest part of the three. We first meet him (I: 3) as simply a gay blade, a good drinker, and a willing fulfiller of the physical duties of marriage. When his wife Gargamelle, in unusually hard labor, utters a half-hearted wish that he had cut off his penis (the cause of her plight), he pronounces himself ready to do so (6, 22), but is readily dissuaded and goes off to drink with the boys. He returns to name his son (7, 25), then only some years later to approve his choice of an ass-wipe (13), get him started on a bad old-style education (14), and correct this (15 ff.) by sending him to Paris to study under Ponocrates (21–24). Grandgousier reappears only with the outbreak of Picrochole's war (28–32), which reveals him as a good neighbor and a pious Christian king, ready to appease his old friend and ally if possible, and to be God's agent, if asked to be, in bringing Picrochole back to sense and conscience. He feasts his son and his followers on their safe arrival (37), takes a milder view of the failings of monks than does his son (40)—but accepts his correction—and preaches an Evangelical sermon to the pilgrims that they receive with wondering delight (45). He treats his prisoner Toucquedillon humanely (46), welcomes his legions in the next chapter, and then completely disappears from the scene and the book. Less of a sage than his descendants will become, he still rivals them in his advice to the pilgrims.

Gargantua is simply a comic giant from his birth to his discovery of the perfect ass-wipe (I: 6–13), and remains basically that under the bad old education (14), through his trip to Paris (16–20) and his bad study habits (21–22), until he comes fully under the tutelage of Ponocrates (23–24). Once educated, as we have noted, he is rarely a giant any more and even more rarely comic (but see 37, 39, 41). From I: 50 on he is the modern Christian sage and king, generous to the vanquished and ready to believe that this pays (50), optimistic about basic human decency in his foundation of Theleme (52–57), worried about the prospects of Evangelism in the prophetic enigma (58), but urging the faithful to hold fast to the true faith. In *Pantagruel* he gives serious concern to his son's education (II: 8).* Translated to the land of the fairies in II: 23, 267—written, of course, two years before he was fully conceived by his author—he reappears, suddenly and mysteriously, late in the *Third Book* (35–36) for the consultation with the Pyrrhonist Trouillogan, comments ruefully on his responses, and leaves the company as suddenly as he had come. Then when Pantagruel agrees to accompany Panurge in quest of the oracle of the Divine Bottle, he goes first (47–48) to seek his father's permission, learns that Gargantua would like to see him married, and is treated to a long and violent denunciation (with which he apparently agrees) of marriages arranged by monks without the parents' consent. In the next book Gargantua exchanges letters with his son early in Pantagruel's voyage (IV: 3–4); and he is apparently still alive at the end of the *Fifth Book* to receive Bacbuc's letter of greeting.

As a grown man he is so constantly kind (to the vanquished and to

---

* Defaux, in *Pantagruel et les sophistes* (pp. 53–59, 74–81, and *passim*), finds him, in *Pantagruel*, comically overimpressed with erudition.

Trouillogan, and in his letter in IV: 3) that his outburst against monks who arrange clandestine marriages (III: 48) must be an expression by Rabelais of righteous indignation against an abomination that threatens the very fabric of a healthy society. Gargantua remains primarily the hero of a single book, more up-to-date than his father in his criticism of monks, much like his son, wise, Evangelical, and in all but one extreme case most benign.

Pantagruel, who gives his name to four of the five books, is much like his father and grandfather but even more developed as a sage and prince. Like Gargantua, he is a comic young giant until his father's letter (II: 8) spurs him to acquire an education. If his Latin still seems weak in the next chapter when he meets Panurge, in the few that follow (10–13) he shows an inspired capacity for both judgment and nonsense in settling the Baisecul-Humevesne lawsuit, then leaves center stage to Panurge for his sayings and exploits and the debate in signs with Thaumaste (18–20).

In the war he does not dominate as his father had done (or more properly, was to do) in *Gargantua*. He lets Panurge and his companions take over the first battle, seems to need encouragement from him before conquering Loup Garou and the other giants, and is ready to kill himself when he thinks Epistémon is dead—until again Panurge takes over. He is still a comic giant in chapter 32, when he covers his army with his tongue and the narrator finds a world inside his mouth, and 33, when his constipation is cured by a mining expedition.

It is only in the *Third Book* that Pantagruel emerges as a benign sage, and Rabelais is at pains from the outset to make his hero's new role clear. Chapter 1 shows him as a model of how to treat a conquered people; in chapter 2, for the only time in his work, Rabelais treats us to a character sketch (p. 335) of the cheerful Christian Stoic whom nothing torments or scandalizes and who takes all things in good part. For the next eleven chapters, until Frère Jean appears, he is still often a somewhat comic foil for Panurge; but mainly he is what he will be henceforth, "the idea and exemplar of all joyous perfection" (III: 51, 506): a constant source of Christian and Stoical counsel for Panurge and his other friends; a tower of strength in danger and affliction (as in the tempest in the *Fourth Book*); a kind of philosopher-king whose wisdom, Pantagruelism, consists in "a certain gaiety of spirit pickled in disdain for fortuitous things" (IV: Prologue, 523). Rabelais's own wisdom may be dispersed in those of Panurge and Frère Jean as well as of Pantagruel; but his highest wisdom is that of Pantagruel.

From the giants we turn to Panurge and Frère Jean. With—or after—Pantagruel, Panurge is the leading character in Rabelais. He first appears (II: 9 ff.) as an ingenious scamp, of middle age (thirty-five) for the time, full of tricks, stories, and plans for the conquest of women, multilingual (ch. 9), hard in his revenge on the lady of Paris (21–22), brave and venturesome in the war (25, etc.), resourceful when Epistémon is thought dead (30). More than his prince and master, it is he who dominates *Pantagruel.*

From the *Third Book* on everything changes. Even as Pantagruel is revealed as a genial sage in chapter 2, Panurge reveals himself in 3 and 4 as a glib proponent of specious causes. Human he is, but pathetically so, eager to marry but only on his own unacceptable terms, ready to consult any oracle on the subject but insisting on reading the answers in his own way. He also appears from the *Third Book* on as a rather old man, a coward, and a heresy-sniffer. Rabelais's vast hospitality keeps Panurge basically congenial to the reader; but now for the first time he makes him the main butt of the comedy. Only at the end of the suspect *Fifth Book,* when Panurge responds joyously in Bacchic verse to the Divine Bottle while Frère Jean does so only grudgingly, does Rabelais give Panurge better play than Frère Jean. Both of course remain less admirable than Pantagruel.

Of the other characters, Frère Jean alone is more than a sketch. Gay, resolutely ignorant except in breviary matter, fearless to the point of rashness, he is above all active, in sharp contrast with the usual rather passive monk. Floyd Gray has called him "the character whose language is immediately an act."[1] When Picrochole's army invades the abbey vineyard, he routs them singlehanded while the other monks mumble prayers (I: 27); when Panurge refuses to return to the dying Raminagrobis (III: 23, 408–11), Frère Jean remains undaunted; his active courage in the tempest contrasts with Panurge's blubbering cowardice (IV: 19); in the *Fifth Book* (15, 785–88) it is he who urges that they return to sack the Furred Cats, whom even Pantagruel finds it wiser to avoid. His lusty humor, never averse to obscenity, is seen when Panurge seeks his advice about marriage (III: 26–28). Frère Jean hails him as 170 kinds of discouraged testicle, twits him about his advancing years and the consolations of his impending cuckoldry, and advises him to use as a remedy Hans Carvel's ring. To me Frère Jean is Rabelais's most fully realized character, the only one whom the reader seems not only to hear but to see.

Of the other characters who appear off and on throughout the book, the narrator, Maistre Alcofribas Nasier, is the most comically attractive. His best scene (II: 32) is when he discovers the world in Pantagruel's mouth, chats congenially with a cabbage-planter along the way, and afterward confesses to his master where he shat ("In your throat, sir") during the six months he was there. His interventions are consistently gay and genial.

Pantagruel's companions are the only others who (for the most part) appear throughout the book. His original team of specialized experts consisted of Eusthenes the strong (appearing in Books II and IV), Carpalim the swift (in II–V), and Epistémon the knowing, wise, or prudent (II–V); of these only the last-named deserves further attention. Gymnaste (I, III, IV) also has his special skill, agility. Eudémon (I–III) holds the stage for a moment (I: 15, 50) as the bright young page whose simple charm puts the still uncouth child Gargantua to shame. Ponocrates (I, III, IV), the tutor who sets Gargantua's education straight, is barely characterized. Rhizotome (III, IV) and the pilot Xenomanes (IV) are hardly even sketched. Other companions of Gargantua appear only once, momentarily (I: 51).

Epistémon (II–V) has his moment of spotlight already in *Pantagruel* (30) when his head is cut off and he is restored to life to report on hell. In the *Third Book* he emerges as the leading minor character, and except for one momentary appearance by Carpalim, he is the only one of these to play a part in the *Fifth Book*. Of the meanings of his name in Greek—"knowing, wise, prudent"—I think the operative one is "knowing." Rarely at a loss for a classical analogue, he helps Pantagruel carry the burden of Rabelais's copious erudition in the *Third* and *Fourth Books*. As we noted before, Rabelais seems once to have nodded, in revising his text between 1548 and 1552, by exchanging two of their speeches with little regard for consistency and sense (III: 44).

For all that, Epistémon is no Pantagruel, but a merely learned type, rather formal and reserved (on terms of *vous*, not *tu*, with all the others), whose limitations are best shown when Panurge consults him about his marriage (III: 24, 414). In reply to the question "Should I marry or not?" he declares his own inadequacy to answer: "Indeed . . . the case is risky: I feel myself much too inadequate to resolve it." And after some discussion of oracles that have ceased, he recommends consulting Her Trippa, who turns out to be a bombastic cuckold.

Of the characters who have only a moment on stage, fully a score deserve passing note. To take them in order of appearance, there is the Limousin student (II: 6), secure and smug in his Latinized French until, frightened by Pantagruel, he lapses into dialectal incoherence; Baisecul and Humevesne (10–13), earnestly delivering their pleas that make no sense; Thaumaste, the modest English sage, happy at the chance to grow in wisdom by arguing in signs (18–20); and the lady of Paris (21–22), perhaps a bit coquettish but hardly deserving the cruel trick played on her by her frustrated would-be lover Panurge. In *Gargantua* we find Janotus de Bragmardo (18–20) seeking to get back the bells of Notre-Dame, slightly tipsy, full of "harrumphs" and delectable pig Latin, but ready to join the others in laughter at himself and to excoriate, as one who knows, his Sorbonne colleagues when they renege on their promised reward. And Picrochole is more than just a sketch; he is a study of a stupid aggressor king, drawn with Emperor Charles V in mind, who takes Grandgousier's offers of appeasement for proofs of his cowardice and lets his advisers gull him into wild dreams of world conquest (32–33).

The *Third Book* offers a number of sketches: the dying poet Raminagrobis (21), serene and courteous even in his death pangs, glad to be rid of the verminous monks, asking only to be let alone; the arrogant and insulting dealer in magic Her Trippa (25), who pronounces Panurge a cuckold, but according to Panurge is an unwitting cuckold himself; the "incredibly modest," wise, and knowing Evangelical theologian Hippothadée (30), who reads Panurge like a book; the learned, pompous, mercenary, and relentlessly discursive Doctor Rondibilis (31–34); the resourceful Pyrrhonistic philosopher Trouillogan (35–36), who fields scores of questions and never gives a positive answer; and the Christian fool Judge Bridoye (39–42), who resolves lawsuits by rolling dice, justifies this by legal precedent, and explains that everyone does just as he does.

In the *Fourth Book*, the main minor character is Dindenault (5–8), whose chief characteristic is his arrogance. From the first he hails Panurge as a cuckold and professes to fear him as a con man trying to pay too little for one of his sheep. While Panurge patiently listens, Dindenault sets forth Panurge's cuckoldry and the incredible virtues of his sheep—until at last Panurge buys one, throws it overboard, and watches the other sheep, the merchant, and his shepherds follow. Quaresmeprenant (29–32) is not really a character but a wildly grotesque sketch. In the land of the Papefigues (45-47), the farmer is fairly shrewd but fearful, his wife tougher and far more resourceful, and the little devil, who is thwarted on all counts, a delightful simpleton. Among the Papimanes (48-54), Bishop Homenaz is their perfect spokesman, virtually drooling with delight at the wondrous things the divine Decretals can do for Rome and against Rome's adversaries. Messere Gaster (57-62), for all the ingenuity that makes him "the first master of arts in the world," is modestly aware that he is no divinity but merely an imperious ruler who knows where to draw the line.

In the *Fifth Book* there is Editus, the quiet and knowing guide who shows the travelers through the Ringing Island (1-8), aware of the faults of those he represents but still loyal. Grippeminault (11-14) is a horrifying figure, dangerous, limited in his talk to "Or sà" ["Well now!" or "Money here!"], a power whom even Pantagruel is reluctant to cross. Queen Quintessence (19-25) does wonders for the sick, and eats and talks in a quintessential way. Bacbuc (42-47) gives a serious and lofty tone to the end of the story.

Although their time on stage is brief, these characters help the main ones keep the book moving and make the story live.

As one would expect, the leading characters affect one another, especially in the last three books, where they all appear together.[2] Already in *Pantagruel*, as Gérard Defaux has shown, the sophistry of Panurge is a temptation to his young giant master.[3] It is Frère Jean whose sudden and apparently unpremeditated appearance one quarter of the way through the *Third Book* (13, 376) has the most striking effect on others. He of course does not "belong" with Pantagruel and Panurge, unless as a senior citizen of Gargantua's generation; he had not appeared in *Pantagruel*, only in *Gargantua*. Now for the first time Rabelais has someone besides Pantagruel to talk to Panurge and respond lustily to his often salacious remarks.

Until Frère Jean comes on the scene, Pantagruel in the *Third Book* had been often free-spoken and sometimes a bit of a wag: in his comment on the preachers of Varenne (6, 350); in his twitting of Panurge for his resolve to marry (7, 352) and for his specious erudition, which leads to his only use of *tu* to Panurge in the last three books (8, 355); in his teasing of Panurge by his "chanson de Ricochet" throughout chapter 9, giving Panurge alternately, in his own words, the conflicting answers that Panurge in effect demands. More striking, when Panurge predicts that he will make love to his wife successfully sixteen times on his wedding night, Pantagruel (11, 365-66) explains this as meaning that on his first attempt he will score a miss (fifteen points in court tennis—or modern lawn tennis), and then succeed on his second try for a total of sixteen.

Once Frère Jean appears, there is no need for a jesting Pantagruel; the monk takes over that function, and Pantagruel is raised above the comic level. In chapter 19 of the *Third Book* (p. 397) he reacts severely to two comic stories of illicit love-making, the second involving a nun and a priest, with these words: "You will never make me laugh at that. I know well enough that all monkhood is less afraid to transgress God's commandments than their provincial statutes."

This elevation of Pantagruel is a continuing process. In the 1548 partial edition of the *Fourth Book*,* Rabelais made Pantagruel and Frère Jean witnesses to Panurge's bargaining with Dindenault and subsequent drowning of the merchant, shepherds, and sheep; in the definitive edition of 1552 Pantagruel is replaced by Epistémon. Similarly in the tempest: in 1552 Rabelais has Pantagruel pray to God twice—at the outset and once later (IV: 19, 594; 21, 601)—as he had not done in 1548 when Pantagruel, like Frère Jean, acted usefully but did not pray. Later in the *Fourth Book* (50, 674–75) Pantagruel sternly rebukes Frère Jean for reporting how beggars at Seuillé referred to one of their legs, made up to look lame or crippled, as "une jambe de Dieu" [a leg of God]:

"When," said Pantagruel, "you tell us such stories, remember to bring a basin: I am almost ready to throw up. To use the holy name of God in such filthy and abominable matters! Fie! I say fie! If such an abuse of words is in usage in your monkery, leave it there, don't transport it outside the cloisters."

Even greater, from III: 13 on, is the impact of Frère Jean on Panurge.[4] In undertaking the bold new venture of the *Third Book*—one with no giants and virtually no story line—Rabelais expresses uneasiness about its reception with his story in the Prologue about Ptolemy I and his two-colored slave and black Bactrian camel (pp. 326–27). For his first thirteen chapters he uses no characters except Pantagruel and Panurge. Then, apparently fearing that with no real plot these two cannot carry the comedy and interest alone, he suddenly introduces Frère Jean, then Epistémon, Ponocrates, Eudémon, Carpalim, "and others."

We have already noted the modest importance of Epistémon from then on and the relative unimportance of the other minor characters.

* IV: 6, 554; "Fac-similé du Quart Livre de 1548," ed. Robert Marichal, in *ER* IX (1971), p. 159.

Frère Jean's impact is great. He had been the leading normal-sized figure in *his* book (*Gargantua*), as Panurge had been in *his* (*Pantagruel*); neither had had much competition. Now they are together, from the *Third Book* on, and as characters they are potential rivals.

To my mind the lusty, dynamic, courageous monk—or antimonk—Frère Jean had from the first been a more three-dimensional, flesh-and-blood character than Panurge, who in *Pantagruel* was rather a stock type in the old tradition of the student scamp. Put them together in a book and they must not be too much alike. Frère Jean, the more solid character, is the more resistant to change. His presence leads Rabelais to make Panurge more different from him than before in three ways: more cowardly, more suspicious of heresy, more comically old.

His cowardice, which leads to his blubbering in the tempest in the *Fourth Book*, shows mainly in his terror at the Sibyl of Panzoust (III: 17, 389) and at the thought of being carried off by devils (23, 408–09) if he returns to try to save the soul of the dying poet Raminagrobis. In the latter episode, incidentally, his fear is in sharp contrast with the quiet courage of Frère Jean (p. 411). His heresy-sniffing, adumbrated in chapter 2 of the *Third Book* though nonexistent in *Pantagruel*, is much clearer after Frère Jean's arrival on the scene, especially in chapters 22 (again apropos of Raminagrobis) and 29, where he remarks that most theologians are heretics (p. 434). He will continue in this vein in the *Fourth Book*, in chapter 18 and elsewhere.

The most striking change in Panurge is the stress on his age. In *Pantagruel* (II: 16, 237) he was portrayed as about thirty-five; and no appreciable time seems to have elapsed in the fiction since then. Frère Jean, a contemporary of Gargantua, should be a full generation older than Panurge. Yet it is Panurge who is several times shown as old, once even by Pantagruel (46, 489); and it is Frère Jean, of all people, who in chapter 28 really rubs in the fact of Panurge's graying beard and advancing years—so successfully that Panurge, for once, admits that he is not getting any younger and that all authorities agree that if he marries he will be a cuckold.

The interaction of characters in Rabelais is not so much a matter of their independent development as of their creator's needs and purposes. Creation of characters is only one of his many gifts, and not his greatest. Yet he endowed his major figures—Gargantua, Pantagruel, Panurge, Frère Jean—and a score of swiftly sketched minor ones with a vivid reality that keeps them alive in the minds of readers to this day.

Fortunes

The full story of Rabelais's literary fortunes has yet to be told. We now have parts of it: Marcel de Grève's valuable work on the interpretation of Rabelais in France, England, and the Netherlands in the sixteenth century and in some French circles in the seventeenth;[1] many studies of Rabelais in England culminating in Huntington Brown's *Rabelais in English Literature*,[2] which goes only through the eighteenth century, claiming that there is little to find later; Marcel Tetel's *Rabelais et l'Italie*;[3] Maurice Lécuyer's *Balzac et Rabelais*;[4] two useful but not exhaustive books on his influence and reputation through the centuries;[5] and a scattering of articles on his impact on individual writers. Much remains to be done.

Rabelais's books were immediate and lasting best sellers; in the sixteenth century alone as many as a hundred thousand copies may have been sold.[6] His influence on contemporary French storytellers was enormous; few escaped his spell.[7] The imprint of his Pantagruelism and of many comic details appears on such eminent craftsmen as Bonaventure des Périers and Noël du Fail,[8] and in various ways on Guillaume Bouchet, Tabourot des Accords, Henri Estienne, Jacques Tahureau, and Béroalde de Verville, author of *Le Moyen de parvenir* [The Way to Succeed]. When the Protestant poet Agrippa d'Aubigné turned to prose satire, Rabelais was a favorite model.[9] As satirist, Pantagruelist, stylist, and above all storyteller, everywhere his influence is strong.

As Grève has shown, his other sixteenth-century French interpreters saw him in different lights at different moments. *Pantagruel* (1532) was generally dismissed as frivolous, but *Gargantua* (1534) was taken seriously and, in the critical years after the Affair of the Placards, seen as dangerous. When the *Third Book* appeared (1546) many had come to regard Rabelais as a pro-Lutheran heretic; and in the next six years others—though not Calvin or his followers—thought him a Calvinist. Although Dupuyherbault in his *Theotimus* (1549) attacks him mainly for gluttony and obscenity, this, argues Grève (*L'Interprétation*, p. 74), is because his heresy is common knowledge. With Calvin's growing influence in France and rejection of Rabelais in *De Scandalis* (1550), Rabelais came to be seen less as a serious Reformist and more as a drunken buffoon. This "legendary view" gains strength after his death from several epitaphs such as that by the great poet Pierre de Ronsard in 1554.

However, the "new Erasmians" of the late 1550s and early 1560s (such as Louis Le Caron and young Estienne Pasquier) clung to the notion of Rabelais's "substantific marrow," and after the outbreak of religious civil war (1562), the enforcement of the decrees of the Council of Trent (1564), and the publication of Rabelais's *Fifth Book* (1564), passed on the notion to the earliest freethinkers. It is especially in the 1580s and 1590s that imitators and disciples of Rabelais abound: not only some of the storytellers already noted, but such writers as Pasquier, Pierre de L'Estoile, and Jean Passerat and other authors of the *Satire Ménippée* [Menippean Satire] (1593), an account of the attempts of the Holy League and the Spaniards to take over not only Paris but all France.

If the main notion of Rabelais which the French sixteenth century passed on to the seventeenth is that of the freethinker, another compatible one goes with it: that of a keen-eyed witness of his time whose book is a *roman à clef* in which Gargantua represents Francis I, Picrochole Charles V, and so on. Especially in the late 1500s, keys to Rabelais's book abound; and the quest for them appealed to readers well into the nineteenth century.

In seventeenth-century France Rabelais still finds a mixed reception.[10] There are a few violent attacks by such churchmen as Father François Garasse, S.J., in 1619–23, who calls his book "the handbook of freethought." The neoclassical concern with regularity and decorum works against Rabelais. However, he attracts many freethinkers—Saint-Amant, Théophile de Viau, Gassendi, La Mothe Le Vayer, Gabriel Naudé, Guy Patin, Samuel Sorbière, and Gilles Ménage—and erudites, many of whom indulged in freethought and continued to seek keys to Rabelais's characters and book. Several great writers cherished his work and drew from it: Racine in his one comedy, *Les Plaideurs*, and three other authors freer of neoclassical ties. Madame de Sévigné was ready to "die laughing" at a reading of his book. Molière referred to him only twice (*The School for Wives*, I: 1, 117–22, and *The Miser*, II: 1) but remembered him often in his comedies. Jean de La Fontaine was steeped in him and drew on him freely in his *Fables* and verse *Contes* for countless details and many subjects: "The Woodcutter and Mercury" (Couillatris), "Hans Carvel's Ring," "The Sick Abbess," "Dindenaut and Panurge," "The Devil of Papefiguière." He knew the older language well and missed its graces, called himself Rabelais's disciple,[11] and, more than anyone else in his century in France, loved him not only wisely but well.

Jean de La Bruyère, however, probably spoke for many if not most of his contemporaries when he wrote in 1690 in his *Caractères*, in the chapter "Of the Works of the Mind," that Rabelais was inexcusable for his filth, incomprehensible, an insoluble enigma,

a monstrous assemblage of a delicate and ingenious morality and a filthy corruption. Where he is bad, he goes far beyond the worst, his is the charm of the rabble; where he is good, he even attains the exquisite and the excellent, he can be the dish of the most delicate readers.

La Bruyère's judgment is mixed but still quite severe.

Meanwhile Rabelais was slowly gaining admirers outside France. In the Netherlands he was widely read and enjoyed from the first,[12] especially in the French-speaking south, by people of all classes. A letter of 1567 tells of a certain Escaubecque who did all his preaching around Lille "with a Paternoster around his neck and a Pantagruel in his hand." The five mentions (one in Latin, four in French) of Rabelais and his book in the *Index of Prohibited Books* published in Antwerp in 1570 by Christophe Plantin suggest a popularity that made such frequent warnings seem necessary. The Dutch blend of humanism and Reform led them to take him seriously. His influence on the Protestant Marnix de Sainte-Aldegonde (1540–98), both in his Flemish *De Biënkorf der H. Roomsche Kerche* [Bee Hive of the Romishe Churche] and in his French *Tableau des différences de la religion*, extends from the whole satirical treatment of religion to countless reminiscences of detail.

In Germany few could read Rabelais in French, but the first foreign translation of *Gargantua*, by Johann Fischart, appeared there in 1575.

("Adaptation" might be the better word; for Fischart, an earnest Protestant, is given to moralizing at length.)[13] In Geneva Rabelais was popular enough to cause concern in the Consistory between 1570 and 1600.[14] Agrippa d'Aubigné was his only (part-time) disciple there, but both Théodore de Bèze and Henri Estienne were criticized for admiring him.

Much has been made of his immediate impact in England,[15] but Grève has convincingly shown that it has been exaggerated.[16] He finds no clear evidence of an influence of Rabelais on Thomas Nashe; a somewhat horrified knowledge of him in Gabriel Harvey; both influence and admiration in John Harington; and genuine enjoyment of him as a model by Ben Jonson after 1600. John Eliot uses Rabelais a great deal in his *Ortho-Epia Gallica*. Randle Cotgrave's valuable *Dictionarie of the French and English Tongues* (1611) is full of Rabelais. Two phrases in Shakespeare[17] recall Rabelais: Hotspur's "tell truth and shame the devil" to Glendower (*Henry IV, Part I*, III: i), which echoes Panurge to Trouillogan: "let us shame the devil in hell, let us confess the truth" (III: 36, 459); and Iago's "making the beast with two backs" (*Othello*, I: i), which echoes both *Gargantua* (3, 13) and *Cent Nouvelles nouvelles* (110, 20). These and other expressions suggest—but are far from proving—that Shakespeare knew Rabelais. In short, Grève finds Rabelais's influence in England, until he was translated in 1653, confined mainly to Bohemian circles, where he was dismissed—in Bacon's phrase—as "the merry jester of France."

In the early seventeenth century, however, we find traces of Rabelais in the theater, and admirers in prose in Francis Bacon, Bishop Joseph Hall, and Sir Thomas Browne. Later came Sir Thomas Urquhart's brilliant translation of the first two books (1653) and his posthumously published *Third* (1693), which naturalized Rabelais in England; then the more pedestrian version of the last two by the French-born Pierre Le Motteux (1694). Urquhart's own original writing was also colored by Rabelais. However, other editions were slow to follow Urquhart's first. There are occasional echoes in Samuel Butler, a considerable debt in Thomas Brown, signs of respect as well as disapproval in Sir William Temple and Thomas Rymer. That was about all in an age when such obscenity as Rabelais's was out of fashion.

In the early eighteenth century Rabelais found one of his greatest admirers—and an independent follower—in Jonathan Swift, who uses him frequently in *A Tale of a Tub* (1704) and abundantly in *Gulli-*

ver's Travels (1727). Like Rabelais, Swift when he borrows is entirely his own man, as we noted apropos of his use of giantism. However, his Academy of Projectors in Lagado (*Book Three*) clearly draws on Rabelais's officers of Quintessence; his account of the dead in Glubb-dubdrib draws on Epistémon's visit to hell (II: 30); and Rabelaisian touches are frequent. Voltaire compares him, and at least for a time much prefers him, to Rabelais.

Of Alexander Pope, Brown says that he viewed Rabelais rather as a cat lover does a dog. In invoking Swift early in *The Dunciad* (I, 19–20) he offers him two alternatives—"Whether thou chuse Cervantes' serious air,/Or laugh and shake in Rab'lais' easy chair"—as ways of avoiding dullness; and Joseph Spence quotes Pope as saying: "Dr. Swift was a great reader and admirer of Rabelais, and used sometimes to scold me for not liking him enough. Indeed there were so many things in his works in which I could not see any manner of meaning driven at, that I could never read him over with patience."[18]

John Arbuthnot, a third member of the Scriblerus Club, was closer to Swift in his fondness for Rabelais and use of him. Joseph Addison cited him a few times. Edward Young, like many of his time, admired him but deplored his indecency.

Later in the century Fielding shows moral disapproval of Rabelais, Goldsmith a good opinion of him, Dr. Johnson a sense of his licentiousness but also of his charm. Smollett draws on him for earthy satire in his late political work, *The Adventures of an Atom*. Most of all, Laurence Sterne is revealed by his correspondence and *Tristram Shandy* as a true disciple. He mentions Rabelais many times, always with affection; his Parson Yorick always carries a volume of Rabelais on him, and reads from it on request; he himself relishes the freedom with which Rabelais treats his story; and he composes a "Fragment in the Manner of Rabelais" that shows his admiration.[19] For all his dilettantism and sentimentality, he embodied a certain Pantagruelism that Rabelais might have enjoyed.

As might be expected of a heterodox Gallican, Rabelais's early fortunes in Italy were not of the best.[20] An Italian living in France, Lodovico Arrivabene, puts him on stage and treats him rather ambiguously in his facetious dialogue in hell, *Sylvius ocreatus* [Dubois in Boots] of 1555. Jacopo Corbinelli, also from France, wrote of him to a friend as the French Aristophanes (1568–69). However, Rabelais's book was on Indexes from 1549 on; and Giovanni Botero probably speaks for many when he calls him an infamous heretical buffoon (1592–95). This view seems to prevail in the seventeenth century, despite the borrowings from Rabelais by the storytelling blacksmith Giulio Cesare Croce and admiring imitation by Francesco Fulvio Frugoni.

In eighteenth-century Italy Rabelais receives a better welcome in treatises on literature and in such burlesque epics as Niccolò Forteguerri's *Il Ricciardetto*. Carlo Gozzi shows clear respect for him. Abbé Galiani, who spent much time in France, admired him greatly, carried his borrowings even to a pastiche, and compared him to a poor man's rear, "fresh, plump, dirty, and healthy." In the nineteenth century Rabelais's popularity grows. Bartolomeo Benincasa writes three articles about him in 1805; the poet Ugo Foscolo knows him well and occasionally imitates his style; the critic Francesco De Sanctis writes of him perceptively as a great humorist and man of sense, a founder of the modern era; Giuseppe Gioachino Belli uses him in his sonnets in Roman dialect; and the avant-garde humorist Carlo Dossi sees him as a learned satirist and creator in the grotesque.

The last hundred years in Italy have seen much Rabelais scholarship since Martinozzi in 1882, and translations by Perfetto (partial) in 1886–87, Passini (complete) in 1930, Bonfantini (complete) in 1953, and Nicoletti (I–III) in 1963. Tetel finds much stress on Rabelais's naturalism (seen as not conflicting with his Catholicism) and on his Italian sources; a sense of his satire as serious; some concern over his obscenity; an esthetic interest primarily in his style and in him as a "pure" comic artist. The futurist leader Marinetti, who learned about Rabelais from Apollinaire, is clearly indebted to him in *Le Roi Bombance* (1905). Carlo Emilio Gadda, the macaronic novelist and humanist, admires his revolt against stupid and dangerous authorities.

French readers of the eighteenth century were generally somewhat repelled by Rabelais's length and obscenity (see Boulenger, pp. 58–76). The first expurgated edition appeared in 1752. Many shared the feelings of La Bruyère. Montesquieu wrote that it always bored him to read Rabelais, but always delighted him to hear him quoted; then he added: "I have since read him with pleasure."[21]

Diderot shows an affectionate sense of Rabelais, mainly as the great champion of the bottle. In the early *Promenade du sceptique* (1747) he compares the ability of priests to wreak havoc on their enemies with that of Frère Jean, "of happy memory."[22] Later on, in his fifties and

ocles, Euripides, Aristophanes, Horace, Virgil are his sons. Dante engendered modern Italy, from Petrarch to Tasso. Rabelais created French letters; Montaigne, La Fontaine, Molière are among his descendants. England is all Shakespeare.[34]

In the early years of the century the pamphleteer Paul-Louis Courier lists Rabelais (with Montaigne, Pascal, and La Fontaine) as old friends, companions, and guides. The Romantic belletrist Charles Nodier knew him extremely well; called him "a buffoonish Homer" and "the most universal and the most profound of the writers of modern times"; is said to have copied out Rabelais's entire book three times; and used to tip his hat every time he passed the house in Paris where Rabelais was thought to have died. The Socialistic churchman Lamennais called him "the man for me. What depth, what verve!"[35] Most critics still clung to rather neoclassical views; even Sainte-Beuve found Rabelais too obscene to be very enjoyable, though he hailed him as a writer and educator.[36] However, poets and prose writers alike read him with enthusiasm as a great and congenial ancestor.

Victor Hugo may not have known Rabelais very well, but he saw in him the monarch of comedy and of the grotesque, which Hugo was eager to restore to serious literature. He salutes him as one of the fourteen geniuses who have honored the human race, the genius of the belly, and a comic giant of incalculable depth. In his *Contemplations* (1856) he calls him one of the "priests of laughter," whom no one understood: "Et son éclat de rire énorme/Est un des gouffres de l'esprit."* Among other poet admirers were Alfred de Vigny and Alfred de Musset. Gérard de Nerval and his friend Théophile Gautier were steeped in Rabelais; Gautier shows this in his perceptive comparison of Villon and Panurge,[37] and draws on him freely in many of his prose works. Late in life Béranger writes of having studied Rabelais for forty years and always learning from him. Banville knew him well, loved him, and cited him often. Jean Moréas loved the rich vigor of his language.[38]

Among the novelists, Prosper Mérimée, once in *Carmen* but mainly in his *Chronique du règne de Charles IX* (1829) and his reception speech in the French Academy (1845), shows great knowledge and appreciation of Rabelais, especially for his language and style. Balzac was a devoted admirer and in his way a disciple.[39] His *Droll Stories* are a pastiche mainly of Rabelais, whom he salutes as "prince of all learn-

---

* [And his enormous burst of laughter / Is one of the abysses of the mind.] Quoted by Boulenger, p. 108; cf. pp. 94–118.

ing and of all comedy" and "the greatest mind of modern humanity."[40] He has him in mind in *The Physiology of Marriage*, and quotes or cites him throughout his work. For comical exuberance and love of the good things of life he found him an unrivaled master. Another one-time Romantic, Gustave Flaubert, worshiped Rabelais as a serene and impassible genius whom he ranks with Homer, Michelangelo, Shakespeare, and Goethe, and above all as a powerful stylist, muscular, substantive, and masculine, whom he reads constantly as he does Montaigne, Régnier, La Bruyère, and Le Sage. As late as 1868 he says he never goes to sleep without having read a chapter of "the sacrosanct, immense, and superlatively beautiful Rabelais."[41]

His friend George Sand had more reservations. Although she resisted Balzac's urging to read Rabelais, she knew him pretty well, and at one time (1847) was planning to collaborate on an expurgated edition in modern spelling—which was never published. His obscenities annoyed her and led her sometimes to want to say: "O divine master, you are a dreadful pig!"[42]

Arthur de Gobineau wrote a youthful potboiler entitled *Les Conseils de Rabelais* in which Master François, consulted by his younger patron Cardinal Odet de Chastillon, advised him not to turn Protestant and marry all for love.[43] Alphonse Daudet used to read Rabelais and Montaigne to himself in the mineral baths and often aloud to his family, with commentary, after dinner. His son Léon, who reports this,[44] adds that these two books never left his side. The same Léon Daudet later wrote an article on Rabelais as a master polemicist.[45]

One of Rabelais's greatest Romantic admirers was the historian Jules Michelet.[46] Already as a youth he rated him with Shakespeare above Aristophanes, Voltaire, and Cervantes, as an incomparable witness to his time. In his *Histoire de France* he placed him far above Montaigne (whom he disliked) and wrote as follows about his book:

> The sphinx or the chimera, a monster with a hundred heads, a hundred languages, a harmonious chaos, a farce of infinite range, a marvelously lucid intoxication, a profoundly wise folly.
>
> What kind of man and what was he? Ask rather what he was not. A man of every study, of every art, of every language, the real *Pan-ourgos*, a universal actor in knowledge and affairs, who was everything and fit for everything, who contained the genius of the century and who overflows it at every moment.[47]

The nineteenth-century French view of Rabelais was largely the Romantic one combining those of Chateaubriand, Hugo, and Michelet:

an infinitely varied and profound comic genius and inspired master of language.

Translation of Rabelais into other languages was slow to start, but has become widespread in recent years. We have already noted some versions: German (Fischart, 1575); Italian (Perfetto, Passini, Bonfantini, and Nicoletti, 1886–1963); English (Urquhart and Le Motteux, W. F. Smith, Putnam, Leclercq, and Cohen, 1653–1955); and Russian (Ljubimov, 1961). In the last half century he has been translated, in full or in part, into at least five other languages: Spanish by Barriobero y Herrán (1923 and 1930); Hungarian by Kémeny Katalin (1936); Polish by Tadeusz Zelenski (1949); Greek by Spyros Skiaderese (1950); Romanian by Romulus Vulpescu (1963). Already in 1682 there had been a Dutch translation published under the pseudonym Gall'Italo. And Germany has outdone England in the warmth of its welcome to Rabelais. The Fischart version has had at least seventeen editions over the years, five of them in this century, and this version was only the first. "Dr. Eckstein" (Christian L. Sander) brought out a new translation in 1785–87; Gottlob Regis an excellent one in 1832–41 which has had at least eight re-editions since 1906; Ferdinand Adolph Gelbcke another in 1880, re-edited in 1970. This century has seen two more: one by "Hegaur" (Wilhelm E. Oestering) and "Owlglass" (Hans E. Blaich) in 1905 (new editions in 1906, 1907–09, 1922, and 1951); and the newest (at least that I have heard of) which Walter Widmer started in 1961, with his *Gargantua* (paperback as well as hardcover), and completed in 1968 in collaboration with Karl August Horst.

A quick glance now at a few high spots of Rabelais scholarship up to the twentieth century. One of the earliest accounts, Antoine Le Roy's *Elogia Rabelaesina* (1649), is little but hagiography; but Le Roy's friend Guillaume Colletet is really Rabelais's first biographer, unsurpassed until Father Jean-Pierre Nicéron in 1735. Important among the older editions is that of 1711 by Jacob Le Duchat, a Protestant refugee in Berlin. Voltaire criticized him for explaining what we do not need to know, but Sainéan notes his contribution to the study of sources. The theory of a key to Rabelais, promoted by Le Motteux, Voltaire, and Ginguené, was consecrated in the Variorum Edition of 1823–26 (9 vols.) by Johanneau and Esmangart, which was highly regarded for almost half a century, until the time of the Marty-Laveaux edition (1868–1903). The nineteenth century produced much good Rabelais scholarship, culminating in Paul Stapfer's *Rabelais* (1881) and Ferdinand Brunetière's chapter on him, first published in 1900, in his *Histoire de la littérature française classique, 1515-1830*.

The beginning of this century saw a new quest led by Abel Lefranc and embodied in his critical edition:[48] a quest for facts relating Rabelais to his time and place—the Picrocholean war to a lawsuit in Chinon, the *Third Book* to the Querelle des Femmes, the *Fourth Book* to voyages of discovery, and so on. When yields from this vein grew meager, later scholars such as Lucien Febvre, V. L. Saulnier, M. A. Screech, and Robert Marichal sought a better understanding of Rabelais by studying his position in the religious, humanistic, and political struggles of his time—a line of investigation that is still proving fruitful.[49]

In the last ten years, however, many have voiced dissatisfaction with this tradition as with the earlier ones, seeing it as too much marked by bourgeois values, too attentive to the voice of Pantagruel rather than to that of Panurge or of Alcofribas, and too concerned with ideas when writing is all that really matters. The first of these criticisms was strongly voiced by Mikhail Bakhtin in *Rabelais and His World*—translated into English in 1968, and into French in 1970—and was picked up by Michel Beaujour in *Le Jeu de Rabelais* (Paris: L'Herne, 1969), and by Denis Hollier in his part of the book he did with Michel Butor, *Rabelais, ou c'était pour rire* (Paris: Larousse, 1972). The heightened concern with Rabelais's language and style, already evident in Manuel de Dieguez, *Rabelais par lui-même* (Paris: Seuil, 1960), appears in Alfred Glauser, *Rabelais créateur* (Paris: Nizet, 1966); Jean Paris, *Rabelais au futur* (Paris: Seuil, 1970) and *Panurge et Hamlet* (Paris: Seuil, 1971); François Rigolot, *Les Langages de Rabelais*, *ER* X (1972); and Floyd Gray, *Rabelais et l'écriture* (Paris: Nizet, 1974). In my view, with the exception of Bakhtin's book, these trends have yet to prove themselves.

We now come to uncharted times and places in the fortunes of Rabelais: the nineteenth century outside France and Italy, and the entire twentieth.

On his fortunes in German-speaking countries little work has been done. The Calvinist Jacob Burckhardt rated him low, but earlier Wieland had hailed him as a great writer; Herder, as a precursor of the French seventeenth century; Jean-Paul (Johann Paul Friedrich Richter), as a model; Chamisso, as a writer to be constantly read; and

Gervinus, as a father and above all a friend. Goethe, who read him often and in his late years, planned a short novel based on Rabelais, *Reise der Söhne Megaprazons.** In the present century the proliferation of translations (new and old) shows Rabelais's great popularity, especially in West Germany; and Rabelais scholarship has been enriched by German contributions, especially those of Ludwig Schrader.

In nineteenth-century England Sainéan (pp. 121–22) points to Robert Southey as an admirer who found Pantagruelism in Shakespeare, Cervantes, and all the great poets; to Browning as another who ranks Rabelais with Molière and Voltaire as representatives of the *gaulois* spirit; and to Coleridge as one who, while regretting what he considered his protective buffoonery and ribaldry,[50] places "the incomparable Rabelais" with Dante, Shakespeare, and Cervantes as minds who created the world. Obviously there were English Romantics who, like the French, worshiped Rabelais; more work needs to be done on them.

Later in the century Rabelais finds a genuine, though genteel, disciple in Charles Kingsley in *The Water-Babies: A Fairy Tale for a Land-Baby* (1863).[51] Five times he refers to "the coming of the Cocqcigrues" (pp. 41, 115, 147, 191, 203; after Rabelais, I: 49, 141; cf. II: 11, 220; IV: 32, 626); he likes to play with the truth or fiction of his tale (p. 47); one of his favorite characters states that the French say of a "finished young gentleman . . . 'Il sait son Rabelais' " (p. 72); and he uses an occasional long composite word (p. 90) and several long lists (pp. 100–03, 117, 200–01) in the manner of the master. Finally, his last chapter offers nonsensical activities (pp. 178–81) reminiscent of Gargantua's games and of the officers of Quintessence; "the great land of Hearsay" (p. 181; cf. Ouyr-Dire); "a poor, lean, seedy, hard-worked old giant" (p. 182) who recalls Quaresmeprenant (but turns out to be rather nice); and a boy (p. 190) whose craving to be frightened suggests the Chiquanous and their eagerness to be beaten (IV: 12–16).

Another warm admirer was Algernon Charles Swinburne, who links Rabelais with Cervantes and Shakespeare as "that divine and human trinity of humourists whose names make radiant for ever the century of their new-born glory."[52] He sets Falstaff morally above Sancho, Sancho above Panurge; and puts also above Panurge "that most irreverend father in God, Friar John"; but he adds that "it is impossible to connect the notion of rebuke with the sins of Panurge." He rejoices in Rabelais's honest championship of the flesh.

* A fragment was published posthumously in 1837.

Rabelais, evangelist and prophet of the Resurrection of the Flesh (so long entombed, ignored, repudiated, misconstrued, vilified, by so many generations of Galilean preachers and Pharisaic schoolmen)—Rabelais was content to paint the flesh merely, in its honest human reality—human at least, if also bestial; in its frank and rude reaction against the half brainless and wholly bloodless teachers whose doctrine he himself on the one hand, and Luther on the other, arose together to smite severally.

I suspect, however, that Walter Besant was more representative of his time and place in his curious judgment of Rabelais.[53] He notes Rabelais's balance of drollery and moral seriousness (pp. 99–100) and his rejection of religious disputes (122–23); finds him clearly a deist, not a Christian (125–26); and gives him high praise as a "glorious wit and satirist" and a "great moral teacher" (126, 128). However, he finds him obscene well beyond the norms of his time, and his ultimate judgment is damning (128):

He destroyed effectually, perhaps for centuries to come, earnestness in France. . . . Great and noble as are many of the passages in Rabelais, profoundly wise as he was, I do believe that no writer who ever lived has inflicted such lasting damage on his country.

In twentieth-century France Rabelais's popularity remains great. Boulenger lists twenty-four editions in the first twenty-two years (1901–22), and they have not ceased to multiply. Scholarly books and articles abound. The *Revue des Etudes Rabelaisiennes* appeared from 1903 to 1912; and now since 1951 we have the *Bulletin de l'Association des Amis de Rabelais et de La Devinière*, and since 1956 thirteen volumes of *Etudes rabelaisiennes*, with more to come. Again, what follows is only a sampling.*

A book that I have not been able to see, by H. M. Durand, published in 1949, bears a title that speaks for itself: *Pastiches de Rabelais, La Bruyère, Anatole France, Giono, Giraudoux, Max Jacob, Henri Michaux, Marcel Proust, Aragon, L.-F. Céline*. Francis Jammes, poet of the people, in 1900 urged a friend to read Rabelais as one whose work (he writes) is born of love of the humble, moving us to tears as well as laughter, singing "a song so grandiose that it is madness" and, in short, "nothing but a grave goodness." The aesthete Pierre Louÿs seems to draw his code for Tryphème [Softness] from the "Do What You Will" of Theleme. Comic author Jules Renard, in his *Journal*, writes admiringly of Rabelais's abundance and use of dialect, and adds this

---

* One which draws on two articles by V. L. Saulnier: "Dix Années d'études sur Rabelais (1939–1948)," *BHR* 11: 105–128, 1949; and "Divers Echos de Rabelais au XXe siècle," *ER* VI (1965), 73–88.

perceptive note (April 16, 1907): "Rabelais is gay: he does not have wit."

Anatole France was drawn to Rabelais from early in his career, reconstructed his *Farce de la femme muette*,[54] and gave a series of lectures on him in Argentina that when posthumously collected filled a whole book.[55] He spoke of him in these lectures as "the great Rabelais" (p. 7), praised his prose for its "abundance, color, movement, and life" (p. 78), and read his conclusion as "Drink in, drink in knowledge; drink in truth; drink in love" (p. 252). Maurice Barrès praised him as one who helped form the French language. Paul Claudel said of him that "the Genius of ironic and biting gaiety has his lyricism too . . . a laughter of the gods, supreme, inextinguishable." Guillaume Apollinaire knew him well and taught his friend Marinetti to enjoy him, too. A friend of Jean Giraudoux testifies to his appreciation of Rabelais. Blaise Cendrars takes "Do What You Will" as one of four epigraphs to his book *Bourlinguer*.

As is seen from some verses of Charles Vildrac, the Unanimist founders of the Abbaye thought of it in terms of Theleme and planned to welcome visitors with some of the same verses. A friend of this movement, Jules Romains, shows Rabelais's influence in *Les Copains*, and in the last volume of *Les Hommes de bonne volonté* represents his hero as thinking that even in the worst moments of history "there is still room for a third party: that of Panurge, of Pantagruel, and also of Voltaire."[56] André Gide's *Journal* offers several references to Rabelais, notably (with Aristophanes and Shakespeare) as one of the male geniuses whom he (Gide) should read more often.[57] Tristan Tzara, founder of Dadaism, once played a game of finding Rabelais's name in an anagram as a concealed "signature" to some verses.[58] Marcel Aymé considers Rabelais's laughter unique and writes that next to him Aristophanes, Boccaccio, and Molière look like undertaker's helpers.[59]

The essayist and teacher Alain (Emile Chartier) marveled at how often Rabelais disregards sense and lets sound lead him, plays with the language like a musician and is intoxicated with it. For him Rabelais's superabundance is part of his wisdom. Students should read him to have a notion of good style. His art is incomparable; even Molière's funniest scenes are only fragments beside him. He delivers his reader from remorse and gives him again "the desire for this joyous crime so easily forgiven."[60]

Louis-Ferdinand Céline of course found his own image in a rebellious, antiacademic Rabelais who wanted a true language, rich, oral, democratic, but who lost out to the academic Amyot:

The Sorbonne, he was against, the doctors and all that. All that was accepted and established, the King, the Church, style, he was against.

No, it wasn't him who won. It was Amyot, the translator of Plutarch. . . . People now still and always want the Amyot, the academic style. That's writing a lot of shit: congealed language.

Thus France has rejected Rabelais and can no longer understand him. And this rejection Céline understands: "In my life I had the same vice as Rabelais. I too spent my time putting myself into desperate situations. Like him, I have nothing to expect from others, like him, I regret nothing."[61]

Another sign of Rabelais's enduring popularity (despite Céline) has been the success of Jean-Louis Barrault's play *Rabelais,* which drew full houses recently not only in Paris (from 1967 on) but also in New York (1970).[62] Barrault follows Jules Michelet as a fervent admirer who also identifies himself with him. His preface to the printed play is full of his enthusiasm:

Rabelais has always been an object of predilection for me. I find in him the presence of the Ancestor. It goes beyond admiration. Each time I sink my teeth into him, my mouth fills with such a juice, my blood receives such a flow, my spinal column such sap that I utter cries, "horrific" cries of enthusiasm.

He is Childhood seizing life with open arms.

Is this peasant atavism? Perhaps. Biologically I feel so French! Now no one is more so than he: defects and qualities, weakness and genius.

Later Barrault stresses Rabelais's naturalness, outgoingness, and fondness for new ideas:

He is a Tree. His roots suck up the loam and the manure. His trunk is stiff as a phallus. His foliage is encyclopedic (the word comes from him). His flowering joins God.

He does not live turned in upon himself, he turns toward the world. Rebellious in mood, an eternal student, obstinate, crafty, a nomad, his temperament makes him inclined, despite his fidelity to traditions, to take his place among those who do battle on behalf of new ideas.

That constitutes our modest encounter with him.[63]

Another devoted reader is the novelist Michel Butor, who, also rejecting the Rabelais of the schoolroom, pronounces the book "probably the most difficult in all French literature"* and finds Mallarmé easy next to him, but is not deterred. For him Rabelais's laughter is largely a disguise (10, 25, 29–31), his apparently Christian statements

* Most of Butor's comments on Rabelais are collected in the Butor–Denis Hollier book *Rabelais, ou c'était pour rire* (Paris: Larousse, 1972), from which are taken this quotation (p. 9) and the following ones indicated in the text.

little more than sops to his churchly protectors (25), allowing him to pursue "his indomitable meditation on religion, politics, and economics" (49). His language is thick, bubbling, full of ferment, caverns, and whirlwinds, drawing the reader on (49, 72); it is of course not dainty or learned but popular. For Butor, Rabelais—like Montaigne, but more so—is steeped in numerology of a sort that often seems largely Butor's (74–85, 101–10, 142–43). Opposed alike to the Sorbonne and to Calvin, to monasticism and a celibate priesthood, Rabelais pleads for the legitimacy of the basic human needs and desires: hunger, thirst, and sex (112–21, 129–35). Rabelais's conclusion in the *Fifth Book* (whose authenticity Butor considers proven) offers hope of an ultimate utopia far in the future; meanwhile let his book be a haven and another Theleme.

As such tributes show, Rabelais remains very much alive in France today.

Rabelais has not lacked for a welcome in Communist countries. His portrait was shown on one of a recent series of Chinese postage stamps "with such other political heroes as Marx and Martí."[64] Mikhail Bakhtin tells of the birth of Soviet Rabelais scholarship after World War II with a monograph by E. M. Evnina (1948), essays by L. E. Pinsky and others, and the excellent translation by N. M. Ljubimov in 1961.[65] He lists several others and notes with pride (p. 143) that "our commentators do not separate Rabelais' artistic vision from his laughter but rather strive to interpret correctly its original traits."

George Saintsbury offers a rather orthodox English view for early in this century in his *Encyclopædia Britannica* article (11th ed., XXII, 1911). For him a discussion of Rabelais poses three questions: "What is the general drift and purpose of *Gargantua* and *Pantagruel*, supposing there to be any? What defence can be offered, if any defence is needed, for the extraordinary licence of language and imagery which the author has permitted himself? What was his attitude towards the great questions of religion, philosophy and politics?" He finds three views of Rabelais prevalent: as earnest Reformist, as a protester against any supernatural explanation of "the riddle of the earth," and as a careless good fellow. Saintsbury's Rabelais is closest to the third of these: "a humorist pure and simple, feeling often in earnest, thinking almost always in jest . . . much less of a mere mocker than Lucian, . . . entirely destitute . . . of the ferocity of Swift." Closer to Lucian than to Swift, "the *rire immense* which distinguishes him is altogether good-natured." He finds "*Gargantua* and *Pantagruel* . . . so little read that no notice of them could be complete without some sketch of their contents."

If Rabelais's book was indeed "little read" by English-speaking people in 1911, that seems hardly true today. His obscenity is no longer the problem it was then. Even when Saintsbury wrote, W. F. Smith and Arthur Tilley (as Saintsbury recognized) had made important contributions to Rabelais scholarship, as have so many English scholars since. Four English translations have appeared in the last eighty-odd years: by W. F. Smith in 1893, Samuel Putnam in 1929, Jacques Leclercq in 1936, and J. M. Cohen in 1955. In the English-speaking countries someone must be reading Rabelais today.

In the sampling that follows we find Henry Adams, early in the century, referring to Rabelais—and to Montaigne!—as virtual anarchists; for he writes of returning to France from England and Germany with a sigh of relief, since "No Frenchman except Rabelais and Montaigne had ever taught anarchy other than as a path to order."[66]

More recently, among the critics, C. S. Lewis calls him a belletrist, not a philosopher, and contrasts him with John Harington: "Rabelais was a fighter, defending humanism and attacking the monks. He was also an inventor in the realm of Nonsense, a follower of Lucian, and a predecessor of Lewis Carroll."[67] Gilbert Highet praises Rabelais's fearlessness, satiric power, and self-made gigantic stature, but finds him "difficult to understand and difficult to admire," a great man but not a great artist:

No one would say that Rabelais was a great artist. His work is often too rough and often too silly. But there can be no doubt that he was a great man; and the two solutions which he applied to his own difficulties and suggested for those of the world were, first, education, and second, enjoyment—gusto—the simple, energetic, life-giving gaiety of the joke and the bottle.[68]

Northrop Frye classifies Rabelais's work as a Menippean satire—"a loose-jointed narrative form"—with a considerable admixture of romance.[69] He is struck by his "disintegration" (p. 325) and his "riotous chaos" in which "satire plunges through to its final victory over common sense" (p. 235). For him, especially in the topics of the topers (I: 5), "Rabelais is one of the greatest masters of *melos* in prose" (p. 266).

Marshall McLuhan, in *The Gutenberg Galaxy*,[70] finds Rabelais living in two worlds (before printing and after) and bearing witness to the new. For him he is "a collective rout of oral schoolmen and glossators suddenly debouched into a visual world, newly set up on individualist and nationalist lines"; this is what makes him seem relevant to us (p. 181). Again, "The celebrated earthy tactility of Rabelais is a massive backwash of receding manuscript cultures" (p. 182). As a prophet and witness to the new age, "Rabelais offers a vision of the future of print culture as a consumer's paradise of applied knowledge." In *Gargantua* he creates the first of "four massive myths of the Gutenberg transformation of society" (p. 179); *Don Quixote,* the *Dunciad,* and *Finnegans Wake* are the others. Seeing that print had begun "the homogenizing of individuals and of talents," Rabelais was "concerned with the democratization of knowledge by the abundance of wines from the printing press" (pp. 179–80). Hence "Rabelais's insistence on *pantagruelion* as the symbol and image of printing from movable types. For this is the name of the hemp plant from which rope is made. From the teasing and shredding and weaving of this plant there came the lineal cords and bonds of greatest social enterprises" (*ibid.*).

Among the poets, T. S. Eliot wrote little but trenchantly about Rabelais, who, he says, like Villon, had a rich *"esprit gaulois"* that Eliot misses in Racine and even Molière, which makes him wonder if even they achieved the full status of a classic.[71] Rabelais lacked the "precise emotional attitude or precise intellectual criticism of the world" that we find in Swift and Molière,[72] but possessed "that slight distortion of *all* the elements in the world of a play or a story" that makes that world "complete in itself" and great farce possible.[73] W. H. Auden hailed Rabelais and Dickens as the great writers about carnival, and criticized Bakhtin (without naming him) for considering parody of religious rites a protest against religious beliefs. This, he finds, is all nonsense since parody, like blasphemy, implies belief.*

In his work aptly titled *A Vision* (1926), an elaborate classification of human personality and outline of history, William Butler Yeats locates Rabelais in Phase Sixteen, in the eighth gyre, which he dates from about 1550 to 1650, together with Blake, Aretino, Paracelsus, and "some beautiful women." In men of this phase he finds opposing natures, capable (his example is Blake) of a hate that "is always close to madness," yet able in the next moment to "produce the comedy of

---

* "They Had Forgotten How to Laugh and How to Pray," in *Columbia Forum,* 13: 46–48, Winter 1970, p. 48. In *The Viking Book of Aphorisms,* which he compiled with Louis Kronenberger (New York: Viking Press, 1966), p. 150, there is just one quotation from Rabelais as against sixteen from Montaigne.

Aretino and of Rabelais or the mythology of Blake, and discover symbolism to express the overflowing and bursting of the mind." "There is always," he goes on, "an element of frenzy, and almost always a delight in certain glowing or shining images of concentrated force." These men may, he says, include "great satirists, great caricaturists, but they pity the beautiful, for that is their *Mask,* and hate the ugly, for that is their *Body of Fate.*"[74] This Rabelais of his appears mainly comical, exuberant, and possessed. Twenty years earlier, more lucidly, he had praised Rabelais as one of the great masters of speech. In his preface to J. M. Synge's *The Well of the Saints,* deploring the recent waning of living individual speech, he rejoices to find it still present in Synge, as once it was in Homer, Cervantes, Racine, and others:

> If one has not fine construction, one has not drama, but if one has not beautiful or powerful and individual speech, one has not literature, or, at any rate, one has not great literature. Rabelais, Villon, Shakespeare, William Blake, would have known one another by their speech. Some of them knew how to construct a story, but all of them had abundant, resonant, beautiful, laughing, living speech.[75]

Many writers of essays and fiction are familiar with Rabelais. Virginia Woolf credits Madame de Sévigné's good sense to the company she kept, which includes "reading Montaigne, Rabelais, Pascal"; and of Sterne she writes, with apparent approval, that "Montaigne, Rabelais, and Cervantes he loved of course."[76]

Aldous Huxley was a devoted admirer of Rabelais and knew him very well. When he writes of modern American literature that "the hopelessness is almost Rabelaisian," he apparently means that "high spirits and a heroic vitality are put into the expression of despair."[77] In two letters of August 12, 1918, he speaks at length of his half-brother Andrew Fielding Huxley as a young Gargantua of heroic appetite—and he gives precise Rabelaisian details.[78] Writing to Philip Wylie in 1949, he speaks of *Pantagruel* as "huge and inordinate," and says: "in order to write *Pantagruel* or Karamazov one has to be a major genius."[79] His strongest and clearest tribute is in a collection of essays from his mid-thirties that he entitled *Do What You Will.** In these he praised the motto of Theleme as designed for his ideal man, the life worshiper; took Rabelais as one of the nine "saints in the life worshiper's calendar"—along with Chaucer, Rubens, Montaigne, Shakespeare, Mozart, Blake, Burns, and Tolstoy before his conversion (pp. 305–08);

* Garden City, N.Y.: Doubleday, Doran, 1929. For more on Huxley, this book, and Rabelais, see the next chapter, p. 192 and fn.

and as regards good taste and scatology, strongly defended Rabelais—against both Voltaire in the past and Orwell in the very near future—in his article on Swift (p. 109):

How instructive, in this context, is the comparison with Rabelais! Both men were scatological writers. Mass for mass, there is probably more dung and offal piled up in Rabelais's work than in Swift's. But how pleasant is the dung through which Gargantua wades, how almost delectable the offal! The muck is transfigured by love; for Rabelais loved the bowels which Swift so malignantly hated. His was the true *amor fati*! he accepted reality in its entirety, accepted with gratitude and delight this amazingly improbable world, where flowers spring from manure, and reverent Fathers of the Church . . . meditate on the divine mysteries while seated on the privy.

George Orwell was more easily shocked. He lists Rabelais with Aristophanes, Boccaccio, Cervantes, and Voltaire among "writers who are remarkable for their brutality and coarseness."[80] He resented the whitewashing of Rabelais's obscenity as "clean dirt," and wrote in 1940 of Albert Cohen's *Nailcruncher* that it was disgustingly scatological and hence hailed in the dust-jacket blurb as "Rabelaisian." Then he went on:

It is curious that this word is invariably used as a form of praise. We are forever being told that whereas pornography is reprehensible, "hearty Rabelaisian humour" (meaning a preoccupation with the W C) is perfectly all right. This is partly, perhaps, because Rabelais is nowadays seldom read. So far from being "healthy" as is always alleged, he is an exceptionally perverse, morbid writer, a case for psycho-analysis. . . . Perhaps the only way of making him respectable [in Victorian times] was to maintain that there was something "normal" and "hearty" in coprophilia, and the legend has survived into an age when few people have glanced at his dirtier passages.[81]

Rabelais has fared much better with English Catholics. In a colorful and cantankerous biography, *Doctor Rabelais*, D. B. Wyndham Lewis, exactly reversing Highet, called him not a great man or thinker but an incomparable writer:

He is no godlike character, but who (barring his worshippers) deems him one? For every pint of wisdom he pours out a quart of nonsense, but who cares? Pen in hand he is incomparable. He is unique. He is magic. He is magnificent. He is gigantic. He dealt with the precise French language as no man has ever done before or since. Rightly is he called the father of modern French prose. His genius is like Niagara. Once having fallen under his spell it is impossible to throw it off.[82]

G. K. Chesterton once called Rabelais "one of the very greatest of the sixteenth-century giants."[83] He contrasts Lewis Carroll with Rabelais and Swift in that "there is no sense in his nonsense," whereas they "had a purpose, and it was, whatever its defects, very largely the serious intellectual purpose of their lives."[84] In his sympathetic essay "Rabelaisian Regrets" in *The Common Man*, he rejects "that horrible fashion of taking sex seriously—of which the true name is Phallic worship," and warns that it may lead the reader to "call upon the shades of Rabelais and Fielding to deliver you out of that foul idolatry."[85] He notes, however, that "sex is the great business of the body," deplores the hypocritical "decency" of much modern speech, observes that the "navvy" in his so-called obscenity "is at one with all the most really masculine poets or romancers . . . at one with Rabelais, with Swift, and even with Browning," and concludes: "It is common enough to talk of the English people speaking; but if ever they do speak they will speak as Rabelais spoke, and as English cabmen speak now" (pp. 129–31).

Of Hilaire Belloc, D. B. Wyndham Lewis wrote that he "loved Rabelais dearly all his life, read him to the end of it, and eulogised him in a memorable essays." I have been unable to find this essay,[86] but have found many appreciative references to "huge Rabelais" and "the great Rabelais," whom Belloc calls a greater man than Ronsard. In *The Path to Rome* (1902), in his section "Praise of This Book," Belloc calls on his "regiments of words" to help him, then addresses Rabelais almost as a muse:

> Rabelais! Master of all happy men! Are you sleeping there pressed into desecrated earth under the doss-house of the Rue St. Paul, or do you not rather drink cool wine in some elysian Chinon looking on the Vienne where it arises in Paradise? Are you sleeping or drinking that you will not lend us the staff of Friar John wherewith he slaughtered and bashed the invaders of the vineyards, who are but a parable for the mincing pedants and bloodless thin-faced rogues of the world?[87]

Where it was Rabelais's joyous gusto that delighted these English Catholics, John Cowper Powys loved his magnanimity and sense of wonder. His *Rabelais* (New York: Philosophical Library, 1951) contains an account of Rabelais's life and story, his own excellent translation of 150 pages, and an insightful interpretation. At the heart of Rabelais's genius he finds the quality of "becoming like a little child literally, in the sense of becoming like an ordinary, harmless, healthy, sense-absorbed, indecently shameless babe or suckling" (p. 283). This helps explain Rabelais's sense of the mystery of the universe, his love of life, bigness, activity, and adventure, his "profound and philosophical refusal . . . to take this world seriously," and his great indulgence. His optimistic views on clemency and benign government are to Powys no pipe dreams but ideas far ahead of his time—and of ours. In religion Powys calls Rabelais a Pelagian, a disbeliever in original sin and the Devil, a "pagan-christian-polytheist" (p. 371), and in short "not *less* but *more* than a Christian" (p. 393), with an unquenchable loving reverence for life. Perhaps it is idle, he remarks, to ask whether he was a Christian or not:

I do not think he was *anything* "at heart," in that particular sense. I think that like Walt Whitman he thought with his intellect, with his reason, with his senses, with his soul, with his spirit, with his skin, blood and bone, and with all his most imponderable instincts, intuitions, urges, feelings, sensations, intimations *at the same time*! (p. 373)

James Joyce would have found Rabelais most congenial, and perhaps he did.[88] He wrote to a friend in 1927 that he never read Rabelais, though nobody would believe it, that he meant to do so soon, and that he has read "a few chapters of a book called *La Langue de Rabelais*."* He did not mention his name in his 1912 examination essay for the University of Padua on the literary influence of the Renaissance.[89] Yet in 1907 he ranked Rabelais with Swift as the best satirists in world literature; and Molly Bloom in her concluding soliloquy speaks of

some of those books he brings me the works of Master Francois somebody supposed to be a priest about a child born out of her ear because her bumgut fell out a nice word for any priest to write and her a—e as if any fool wouldnt know what that meant I hate that pretending of all things with the old blackguards face on him anybody can see its not true . . .[90]

It is of course Rabelais that she refers to (I: 6); and it is hard to see how Molly could know the story if her creator did not.

Finnegans Wake (1939), with its extraordinary wordplay, is the work of Joyce's that is most like Rabelais. There are many long words that recall some of Rabelais's coinages;[91] long lists of names (some abusive) and of games (pp. 71–72, 104–07, 176, 183–84, 306–08); an allusion to the Sortes Virginianae (p. 281; cf. Rabelais's "sors virgilianes," III: 12–13); a dialogue between Mutt and Jule (pp. 16 ff.) that reminds one of the Limousin schoolboy (II: 6); and a list of books (p. 440) not unlike those of St.-Victor (II: 7). Moreover, in recently published workbooks for *Finnegans Wake*, Claude Jacquet has found a number of words—such as *encornifistibuler, lifrelofre, papefigue, papimane*—

* By Lazare Sainéan; 2 vols. (Paris: Boccard, 1922–23).

which come from Rabelais and appear to be taken directly from him, but in an order that virtually proves that Joyce took them out of Sainéan.[92]

Now Joyce could have praised Rabelais highly as a satirist, and known his story of a baby born through the ear, without having read him; he could not, in my judgment, have written *Finnegans Wake* after reading Rabelais without making some clearer borrowings than he does. Rabelais's example, as seen through Sainéan's book, may have encouraged him to write *Finnegans Wake* as he did; but to me the evidence suggests that here we are dealing not with influence but with affinities. This conclusion does not keep Joyce from being one of the most Rabelaisian of writers.

And it should be clear from these last pages that, not only in France but in English-speaking countries, Rabelais remains very much alive today.

Theleme in the World
of Today

In the present century and especially the last thirty to fifty years—no doubt in reaction against the sense of being lost amid the masses of men and machines—our age-old human aspiration to become ourselves by doing what we will has come very much alive. A few writers noted in the last chapter showed a certain wistfulness or even hope for the "Do What You Will" of some new Theleme: witness Pierre Louys's similar code for a somewhat similar utopia (1901);[1] the dream of Charles Vildrac and others around 1905 that their Abbaye might be a new Theleme; and the choice of "Do What You Will" as one of four epigraphs in Blaise Cendrars's *Bourlinguer* (1948).[2]

As we also noted, Aldous Huxley in 1929 gave the title *Do What You Will* to a volume of essays in which he hailed "the 'Do what thou wilt' of Thelema"—within the limits set by Rabelais—as the proper rule for his ideal man, the "life worshipper."* And just a few years ago Michel Butor concluded the book he wrote with Denis Hollier on

* *Do What You Will* (Garden City, N.Y.: Doubleday, Doran), p. 307. He notes that this rule was addressed only to free, well-born, and well-bred persons, recognizes that others will need restraints, and goes on to identify himself (I fancy) with his ideal: "The best life worshippers are probably those who have been strictly educated in Christian or bourgeois morality, in the philosophy of common sense tempered by religion, and have afterward revolted against their upbringing." To be sure, the loss of his faith may lead one of these to neurasthenia or even suicide. "But if he were tough enough to survive, he could be confidently left to do what he liked." Huxley again invokes Rabelais's limits in replying to those who charge that the rule of Theleme will let a person behave like a pig. "If one is well-born and well-bred one does not behave like a pig; one behaves like a human being. In the case, moreover, of a sincere life worshipper, his religion is a guarantee against swinishness. For swinishness is not a manifestation of life, but a blasphemy against it" (pp. 307–08).

Rabelais by quoting his invitation to the Evangelical preachers to enter Theleme, which follows these final words of his own: "By the intermediary of our descendants we shall at last do what we will. In the meantime . . . may this book be an abbey to us."[3]

These writers generally confined themselves to aspiring to the rule of Theleme. The first person I know of to apply it successfully was the Scotsman A. S. Neill, in Summerhill, the school he founded in Suffolk in 1921 and guided for well over forty years.* By offering children love and freedom—but not license—he let them learn self-regulation and through it become fully and happily themselves. He preached his doctrines—often rather pugnaciously—in his books from the 1920s on,† but to a rather limited public until the great success of his *Summerhill: A Radical Approach to Child Rearing* in 1960. A similar faith in the basic goodness of the child—and (unlike Neill) in that of the parent as well—and in a healthy degree of freedom for each, fills the book that has guided so many millions of American and other recent parents, Dr. Benjamin Spock's *Baby and Child Care* (1946).†

For all his insight and experience, Neill could not claim the authority of science for his doctrines; and his faith in basic human goodness was (at least in recent history) ahead of his time. Thirty or forty years ago any optimism about human nature such as his—or as Rabelais's in his first two books and notably in Theleme—was bound to strike most readers as charming but naïve. (Even Huxley in 1929 limited the rule to the elect.) These readers had learned in theory from Freud of the powerful dangers that lurked in the subconscious, and in history from Nazism and Stalinism (to mention only those two) that man was marked by a monstrous propensity for evil.

However, already in the 1930s and 1940s some of the most distinguished psychotherapists were beginning to follow the lead of Jung

---

* As may be apparent already, this entire chapter cannot pretend to thoroughness and seeks only to break ground in an area in which more work is needed. I am sure there are omissions, and sorry only if some of these are major.

As regards priority, Neill acknowledges the influence on him of Homer Lane, who in his *Little Commonwealth* "gave delinquent children the freedom to be themselves, and they became good." A. S. Neill, *The Problem Family* (London: Jenkins, 1949), p. 155; *Summerhill: A Radical Approach to Child Rearing* (New York: Hart, 1960), p. 274.

† Such as *The Problem Child*, 1926; *The Problem Parent*, 1932; *The Problem Family*, 1949; *The Free Child*, 1953.

‡ Neill has high praise for Spock (*The Problem Family*, p. 144), as does Erich Fromm for Neill, for whose *Summerhill* he wrote the Foreword.

(*Modern Man in Search of a Soul*, 1933) and to criticize Freud—as had Neill—for generalizing from the psychically ill while ignoring the healthy, and thus finding human nature basically evil rather than either neutral or balanced between good and evil. They saw man's best hope in the self-actualization of the individual, the fullest possible development of his inner nature, and the necessary condition for this in freedom. Among the first of these were Kurt Goldstein (*Human Nature in the Light of Psychopathology*, 1940), Karen Horney (*Neurosis and Growth: The Struggle toward Self-Realization*, 1950), and Erich Fromm (*Escape from Freedom*, 1941; *The Sane Society*, 1955; and especially *Man for Himself*, 1947). These were soon followed by such others as Rollo May (*Man's Search for Himself*, 1953; *Love and Will*, 1969) and Abraham H. Maslow (*Motivation and Personality*, 1954; *Toward a Psychology of Being*, 1968).

Like Neill, the last three of these in particular—Fromm, May, and Maslow—seek in healthy human nature, apart from religious dogma, a "humanistic" (in the modern sense of man-based) psychology and science of ethics. This psychology and ethics are grounded on our need for growth, for a free self-actualization—mainly through love, perception of reality, and creativity—that is the best that we as individuals can achieve, not only for ourselves but also for others.*

All four show an optimism about human nature that recalls both Rabelais and Montaigne.† All four, though they do not quote Rabelais and appear not to have read him,‡ express ideas and attitudes found in

---

* Some of the key terms in this psychology that seeks to be a "science of ethics" (Maslow) are "self-regulation" (Neill) as the path to "self-actualization" (Goldstein, Maslow) and "self-realization" (Fromm, Horney, May); "morality of evolution" (Horney), "humanistic ethics," "humanistic psychoanalysis," and "normative humanism" (Fromm); "normative social psychology" (Maslow); and "humanistic psychology," of which Calvin Tomkins (*New Yorker*, January 5, 1976, pp. 41–42) calls Maslow "the real father."

† For the relation to Rabelais of Fromm and especially Maslow, I am indebted to Lloyd Bishop's article "Rabelais and the Comic Catharsis," submitted to *French Forum* but unpublished as I write.

I shall treat elsewhere the relation of these men to Montaigne and to his optimism about human nature, which some of his readers overlook.

‡Whereas Maslow cites scientists almost exclusively, Fromm and May draw freely on theologians, philosophers, and other writers in their opposition to such figures as Luther and Calvin (Fromm), Descartes and Pascal (May), and in their admiration for Spinoza. In my limited reading in all these psychologists, I have found only two references—and these indirect and somewhat unfavorable—one to Montaigne (Goldstein, *Human Nature*, p. 249; cf. p. 227) and one to Rabelais (Neill, *Summerhill*, p. 206). Of course even Montaigne dismissed Rabelais's book as "simply entertaining" (*Essays*, II: 10).

him, especially in *Gargantua*, 50–57. Rabelais, who hated Calvin, would have agreed with Fromm's view that Calvin, like his God, hated man;[4] with Neill and May in welcoming the body back into the union with the self;[5] and with all four in their strong and central sense that we need freedom and spontaneity to be happy and to realize ourselves. Neill, Fromm, and May point out that freedom is needed for love as well as for spontaneity, and May sharply rejects any ethics of obedience as self-mutilating.[6] Neill writes of hate and love in exactly the spirit of Theleme: "Human beings are good; they want to do good; they want to love and be loved. Hate and rebellion are only thwarted love and thwarted power."[7] Both Fromm and May find an element of growth and self-realization even in Adam's original sin.[8] Had he lived in an age such as ours, more secular than his own, I could imagine Rabelais welcoming this man-centered version of Augustine's *felix culpa*.

It is Maslow who most puts me in mind of Rabelais. A reasoned optimist about human nature, he sees good in joy and happiness, not merely in suffering: with unwonted disdain he puts down the angst of Sartrian Existentialists as "high I.Q. whimpering on a cosmic scale."[*] He finds our basic inner nature "not to be intrinsically or primarily or necessarily evil . . . not nearly as bad as it has been thought to be . . . good or neutral rather than bad. . . . If it is permitted to guide our life, we grow healthy, fruitful, and happy." If however it is denied or suppressed, sickness follows (3–4). Like Fromm (*Man for Himself*, pp. 218–19), who finds much of man's destructiveness "a secondary potentiality" manifested only if he fails to realize his primary ones, Maslow calls it "reactive," not spontaneous, the result of a frustrated drive for good (195; *MP*, 173). Again, Neill is in close agreement, as when he writes that "all crimes, all hatreds, all wars can be reduced to unhappiness." (*Summerhill*, p. xxiv.) Perhaps even closer to Rabelais's view, in the chapter on "Do What You Will" (I: 57), that freedom breeds goodness, and constraint, rebellion, is Rollo May's statement that *eros*, our daimonic, creative form of love, will destroy if it is not given freedom to construct.[9]

Maslow's ideal persons, the self-actualizers, often seem much like Rabelais himself, at least as he appears to us. They put me in mind of

* *Toward a Psychology of Being*, 2nd ed. (New York, etc.: Van Nostrand, 1968), p. 16; cf. p. 12. Hereafter all quotations from Maslow will be by page numbers from this book and edition except those introduced by *MP*, which are from his *Motivation and Personality* (New York: Harper, 1954).

John Cowper Powys's sympathetic and perceptive portrait of him.[10] They tend, says Maslow (*MP*, 207), "to be good and lusty animals hearty in their appetites and enjoying themselves mightily without regret or shame or apology." He finds in them a "kind of godlike gaiety" (106), a "healthy childishness" that lives happily with great maturity (96, 140), a playfulness that "has a cosmic or a godlike, good-humored quality, certainly transcending hostility of any kind" (112). Though Rabelais has his share of hostility, he often transcends it, especially in *Gargantua*, as in the account of Janotus de Bragmardo, (ch. 18–20). In all these points Neill and Maslow are very close. Maslow's growth-motivated people are not sated but only further motivated by gratification: "The appetites become intensified and heightened. They grow upon themselves and instead of wanting less and less, such a person wants more and more of, for instance, education. The person rather than coming to rest becomes more active" (p. 30).

Last and perhaps most important, Maslow's self-actualizers in many ways resemble those Rabelaisian Utopians, the Thelemites—insofar as Rabelais allows us to know them. Basically decent and attractive people, the Thelemites naturally and happily choose to be good as long as the free choice is theirs. Each freely decides to join in the activities of the others; even as the ladies have chosen to dress alike each day, so each day the men select their apparel to match the women's. Although active productivity and growth are manifest mainly in Gargantua's education, and in Theleme are secondary to freedom and to sumptuous dress and lodging (Rabelais's problems were not the same as ours), his Thelemites can all read, write, sing, play musical instruments, speak and write (both verse and prose) in five or six languages; and at their disposal he puts six fine big libraries, one for each of six languages: Greek, Latin, Hebrew, French, Tuscan, and Spanish. It seems reasonable to assume that, like their creator, they knew the joy of learning and with it that of growth.

The self-actualizers enjoy the freedom that allows them to practice their natural goodness, for what the healthy human, child or adult, enjoys is generally good for him—and also for others.[11] For the self-actualizer duty and pleasure become interchangeable (Maslow, 140); self-discipline becomes easy (163); and he or she moves from lower to higher needs and values as the lower ones are gratified (153–59). In virtually all these findings, Neill in his schoolhouse anticipated the psychotherapists—even as Rabelais, in imagination and hope, anticipated them all.

Of course Rabelais is not the classic author who best expresses the main values of modern growth psychology. That author is Goethe, the Goethe of *Faust*, Part II, and specifically of Faust's dying words—

> Nur der verdient sich Freiheit wie das Leben,
> Der täglich sie erobern muss.
>
> [He only earns his freedom and his life
> Who takes them every day by storm.][12]

—when he has created the perfect environment to keep his people active and, if they are to live, presumably ever growing. Fromm quotes and discusses this example at length (*Man for Himself*, pp. 99–100), and May does so twice (*Man's Search for Himself*, pp. 168, 264–65). This Faust is clearly their most direct and important literary ancestor.

Nevertheless, the basic optimism about the nature of man that is so striking in Rabelais—and must be one reason why he and Calvin hated each other—is, in however modified a form, indispensable for any psychology of growth. For Rabelais (in the *Third Book* as well as in Theleme) and for any ethic of self-actualization, the freedom of an enlightened will is essential. It is therefore not surprising that Dr. Rabelais's *Fay ce que vouldras* finds an implicit echo in Dr. Fromm and an explicit one in Drs. May and Maslow; while Neill, in whose school a Thelemite would feel at home, says that at Summerhill, as long as he is not trespassing on the freedom of others, "Each individual is free to do what he likes" (*Summerhill*, p. 155). May's statement is conditional and indirect, but still—to me at least—illustrative: "If wish and will can be seen and experienced in this light of autonomous, imaginative acts of interpersonal mutuality, there is profound truth in St. Augustine's dictum: 'Love and do what you *will*'" (*Love and Will*, p. 214). But again it is Maslow who comes closest, and—what is more striking—apparently without knowing it. In discussing "The Problems of Control and Limits," he points out that while self-actualized persons will set their own limits, all others will need to have limits set for them: "Only to the self-disciplined and responsible person can we say, 'Do as you will, and it will probably be all right'" (pp. 163–64).

In short, in this troubled century of ours, both early and late, a number of excellent minds of varied training and expertise have been—

and still are—coming to very much the same conclusion: that for the healthy person who truly loves life, for inner as well as outer freedom Rabelais's "Do What You Will" remains the best rule. It is heartening to hear its accents in Western Europe and America today.

Conclusion

As was seen in chapter 16, Rabelais has meant—and still means—many things to many people: from drunken buffoon to cosmic jester, from a perverse and morbid case for psychoanalysis to master of all happy men. As was also noted, most scholars of the last forty years differ sharply from those of Lefranc's generation in their view of Rabelais, and considerably from one another in their sense of what in him is great. Many today, reacting against the earlier emphasis on his ideas, play these down and find his sole greatness in his mastery of words. The main cleavage today seems to lie in the centrality attributed to either Pantagruelism or what has been called Rabelaisianism and I would prefer to call the voice of Panurge or of Alcofribas. Everyone recognizes the presence of both elements or voices, but whereas Marichal, Saulnier, and Screech stress that of Pantagruel, Keller finds that of Panurge or Alcofribas greater, while Bakhtin almost ignores Pantagruelism entirely.

I see great danger in sacrificing either element; for the balance between them seems fairly even, and Rabelais would simply not be Rabelais without both. I know of no writer, with the possible exception of Aristophanes, who has so successfully combined the serious and lofty with the comical and grotesque. To me it is the blend, not either component element, that alone deserves the name Rabelaisian; it is neither Pantagruel's moving speech on the death of Jesus (IV: 28), nor the tears the size of ostrich eggs that it elicits, but the juxtaposition of the speech with the tears. His mastery of each voice is indeed remarkable, but not, I think, unique; many other writers have excelled in one or the other. For me his uniqueness lies in the magic with which he blends these two disparate voices into a single unified work of art that has delighted readers for over four centuries, even as it seems sure to do for many more.

Notes

Introduction

1. See Barbara C. Bowen, *The Age of Bluff* (Urbana, Chicago, London: University of Illinois Press, 1972), pp. 38–102.

2. Leo Spitzer protested eloquently against the resulting notion of a "realistic" Rabelais. See "Le Prétendu Réalisme de Rabelais," *Modern Philology* 37: 139–50, 1939–40.

3. *Rabelais: A Study in Comic Courage* (Englewood Cliffs, N.J.: Prentice-Hall, 1970), p. 11.

4. *The Telling of Tales in Rabelais: Aspects of His Narrative Art*, Analecta Romanica, Heft 12 (Frankfurt am Main: Klostermann, 1963), pp. 76–80.

Chapter 1: The Times

1. Lucien Febvre, *Le Problème de l'incroyance au XVIe siècle. La Religion de Rabelais* (Paris: Michel, 1942), pp. 361–490, *passim*.

2. See Jean Larmat, *Le Moyen Age dans le Gargantua de Rabelais* (Paris: Les Belles Lettres, 1973).

3. For Rabelais as witness to the age of printing, see Marshall McLuhan, *The Gutenberg Galaxy* (1962; New York: New American Library, 1969 ed.), pp. 179–84, 223, 233–34, 309.

4. See A. C. Keller, *The Telling of Tales in Rabelais*, pp. 10, 18, 21, and *passim*.

5. See Leo Spitzer, "Le Prétendu Réalisme de Rabelais," pp. 141, 145; and *Linguistics and Literary History* (Princeton, N.J.: Princeton University Press, 1948), pp. 15–18.

Chapter 2: The Life

1. The best book on Rabelais's life is still Jean Plattard, *Vie de François Rabelais* (Paris and Brussels: Van Oest, 1928). There is a shorter version:

François Rabelais (Paris: Boivin, 1932). Both sometimes accept possibility as probability and probability as fact.

2. V. L. Saulnier has refuted the argument, used against the birth date of 1483, that André Tiraqueau congratulates Rabelais in 1524, when Rabelais would have been forty-one, on being "vir supra aetatem" [a man above his years], pointing to contemporary uses of the term about still older men. It seems unlikely to me, however, that Tiraqueau, born in 1488, would have used the phrase about a man older than himself. See Saulnier, "Rabelaesiana: Sur la date de naissance de Rabelais," *BHR* 7, 245–46, 1945; but cf. Plattard, *Rabelais* (1932), p. 11.

3. See Louis Delaruelle, *Répertoire analytique et chronologique de la correspondance de Guillaume Budé* (1907); reprinted, New York: Burt Franklin, n.d., pp. 140–41.

4. A. J. Krailsheimer, *Rabelais and the Franciscans* (Oxford: Clarendon Press, 1963), pp. 7–9.

5. See Henri Busson, "Les Dioscures de Fontenay-le-Comte: Pierre Amy-François Rabelais," in *ER* VI (1965), pp. 1–50, especially 1–10.

6. Jean Bouchet, *Epistres morales et familieres* (1545); reprinted, The Hague: Mouton, 1969. (In *Epistres familieres*, no. 48.) See Rabelais (Pléiade ed.), pp. 951–53.

7. This is clearly implied by two of his autographs in books of his, one of 1521, one of 1525. See Roland Antonioli, *Rabelais et la médecine*, *ER* XII (1976), p. 6.

8. *Ibid.*, pp. 9–11.

9. V. L. Saulnier, "Médecins de Montpellier au temps de Rabelais," *BHR* 19: 441, 1957.

10. *Ibid.*, pp. 426–35, 441.

11. *Ibid.*, pp. 442–43.

12. Mikhail Bakhtin (*Rabelais and His World*, p. 68) notes that two books by another Montpellier doctor, Laurent Joubert's *Traité du ris . . .* (1560) and *La Cause morale du ris* (1579), suggest that the curative value of laughter may have been much discussed there in Rabelais's time.

13. Letters (dedicatory and missive) of Rabelais's are also found, with a French translation of those in Latin, on pp. 943–94 of the Pléiade ed. of Rabelais, our edition of reference. This Preface is on pp. 954–58.

14. *Le Problème de l'incroyance.* For the limits of Rabelais's debt to Erasmus see M. A. Screech, "Some Stoic Elements in Rabelais's Religious Thought," *ER* I (1956), p. 75; and *L'Evangélisme de Rabelais*, *ER* II (1959), *passim.*

15. In the Prologue to *Pantagruel* Rabelais deletes the "grant et" (the second "Great and") when he mentions this title.

16. See Marcel Françon's edition of *Le Vroy Gargantua* [The Real Gargantua] (Paris: Nizet, 1949), pp. 19–44.

17. See Françon, *Le Vroy Gargantua,* and many articles; Paul Sébillot, *Gargantua dans les traditions populaires* (Paris: Maisonneuve, 1883); Henri Dontenville, *Histoire et géographie mythiques de la France* (Paris: Maisonneuve et Larose, 1973).

18. J. Lesellier, "L'Absolution de Rabelais en cour de Rome. Ses Circonstances. Ses Résultats," *HR* 3: 239, 1936.

19. But perhaps not until the summer of 1535; see below, ch. 4, p. 29.

20. J. Lesellier, "L'Absolution de Rabelais en cour de Rome. Ses Circonstances. Ses Résultats," *HR* 3: 239, 1936.

21. See Rabelais III: 21, 402–03; IV: 27, 615–16.

22. Some have claimed that in 1543 he was made a *maître des requêtes,* but this seems unlikely. See R. Marichal, "Rabelais fut-il maître des requêtes?" in *BHR* 10: 169–78, 1948.

23. However, Screech stresses Rabelais's boldness in this book in his edition of the *Tiers Livre* (Geneva: Droz, 1964), p. 162.

24. We know that Rabelais was in Metz on June 24, 1547, and in Rome on June 18, 1548, but not where he was in between. See Marichal, "Le Quart Livre de 1548," p. 142.

25. As well as the definitive conclusion to *Pantagruel* (II: 34, end) in the 1542 edition.

26. Henri Busson has shown that the attack was probably prompted by Dupuyherbault's friend François Le Picart. See "Les Églises contre Rabelais," in *ER* VII (1967), pp. 1–81.

27. See Rabelais's addition of 1542 ("prestinateurs, emposteurs") to the Prologue to *Pantagruel* (p. 168).

Chapter 3: *Pantagruel: Book Two*

1. *Linguistics and Literary History,* pp. 15–18.

2. For a good linguistic analysis of these chapters see François Rigolot, *Les Langages de Rabelais, ER* X (1972), pp. 41–48.

3. For shock and surprise, see Bowen, *The Age of Bluff,* pp. 38–102; for other phenomena noted, Gerard J. Brault, "The Comic Design of Rabelais' Pantagruel," *Studies in Philology* 65: 140–46, 1968; and especially Raymond C. La Charité, "The Unity of Rabelais's *Pantagruel,*" *French Studies* 26: 257–65, 1972.

4. *Pantagruel et les sophistes* (The Hague: Nijhoff, 1973).

5. "'Ung Abysme de Science': On the Interpretation of Gargantua's Letter to Pantagruel," *BHR* 28: 615–32, 1966.

6. *Rabelais au futur* (Paris: Seuil, 1970), pp. 147–57.

7. *Pantagruel et les sophistes,* p. 80; cf. pp. 59–81.

8. Jean Larmat in his *Rabelais* (Paris: Hatier, 1973), pp. 40–42, seems also to find the letter suspect as a serious document.

9. Some scholars, including Charles Béné, Marcel Françon, and M. A. Screech, consider the letter a late interpolation. For a treatment of this see Rigolot, *Les Langages de Rabelais*, pp. 55–57.

Chapter 4: *Gargantua: Book One*

1. "The Sense of Rabelais's Enigme en prophétie (*Gargantua* LVIII)," *BHR* 18: 399, 1956.

2. See his Introduction to the Calder-Saulnier-Screech edition of *Gargantua*, Textes Littéraires Français (Geneva: Droz; Paris: Minard, 1970), pp. XL–I; "Some Reflexions on the Problem of Dating 'Gargantua, "A" and "B,"' in *ER* XI (1974), pp. 9–56; and "Some Further Reflexions on the Dating of Gargantua (A) and (B) and on the Possible Meaning of some of the Episodes," in *ER* XIII (1976), pp. 79–111.

3. "Les Dates de composition et de publication du *Gargantua*. Essai de mise au point," in *ER* XI (1974), pp. 137–42.

4. *ER* XI (1974), pp. 81–82.

5. "Rabelais et les cloches de Notre-Dame," in *ER* IX (1971), pp. 1–28.

6. Preface to *ER* IX (1971), p. viii.

7. Preface to *ER* XI (1974), pp. vii–xv.

8. See Marcel de Grève, *L'Interprétation de Rabelais au XVIe siècle*, *ER* III (1961), pp. 12–23.

9. See Lucien Febvre and Henri-Jean Martin, *L'Apparition du livre* (Paris: Michel, 1958), pp. 414–15.

10. Lucien Febvre (*Le Problème de l'incroyance*, p. 95) regarded this poem as *quite possibly* addressed to Rabelais; Marcel de Grève (*L'Interprétation*, p. 17) quotes it as addressed to him.

11. Two apparent objections arise. *Pantagruel* begins with a *dizain* by Hugues Salel praising Rabelais for "mixing profit with sweetness," combining understanding and utility like another Democritus, and urges him to continue and reap his due reward, if not here below, then above. This poem, however, appeared not in 1532 with the original *Pantagruel*, but only in 1534, the year of *Gargantua*.

Gargantua opens with Rabelais's own *dizain* "Aux lecteurs," claiming that the book is harmless and should not scandalize them. True, it is far from perfect; but by laughter it may console their grief:

> Mieux est de ris que de larmes escripre,
> Pour ce que rire est le propre de l'homme.

> [Better to write of laughter than of tears,
> Since laughter is the proper role of man.]

This invites us not to seek serious meaning in the book; but its first known publication was in 1535, when Rabelais, after the Affair of the Placards, was presumably eager to appease his critics. It may have appeared in the undated first edition, on the verso of the missing title page; but it may have been added only in the second edition to try to ward off the Sorbonne.

(For a different reading of these facts see Rigolot, *Les Langages de Rabelais*, pp. 19–22, who considers all this to be deliberate ambiguity on Rabelais's part.)

12. See Jean Bichon, "Rabelais et 'la vie œconomicque,'" in *ER* VII (1967), pp. 105–17.

13. For a good discussion see Floyd Gray, "Ambiguity and Point of View in the Prologue to *Gargantua*," *Romanic Review* 56: 12–21, 1965.

14. Florence Weinberg, "Frère Jean, Evangélique: His Function in the Rabelaisian World," *Modern Language Review* 66, 298–305, 1971.

15. *Essais:* I: 26; in the 1962 Pléiade edition, pp. 158–59.

16. Liddell and Scott, *Greek-English Lexicon*, 7th ed. (New York: Harper, 1883).

17. "Thélème, Panurge et la Dive Bouteille," *Revue d'Histoire Littéraire de la France* 65: 385–97, 1965.

18. In ch. 52 the admissible are "les belles, bien formées et bien naturées, et les beaulx, bien forméz et bien naturéz" (p. 148) [the beautiful, well-formed, and well-natured women and the handsome, well-formed, and well-natured men], with no suggestion of social rank. In ch. 54 the men welcomed are first "tous nobles chevaliers" [all noble knights] but then "en général tous gentilz compaignons" (p. 153) [in general all nice companions], and, in the summarizing sestet, "compaignons gentilz." The women, "dames de hault paraige" (p. 154), seem to be clearly noble.

I find it hard to know just what to make of this. I think it means that Rabelais is not categorical about nobility; that he wants nice people, and thinks that these are most likely to be found among the nobles.

19. Much debated, and apparently unanswerable still, is the question whether or not each room has its own little chapel or oratory. The problem is the meaning of the word "chapelle" (53, 150). See Robert Marichal, "Quart Livre. Commentaires," in *ER* V (1964), pp. 65–78.

20. To quote Screech: "This optimistic abbey is really set under the aegis of Socrates, not that of the gay and unbeautiful Benedictine who drops snot from his nose." "Some Reflexions on the *Abbey of Thelema*," in *ER* VIII (1969), p. 112; cf. pp. 109–10.

21. Screech explains a number of these by his theory of different moments of composition, before and after the Affair of the Placards. I find his theory impressive but not wholly convincing, partly for reasons already noted (p. 29) and partly because it does not deal with the learning of the young Thelemites.

12. "Le Silence de Rabelais et le mythe des paroles gelées," *FR*, pp. 233–47. For a different reading, also cogently argued but more poetic and linguistic, see Jean Guiton, "Le Mythe des paroles gelées," *Romanic Review* 31: 3–15, 1940.

13. "Commentaires du *Quart Livre*, VIII. Messere Gaster (Ch. LVII–LXII)," in *ER* I (1956), pp. 183–202.

14. Ch. 3, Oratio 3, "Quod sit Amor Magister Artium."

15. "Pantagruel au large de Ganabin, ou La Peur de Panurge," *BHR* 16: 58–81, 1954.

16. R. Marichal, "L'Attitude de Rabelais devant le néoplatonisme et l'italianisme. *Quart Livre*, ch. IX à XI," in *FR*, pp. 181–209; see especially pp. 204, 209.

Chapter 7: The *Fifth Book*

1. Three recent examples are Marcel Tetel, *Rabelais* (New York: Twayne, 1967); Mikhail Bakhtin, *Rabelais and His World*, tr. Helene Iswolsky (Cambridge, Mass., and London: The M.I.T. Press, 1968); and Dorothy G. Coleman, *Rabelais: A Critical Study in Prose Fiction* (Cambridge: The University Press, 1971). See also Pierre Villey, *Marot et Rabelais* (Paris: Champion, 1923), pp. 295–96, 325; M. A. Screech, critical edition of *Tiers Livre*, p. xi. Just lately Alfred Glauser has spent a whole book arguing the inauthenticity of the *Fifth Book: Le Faux Rabelais, ou de l'inauthenticité du Cinquième Livre* (Paris: Nizet, 1975). But George A. Petrossian, in his "stylo-statistical" study *The Problem of the Authenticity of the Cinquiesme Livre de Pantagruel: A Quantitative Study*, *ER* XIII (1976), pp. 1–64, claims to have shown beyond a doubt that Rabelais is indeed the author.

2. Jourda gives an excellent summary in his edition of the *Œuvres complètes*, II, 263–72. A full account is in Lazare Sainéan, "Le Cinquième Livre de Rabelais. Son Authenticité et ses parties constitutives," in *Problèmes littéraires du seizième siècle* (Paris: Boccard, 1927), pp. 1–98. Sainéan considered the book almost completely authentic.

3. The complete Prologue is full of borrowings from the Prologues to the *Third* and *Fourth Books*. See also V: 1, 751; 3, 757; 22, 810; etc.

4. However, Robert J. Clements argues strongly for the authenticity of chapters 24–25 in "The Chess Ballet: A Faraway Vision of Pantagruel and Polifilo," in *Connaissance de l'étranger. Mélanges offerts à la mémoire de Jean-Marie Carré* (Paris: Didier, 1964), pp. 224–39.

5. *Prosopographie* (Lyons: Frelon, 1604), III, 2,452; quoted by Jourda in his edition of Rabelais, II, 264, fn. 4. Sainéan, "Le Cinquième Livre de Rabelais," p. 3, dates the work at 1603 and, after Le Duchat, says that Du Verdier was confusing the *Isle sonante* with Guillaume des Autels's *Mytistoire barragouine de Fanfreluche et Gaudichon* (1574).

6. *Les Diverses Leçons de Loys Guyon* . . . (Lyons: Morillon, 1604), Book II, ch. 30; also quoted by Jourda, II, 264–65, fn. 5. Sainéan questions Guyon's pronouncement and points to two references to a much earlier work, the *Bigarrures* of Estienne Tabourot des Accords (1572), that assume Rabelais's authorship of the *Fifth Book* ("Le Cinquième Livre de Rabelais," pp. 4–5).

7. On the supper served to the Lady Lanterns—a chapter appearing only in the manuscript.

8. Nan Cooke Carpenter, *Rabelais and Music* (Chapel Hill: University of North Carolina Press, 1954), pp. 97–119; also in *Modern Language Quarterly* 13: 299–304, 1952. Sainéan, in *L'Histoire naturelle et les branches connexes dans l'œuvre de Rabelais* (Paris: Champion, 1921), stresses the resemblances between the *Fifth Book* and earlier ones in technical vocabulary. G. Mallary Masters, in *Rabelaisian Dialectic and the Platonic-Hermetic Tradition* (Albany: SUNY Press, 1969), urges the authenticity of the *Fifth Book*, but seems less to prove it than to assume it from the start.

9. In the Prologue to the *Third Book* (pp. 325–26) he announces only the *Third* and *Fourth Books*.

10. For a very brief summary see the Jourda edition, II, 271–72.

11. Several exceptions have already been noted.

12. *Rabelais: A Study in Comic Courage* (Englewood Cliffs, N.J.: Prentice-Hall, 1970), p. 106.

13. The name "Fredon" (Cotgrave, *Dictionarie*: "Semie-quaver, or Semie-semie-quaver") rests on an analogy between musical terms and names of certain religious orders. First came the Little Brothers; then the Minors founded by Saint Francis of Assisi; then the Minims founded by Saint François de Paule. What could be smaller or more modest than a *minime* in music? Only a *fredon*. However, except as a satiric comment on the friars' professed modesty, the name has little to do with the comedy of these chapters.

14. Des Périers died in 1544; his book was published in 1558. Rabelais died in 1553; this part of his book was published in 1564. Des Périers could hardly have borrowed from Rabelais; Rabelais might have known Des Périers's work in manuscript and used it as a starting point. It seems more likely that they had a common source.

15. $1 + 2 + 3 + 4 = 10$. $10 \times (1 + 2 + 3 + 4) = 10 + 20 + 30 + 40 = 100$. $100 +$ the first cube $(8) = 108$. Of course 108 is also $2^2 \times 3^3$ (4×27).

16. See for example Bakhtin, *Rabelais and His World*, pp. 138, 439, 453–454.

17. Henri Lefebvre, in his Marxist *Rabelais* (Paris: Les Editeurs Français Réunis, 1955), p. 39, places Rabelais squarely (and rightly) in "the first youth, the adolescence of the bourgeoisie."

18. Pierre Villey, *Marot et Rabelais* (Paris: Champion, 1923), pp. 276–83, explains parts of this movement by the general situation and Rabelais's needs at the various moments of composition.

19. "On me feroit desplaisir de me desloger de cette creance." *Essais*, I: 40, 243 in the Pléiade edition.

20. Per Nykrog, "Thélème, Panurge et la Dive Bouteille," *Revue d'Histoire Littéraire de la France 65*: 1965, 395.

Chapter 8: Comedy and the Carnivalesque

1. *Tvorchestvo Fransua Rable* (Moscow, 1965); tr. Helene Iswolsky (Cambridge, Mass., and London: The M.I.T. Press, 1968). A French translation was published in 1970.

2. *Rabelais and His World*, pp. 441, 337, and 325 (cf. p. 338).

Chapter 9: Obscenity

1. *L'Interprétation de Rabelais au XVIᵉ siècle, ER* III (1961).

2. "Cynical," p. 176. "Naïve" (apropos of language), p. 471; cf. p. 271 and *passim*.

3. The first I know of to do so was the poet Joachim du Bellay in 1549 in his *Deffence et Illustration de la langue françoyse*, Book II, ch. 12.

4. In *Renaissance and Other Studies in Honor of William Leon Wiley*, ed. George B. Daniel, Jr. (Chapel Hill, N.C.: The University of North Carolina Press, 1968), pp. 167–89.

5. Another example, also already noted, shows that this example of didactic obscenity is not unique: the reminder (III, Prologue, p. 328) of the "four buttocks" that engendered us, and that we would not be here if Mom and Dad had not copulated.

6. Facsimile edition (Paris: Silvestre, 1845), pp. Aiii recto and verso; also Huntington Brown, ed., François Girault, *The Tale of Gargantua and King Arthur* (Cambridge, Mass.: Harvard University Press, 1932), pp. 107–08. Some spelling and punctuation have been modernized.

7. For two sharply contrasting recent reactions to the scatological side of Rabelais's obscenity, see the remarks by George Orwell and Aldous Huxley in chapter 16 below (pp. 187–88). Where Orwell calls it "a preoccupation with the W C" and finds Rabelais (apparently because of it) "an exceptionally perverse, morbid writer, a case for psycho-analysis," Huxley, contrasting Rabelais with Swift, sees as pleasant "the dung through which Gargantua wades," since "the muck is transfigured by love; for Rabelais loved the bowels which Swift so malignantly hated."

Chapter 10: Satire and Fantasy

1. There is fantasy of a different kind in the account of the sumptuous lodgings, dress, and life of the Thelemites (53, 55–56); but this is not of the sort I am talking about here.

Chapter 11: Storytelling

1. For the following references, see Selected Bibliography.

Chapter 12: The Exuberant Style

1. Leo Spitzer, *Die Wortbildung als stilistisches Mittel, exemplifiziert an Rabelais* (Halle: Niemeyer, 1910); "Rabelais et les rabelaisants," *Studi Francesi* 12: 401–23, 1960; and pp. 15–23 of *Linguistics and Literary History* (Princeton: Princeton University Press, 1948). Erich Auerbach, "The World in Pantagruel's Mouth," in *Mimesis*, pp. 229–49. Floyd Gray, "Ambiguity and Point of View in the Prologue to *Gargantua*," *Romanic Review* 56: 12–21, 1965; "Structure and Meaning in the Prologue to the *Tiers Livre*," *L'Esprit Créateur* 3: 57–62, 1963; and *Rabelais et l'écriture* (Paris: Nizet, 1974). Dorothy Gabe Coleman, *Rabelais. A Critical Study in Prose Fiction* (Cambridge: The University Press, 1971). François Rigolot, *Les Langages de Rabelais, ER* X (1972).

2. See for example his absent-minded exchange of Epistémon and Pantagruel as speakers in III: 44, which we noted already in chapter 5.

3. I am indebted to Dorothy Coleman, *Rabelais*, pp. 232–33, for the distinction between the *paratactic* structure—simple sentences connected, if at all, by such conjunctions as *and*, *but*, or *so*—and the *hypotactic*, which involves complex sentences, subordinate clauses, and often "a network of participles."

Chapter 13: Giantism

1. John Cowper Powys stresses Rabelais's childlike quality in his *Rabelais* (New York: Philosophical Library, 1951), pp. 283–94.

Chapter 14: Humanism and Evangelism

1. Critical edition (1913–55), preface to Vol. III.

2. Notably "Some Stoic Elements in Rabelais's Religious Thought (The Will—Destiny—Active Virtue)," in *ER* I (1956), pp. 73–97; and "The Death of Pan and the Death of Heroes in the Fourth Book of Rabelais: A Study in Syncretism," *BHR* 17: 36–55, 1955.

3. Textes Littéraires Français (Geneva: Droz; Paris: Minard): *Gargantua* (1970), *Tiers Livre* (1964).

4. Lucien Febvre has rightly called this chapter "the protest of an impenitent old Evangelical." *Le Problème de l'incroyance*, p. 358.

5. At least if we follow, as I do, Saulnier's reading of this episode in "Pantagruel au large de Ganabin . . . ," *BHR* 16: 58–81, 1954. One might also list the "hésuchisme" of the episode of the Frozen Words (55–56); see

Saulnier, "Le Silence de Rabelais et le mythe des paroles gelées," in *FR*, pp. 233–47.

6. "*Quart Livre*: Commentaires: L'Isle des Papimanes," in *ER* V (1964), pp. 100–33, especially 123–27.

7. Thomas M. Greene, *Rabelais: A Study in Comic Courage*, Landmarks in Literature (Englewood Cliffs, N.J.: Prentice-Hall, 1970).

Chapter 15: Characters and Their Interaction

1. *Rabelais et l'écriture* (Paris: Nizet, 1974), p. 108.

2. See my "Interaction of Characters in Rabelais," *Modern Language Notes* 87: 12–23, 1972.

3. *Pantagruel et les sophistes*, pp. 165–69 and *passim*.

4. See my article "The Impact of Frère Jean on Panurge in Rabelais's *Tiers Livre*," in *Renaissance and Other Studies in Honor of William Leon Wiley*, ed. George B. Daniel, Jr. (Chapel Hill: The University of North Carolina Press, 1968), pp. 83–91.

Chapter 16: Fortunes

1. *L'Interprétation de Rabelais au XVIe siècle*, *ER* III (1961); "Limites de l'influence linguistique de Rabelais en Angleterre au XVIe siècle," *Comparative Literature Studies* 1: 15–30, 1964; and articles on the seventeenth-century French freethinkers in *ER* I (1956), pp. 120–50, and on erudites in *ER* V (1964), pp. 41–63.

2. Harvard University Press, 1933; reprint ed., New York: Octagon, 1967.

3. Florence: Olschki, 1969.

4. Paris: Les Belles Lettres, 1956.

5. Jacques Boulenger, *Rabelais à travers les âges* (Paris: Le Divan, 1925); Lazare Sainéan, *L'Influence et la réputation de Rabelais* (Paris: Gamber, 1930).

6. Lucien Febvre and Henri-Jean Martin, *L'Apparition du livre* (Paris: Michel, 1958), pp. 414–15.

7. Sainéan, *L'Influence*, pp. 127–39.

8. For Des Périers, see also Françoise Charpentier, "Une Page rabelaisienne de Des Périers: La Première Nouvelle en forme de Préambule," *Revue d'Histoire Littéraire de la France* 67: 601–05, 1967.

9. Jacques Bailbé, "Rabelais et Aubigné," *BHR* 21: 380–419, 1959.

10. See the books by Boulenger and Sainéan, and especially the Grève articles.

11. In a letter to Saint-Evremond dated Dec. 18, 1687. *Œuvres diverses*, ed. Pierre Clarac (Paris: Gallimard, Pléiade ed., 1958), p. 674; see Sainéan, p. 174.

12. Marcel de Grève, "Rabelais au pays de Brueghel. Réflexions sur la popularité de Rabelais dans les Pays-Bas du XVIᵉ siècle," *BHR* 17: 154–87, 1955.

13. See especially Grève, *L'Interprétation*, pp. 204–08.

14. *Ibid.*, pp. 208–17; cf. pp. 125–29.

15. By Charles Whibley, W. F. Smith, A. H. Upham, Sidney Lee, Alan D. McKillop, and especially Huntington Brown, whose book sums up and adds to the work of his predecessors but goes only through the eighteenth century.

16. *L'Interprétation*, ch. 8 ("The Merry Jester of France"), pp. 218–43; and "Limites de l'influence."

17. Brown treats Shakespeare only in passing; Grève treats him not at all.

18. Joseph Spence, *Observations, Anecdotes, and Characters of Books and Men, Collected from Conversation*, ed. James M. Osborn, new ed. (Oxford: Clarendon Press, 1966), I, 55 (February or March, 1735).

19. See Melvyn New, "Sterne's Rabelaisian Fragment: A Text from the Holograph Manuscript," *Publications of the Modern Language Association of America* 87: 1083–92, 1972.

20. For all this part see Marcel Tetel, *Rabelais et l'Italie*.

21. *Cahiers*, ed. B. Grasset (Paris, 1942), p. 83; quoted by V. L. Saulnier in "Dix Années d'études sur Rabelais (1939–1948)," *BHR* 11: 119, 1949.

22. *Œuvres complètes*, eds. Assézat and Tourneux, 20 vols. (Paris: Garnier, 1875–77), I, 195.

23. *Œuvres romanesques*, ed. Bénac (Paris: Garnier, 1959), pp. 716–17.

24. *Ibid.*, p. 400.

25. *Ibid.*, p. 450.

26. *Ibid.*, p. 487.

27. See his earlier remark (p. 397) on the Nephew: "He makes the truth come out."

28. *Correspondance*, eds. Roth and Verloot, 16 vols. (Paris: Editions de Minuit, 1955–70), XIV, 28–33; noted by Arthur Wilson on p. 654 of his *Diderot* (New York: Oxford University Press, 1972).

29. Boulenger, pp. 58–68; Jean Sareil, "Voltaire juge de Rabelais," *Romanic Review* 56: 171–80, 1965.

30. *Lettres philosophiques*, in *Œuvres complètes*, Moland ed., 52 vols. (Paris: Garnier, 1877–85), XXII, 174.

31. *Correspondance*, ed. Bestermann, 107 vols. (Geneva: Institut et Musée Voltaire, 1953–65), XXXVII, 136–37; XLI, 195.

32. *Lettres à S. A. Mgr. le Prince de^{xxx} sur Rabelais*, in *Œuvres complètes*, XXVI, 470.

33. Here Boulenger is our best guide, and Sainéan often a help.

34. *Essai sur la littérature anglaise*, in *Œuvres complètes*, Garnier ed., XI, 614; cf. pp. 545, 606; quoted by Boulenger, p. 79. Chateaubriand repeated this passage in his *Mémoires d'Outre-Tombe*.

35. As quoted by Sainéan, p. 116.

36. "Rabelais," in *Causeries du lundi*, III (Paris: Garnier, n.d.), 1–18 (October 7, 1856).

37. *Les Grotesques* (Paris, 1897; Geneva: Slatkine Reprints, 1969), pp. 31–33.

38. V. L. Saulnier, "Divers Echos de Rabelais au XXe siècle," *ER* VI (1965), p. 74.

39. See Maurice Lécuyer, *Balzac et Rabelais* (Paris: Les Belles Lettres, 1956).

40. From *Le Cousin Pons*, in *Œuvres complètes*, 27 vols. (Paris: Les Bibliophiles de l'Originale, 1965–73), XVII, 478.

41. Quoted by Boulenger, p. 159; cf. pp. 156–58.

42. Boulenger, pp. 127–31.

43. A. B. Duff, ed. (Paris: Mercure de France, 1962); reprinted from *Le Courrier Français*, October 22–23, 1847.

44. Quoted by Boulenger, p. 162.

45. "Le plus grand de nos polémistes: François Rabelais," in *Flambeaux* (Paris: Grasset, 1929).

46. Boulenger, pp. 134–38.

47. *Histoire de France*, 16 vols. (Paris: Flammarion, 1898), VIII, 361.

48. *Œuvres* (Paris: Champion; Geneva: Droz, 1913–55), 6 vols., incomplete (I–IV: 17).

49. See for example the work of Defaux and of Larmat, noted in the Selected Bibliography.

50. See *Coleridge's Miscellaneous Criticism*, ed. Thomas M. Raysor (London: Constable, 1936), pp. 113–14, 127–28, 286, 407, 419.

51. References are to the Everyman ed. (London: Dent, 1908; New York: Dutton, 1949).

52. "A Study of Shakespeare," in *Complete Works*, eds. Gosse and Wise, 20 vols. (London: Heinemann; New York: G. Wells, 1925–27), XI, 1–222; see pp. 78–80.

53. *The French Humorists from the Twelfth to the Nineteenth Century* (Boston: Roberts, 1877), pp. 89–131. See also his *Rabelais* (Philadelphia: Lippincott, 1879), which offers much high praise but concludes: "The pity of it!" (p. 184).

54. *Œuvres complètes illustrées*, 25 vols. (Paris: Calmann-Lévy, 1925–35), XVIII, 423–81.

55. *Ibid.*, XVII (1928).

56. *Les Hommes de bonne volonté*, XXVII: *Le Sept octobre* (Paris: Flammarion, 1946), p. 231.

57. *Journal*, Bibliothèque de la Pléiade (Paris: Gallimard, 1948), p. 21; cf. pp. 241, 1133.

58. See M. Puisségur, "Rabelais, Dada et les probabilités," *Bulletin de l'Association des Amis de Rabelais et de La Devinière*, 2: 335–40, 1971.

59. Quoted by Michaël Baraz, "Le Sentiment de l'unité dans l'œuvre de Rabelais," *Etudes Françaises* 8: 44, Feb. 1972.

60. *Humanités* (Paris: Presses Universitaires de France, 1960), pp. 3–13.

61. "Rabelais, il a raté son coup," *L'Herne* 5: 19–21, 1965; quoted in part by Michel Beaujour in *Le Jeu de Rabelais* (Paris: L'Herne, 1969), p. 17, fn. 2.

62. Robert J. Clements notes the performance in 1968 at the Vieux Colombier in Paris of an antiwar play called *The Picrocholean Wars*. "The Modernity of Rabelais," *American Society Legion of Honor Magazine*, 40: 41, 1969.

63. *Rabelais. "Jeu dramatique" en deux parties tiré des cinq livres de François Rabelais* (Paris: Gallimard, 1968), pp. 9, 12, and *passim*.

64. Clements, "The Modernity of Rabelais," p. 44.

65. *Rabelais and His World*, pp. 139–44.

66. *The Education of Henry Adams* (1906; New York: Modern Library, 1931), p. 454.

67. *English Literature in the Sixteenth Century Excluding Drama* (Oxford: Clarendon Press, 1954), pp. 30, 417; cf. p. 468.

68. *The Classical Tradition* (Oxford: Clarendon Press, 1949), pp. 178, 185, 193, 311, 320, and pp. 178–93 *passim*.

69. *Anatomy of Criticism* (Princeton, N.J.: Princeton University Press, 1957), pp. 308–09.

70. 1962; New York: New American Library, 1969.

71. *What Is a Classic?* (London: Faber and Faber, 1945), p. 27.

72. *Essays on Elizabethan Drama*, Harvest Book (1932; New York: Harcourt, Brace, 1956), p. 71.

73. *Ibid.*, p. 160.

74. *A Vision* (London: Macmillan, 1937 ed.), pp. 137–40, 293–94.

75. Dated January 27, 1905. Quoted from *The Cutting of an Agate* (New York: Macmillan, 1912), p. 40; cf. pp. 41–44. My thanks go to Professor Jean Bruneau of Harvard for calling my attention to this quotation.

76. *Collected Essays*, 4 vols. (London: The Hogarth Press, 1966–67), III, 68, 89; cf. 88.

77. "Vulgarity in Literature," from *Music at Night*, in *Collected Essays* (New York: Harper, 1959), p. 107.

78. *Letters of Aldous Huxley,* ed. Grover Smith (London: Chatto and Windus, 1969), pp. 160–61. On p. 215 he writes of the "exuberant and rather tormented style" of Le Motteux's translation.

79. *Ibid.,* p. 600.

80. *The Collected Essays, Journalism and Letters of George Orwell,* eds. Sonia Orwell and Ian Angus, 4 vols. (New York: Harcourt, Brace, and World, 1968), III, 285.

81. *Ibid.,* II, 45–46.

82. *Doctor Rabelais* (New York: Sheed and Ward, 1957), p. 258.

83. "Chaucer and the Renaissance," in *G. K. Chesterton: A Selection from His Non-Fictional Prose,* selected by W. H. Auden (London: Faber and Faber, 1970), p. 29.

84. "Lewis Carroll," in *A Handful of Authors* (1953; New York: Kraus Reprint Co., 1969), p. 118.

85. New York: Sheed and Ward, 1950, pp. 122–31.

86. This must be the one, however, from which Wyndham Lewis quotes at length in his Introduction (I, xv) to the 1929 Everyman edition of the Urquhart-Le Motteux translation when he hails "my master Rabelais" as "the past-master of all arts and divinations . . . , the Teacher of wise men, the comfort of an afflicted world, the uplifter of fools, the energiser of the lethargic, the doctor of the gouty, the guide of youth, the companion of middle age, the *vade mecum* of the old, the pleasant introducer of inevitable Death, yea, the general solace of mankind."

87. London: Allen and Unwin, 7th printing, 1949, p. 60. See also *Hilaire Belloc. An Anthology of His Prose and Verse* (Philadelphia and New York: Lippincott, 1951), pp. 26, 50–51; *Avril* (London: Duckworth, 1904), pp. xiv, 5, 42, 133, 135; and *How the Reformation Happened* (1928; New York: Dodd, Mead, 1954 ed.), p. 64.

88. See Alfred G. Engstrom, "A Few Comparisons and Contrasts in the Word-Craft of Rabelais and James Joyce," in *Renaissance and Other Studies in Honor of William Leon Wiley,* ed. G. B. Daniel, Jr. (Chapel Hill, N.C.: The University of North Carolina Press, 1968), pp. 65–82; Claude Jacquet, *Joyce et Rabelais: Aspects de la création verbale dans Finnegans Wake,* Etudes Anglaises; 4 (Paris: Didier, 1972).

89. Ed. and tr. Louis Berrone, *Journal of Modern Literature,* 5: 14–18, 1976.

90. *Ulysses,* The Modern Library (New York: Random House, 1934), p. 736. See Engstrom, "A Few Comparisons," pp. 65–66.

91. New York: Viking, 1939, pp. 3, 23, 44, 90, 113, 154, 157, 314, 332, 414, 424.

92. *Joyce et Rabelais,* p. 11.

Chapter 17: Theleme in the World of Today

1. In *Les Aventures du roi Pausole*, ch. 1; cited in V. L. Saulnier, "Divers Echos de Rabelais au XXᵉ siècle," in *ER* VI (1965), p. 77.

2. Saulnier, "Divers Echos," pp. 85–88.

3. *Rabelais, ou c'était pour rire* (Paris: Larousse, 1972), p. 143.

4. *Escape from Freedom* (1941; New York: Avon, 1966), pp. 115–18; cf. pp. 103–07. Neill comes close to this in *Summerhill*, pp. 205, 214.

5. Neill, *Summerhill*, p. 206 and *passim*; May, *Man's Search for Himself* (New York: Dell, Delta Books, 1953), p. 109.

6. *Man's Search for Himself*, pp. 186–87.

7. *Summerhill*, p. 316.

8. Fromm, *Escape from Freedom*, p. 50; May, *Man's Search for Himself*, pp. 180–84.

9. *Love and Will* (New York: Dell, Laurel Editions, 1969), p. 129.

10. *Rabelais* (New York: Philosophical Library, 1951), pp. 283–315 and *passim*. See above, ch. 16, pp. 189–90.

11. Neill, *passim*; Fromm, *Escape from Freedom*, pp. 135–36; May, *Love and Will*, p. 82; Maslow, pp. 158–59.

12. *Faust*, Part II, Act V, lines 11,575–11,576; tr. Louis MacNeice, abridged version (New York: Oxford University Press, 1951), p. 287.

Selected Bibliography

Editions

Œuvres. Critical edition by Abel Lefranc *et al.* 6 vols., incomplete (includes I–IV: 17). Paris: Champion; Geneva: Droz, 1913–55.
Valuable edition that gives all variants. Many editorial views now outdated.

Œuvres complètes. Edited by Jacques Boulenger and Lucien Scheler. Bibliothèque de la Pléiade. Paris: Gallimard, 1959.
Excellent and handy scholarly reader's edition. All known writings but few variants. Follows *L'Isle sonante*, then MS for *Fifth Book*. Our edition of reference.

Œuvres complètes. Edited by Pierre Jourda. 2 vols. Paris: Garnier, 1962.
Excellent scholarly reader's edition. All known writings but few variants. Follows *L'Isle sonante*, then 1564 ed. for *Fifth Book*.

Pantagruel, Gargantua, Tiers Livre, Quart Livre, Cinquiesme Livre. Edited by Pierre Michel. 5 vols. Paris: Gallimard, Livre de Poche, 1965; and Folio, undated.
Excellent edition, especially for reader who wants just one book or two.

Few variants. Notes on facing pages.

Pantagruel, ed. Saulnier, 1946; *Gargantua*, eds. Saulnier, Screech, and Calder, 1970; *Tiers Livre*, ed. Screech, 1964; *Quart Livre*, ed. Marichal, 1947; *Pantagruéline Prognostication*, ed. Screech, 1974. Textes Littéraires Français. Geneva: Droz, and other publishers.
The best critical texts we have, giving all variants, glossaries, indexes, excellent notes.

Le Quart Livre de Pantagruel (Edition dite partielle, 1548). Edited by Jean Plattard. Paris: Champion, 1910.
Good critical edition of the eleven chapters of the incomplete 1548 text.

"Fac-similé du Quart Livre de 1548," edited by Robert Marichal. In *ER* IX, 1971, pp. 151–74.
Clear reproduction without notes or commentary.

L'Isle sonante. Edited by Abel Lefranc and Jacques Boulenger. Paris: Champion, 1905.
Sound edition with useful introduction.

Translations

Gargantua and Pantagruel (Books I–V). Translated by Thomas Urquhart and Pierre Le Motteux. I–II (1653) and III (1693) by Urquhart; IV–V (1694) by Le Motteux. Many editions, including Everyman's Library, 2 vols. London: Dent; New York: Dutton, 1929.
The classic English translation: I–III (Urquhart) is imaginative, racy, excellent; IV–V is generally good. Must be used with caution, since both translators add to and "improve on" the original.

The Five Books and Minor Writings. Translated by W. F. Smith. 2 vols. London: Watt, 1893. 2nd ed. of Vol. I: *Gargantua,* Cambridge: University Press, 1934.
Scholarly and accurate, but somewhat stately and academic. In 1st ed., some chapters are left in French.

All the Extant Works of François Rabelais. Translated by Samuel Putnam. 3 vols. New York: Covici-Friede, 1929. Parts available in *The Portable Rabelais,* New York: Viking Press, 1946.
The best modern English translation: lively, imaginative, generally accurate.

Gargantua and Pantagruel: The Five Books by François Rabelais. Translated by Jacques Leclercq. 5 vols. New York: The Limited Editions Club, 1936. Also the Modern Library, New York: Random House, 1944.
Often brilliant, but regularly adds words, and in effect puts footnotes into the text by explaining, in the text, words unexplained by Rabelais.

Gargantua and Pantagruel. Translated by J. M. Cohen. Harmondsworth: Penguin Books, 1955.
The best readily available modern English translation, resourceful and generally accurate.

Rabelais Studies: Books

Antonioli, Roland. *Rabelais et la médecine. ER* XII. Geneva: Droz, 1976.
Rich and rewarding study of a very important subject.

Bakhtin, Mikhail. *Rabelais and His World* (1965). Translated by Helene Iswolsky. Cambridge, Mass., and London: The M.I.T. Press, 1968.
Seminal treatment of the carnivalesque in Rabelais. Some populist bias; some repetition, especially in second half of book.

Boulenger, Jacques. *Rabelais à travers les âges.* Paris: Le Divan, 1925.
Rich sampling of Rabelais's fortunes in France, especially in the nineteenth century.

Bowen, Barbara C. *The Age of Bluff: Paradox and Ambiguity in Rabelais and Montaigne.* Urbana, Chicago, London: University of Illinois Press, 1972.
Perceptive study of paradox, ambiguity, and shock; good on Rabelais, less so on Montaigne.

Carpenter, Nan C. *Rabelais and Music.* Chapel Hill, N.C.: University of North Carolina Press, 1954.
Thorough, knowledgeable treatment of an important subject.

Coleman, Dorothy Gabe. *Rabelais: A Critical Study in Prose Fiction.* Cambridge: The University Press, 1971.
Rabelais as a prose artist, especially his personae and the genre in which he wrote.

Defaux, Gérard. *Pantagruel et les sophistes.* The Hague: Nijhoff, 1973.
Important study of the temptation of sophistry, incarnated in Panurge, for Pantagruel in *Book Two.*

Etudes rabelaisiennes. 13 vols. Geneva: Droz, 1956–76. (*ER*)
Composed partly of volumes of articles, partly (II–IV, X, XII) of whole books. Some of the books and articles are also listed here by authors. Somewhat uneven, they contain much of the best Rabelais scholarship of the last twenty years.

Febvre, Lucien. *Le Problème de l'incroyance au XVIe siècle: La Religion de Rabelais.* Paris: Michel, 1942.
The first book to show Rabelais solidly rooted in his own time, as an Evangelical, Erasmian Christian. Well written; sometimes extreme. Still the best general introduction to Rabelais and his time.

Febvre, Lucien, and Martin, Henri-Jean. *L'Apparition du livre.* Paris: Michel, 1958.
Superb treatment of how, in Rabelais's time, the book came about.

François Rabelais: Ouvrage publié pour le quatrième centenaire de sa mort. 1553–1953. Geneva: Droz; Lille: Giard, 1953. (*FR*)
Valuable collection of articles (some listed here by authors) by leading scholars.

Gray, Floyd. *Rabelais et l'écriture.* Paris: Nizet, 1974.
Rabelais as a great and conscious artist in both speech and writing.

Greene, Thomas M. *Rabelais: A Study in Comic Courage.* Landmarks in Literature. Englewood Cliffs, N.J.: Prentice-Hall, 1970.
Well written, perceptive; the best short introduction to Rabelais.

Grève, Marcel de. *L'Interprétation de Rabelais au XVIe siècle.* ER III. Geneva: Droz, 1961.
Valuable, thorough study of Rabelais's reception in his time.

Kaiser, Walter. *Praisers of Folly: Erasmus, Rabelais, Shakespeare,* Part II, pp. 101–92. Cambridge, Mass.: Harvard University Press, 1963.
Thoughtful treatment of the *Third Book,* stressing Rabelais's debt to Erasmus.

Keller, Abraham C. *The Telling of Tales in Rabelais: Aspects of His Narrative Art.* Analecta Romanica, Heft 12. Frankfurt am Main: Klostermann, 1963.
Opens up a central subject with good questions and answers.

Krailsheimer, A. J. *Rabelais.* Les Ecrivains devant Dieu. Paris: Desclée de Brouwer, 1967.
Brief portrait of a thoroughly religious Rabelais.

——. *Rabelais and the Franciscans.* Oxford: Clarendon Press, 1963.
Valuable demonstration of Rabelais's debt to his Franciscan training.

Larmat, Jean. *Le Moyen Âge dans le Gargantua de Rabelais.* Paris: Les Belles Lettres, 1973.
Impressive demonstration of medieval influences and affinities in *Gargantua* and elsewhere.

——. *Rabelais.* Connaissance des Lettres. Paris: Hatier, 1973.
A very good introduction.

Lote, Georges. *La Vie et l'œuvre de Rabelais.* Aix-en-Provence: Fourcine; Paris: Droz, 1938.
Rabelais as an optimistic theist, vehement patriot, and admirable master of language.

Plattard, Jean. *Vie de François Rabelais.* Paris and Brussels: Van Oest, 1928.
Still our best biography of Rabelais; but sometimes inflates possibilities into probabilities and probabilities into facts.

Rigolot, François. *Les Langages de Rabelais.* ER X. Geneva: Droz, 1972.
Perceptive study of Rabelais's voices and languages.

Sainéan, Lazare. *La Langue de Rabelais.* 2 vols. Paris: Boccard, 1922–23.
Thorough but not always fruitful analysis of aspects of Rabelais's language.

Saulnier, V. L. *Le Dessein de Rabelais.* Paris: SEDES, 1957.
Valuable attempt to find a deeper unifying pattern in *Third* and *Fourth Books.*

Screech, M. A. *L'Evangélisme de Rabelais: Aspects de la satire religieuse au XVIᵉ siècle.* ER II. Geneva: Droz, 1959.
Searching studies of Evangelical texts in Rabelais, showing his wide theological reading and independent eclecticism.

——. *The Rabelaisian Marriage.* London: Arnold, 1958.
The best study of the *Third Book*; Rabelais as a philogamic feminist.

Spitzer, Leo. *Die Wortbildung als stilistisches Mittel, exemplifiziert an Rabelais.* Zeitschrift für Romanische Philologie, Beiheft 29. Halle: Niemeyer, 1910.
Pioneering study of Rabelais as artist by a leading linguistic critic.

Tetel, Marcel. *Rabelais et l'Italie.* Florence: Olschki, 1969.
Sound treatment of a broad subject.

Villey, Pierre. *Marot et Rabelais*. Paris: Champion, 1923.
  Still useful for Rabelais's evolution.

Rabelais Studies: Articles

Auerbach, Erich. "The World in Pantagruel's Mouth." In *Mimesis*, tr.
  Willard Trask, pp. 229–49. Garden City: Doubleday, Anchor Books, 1957.
  Generally excellent analysis of Rabelais's mixed styles and worlds.

Baraz, Michaël. "Le Sentiment de l'unité dans l'œuvre de Rabelais." *Etudes
  Françaises* 8: 3–53, 1972.
  Finds sense of unity everywhere in Rabelais and essential to his laughter.

Brault, Gerard J. " 'Ung Abysme de Science': On the Interpretation of
  Gargantua's Letter to Pantagruel." *BHR* 28: 615–32, 1966.
  II: 8 seen as a parody.

Busson, Henri. "Les Dioscures de Fontenay-le-Comte: Pierre Amy-François
  Rabelais." In *ER* VI (1965), pp. 1–50.
  Solid article on Rabelais's early friendship with Pierre Amy.

———. "Les Eglises contre Rabelais." In *ER* VII (1967), 1–81.
  Thorough study of the attacks on Rabelais by Gabriel Dupuyherbault
  (and his friend François Le Picart) and by Calvin.

Defaux, Gérard. "Rabelais et son masque comique: *Sophista loquitur*." In
  LR XI (1974), 89–136.
  Alcofribas Nasier seen as sophist and as independent character and story-
  teller.

Frautschi, R. L. "The 'Enigme en Prophétie' (*Garg*. LVIII) and the Question of Authorship." *French Studies* 17: 331–40, 1963.
  The "Enigme" may be by Rabelais, not by Saint-Gelais.

Gilson, Etienne. "Rabelais franciscain." In *Les Idées et les lettres*, pp. 197–
  241. Paris: Vrin, 1932.
  Rabelais as a good, though not always reverent, Franciscan.

Gray, Floyd. "Ambiguity and Point of View in the Prologue to *Gargantua*." *Romanic Review* 56: 12–21, 1965.
  Sensitive and searching study.

———. "Structure and Meaning in the Prologue to the *Tiers Livre*."
  L'Esprit Créateur 3: 57–62, 1963.
  Persuasive treatment of this Prologue as a "defense and illustration of
  creative writing."

Grève, Marcel de. "Les Erudits du XVIIe siècle en quête de la clef de
  Rabelais." In *ER* V (1964), pp. 41–63. "François Rabelais et les libertins
  du XVIIe siècle." In *ER* I (1956), pp. 120–50.
  Sound and searching studies.

Jourda, Pierre. "François Rabelais." In Bédier and Hazard, *Littérature française*, revised ed., directed by Pierre Martino, Vol I, 201–18. Paris: Larousse, 1948–49, 2 vols.
  Excellent brief introduction to Rabelais.

La Charité, Raymond C. "An Aspect of Obscenity in Rabelais." In *Renaissance and Other Studies in Honor of William Leon Wiley*, ed. George B. Daniel, Jr., pp. 167–89. Chapel Hill, N.C.: The University of North Carolina Press, 1968.
Revealing study of Rabelais's many terms for copulation.

———. "The Unity of Rabelais's *Pantagruel*." *French Studies* 26: 257–65, 1972.
Shows the unity and strength of the first book Rabelais wrote.

Lefranc, Abel. "Le Platon de Rabelais." *Bulletin du Bibliophile et du Bibliothécaire*, 105–14, 169–81, 1901.
Rich, still valuable study of an important subject.

Lesellier, J. "L'Absolution de Rabelais en cour de Rome. Ses circonstances. Ses résultats." *HR* 3: 237–70, 1936.
Rabelais a clumsy but successful petitioner for absolution.

———. "Deux enfants naturels de Rabelais légitimés par le Pape Paul III." *HR* 5: 549–70, 1938.
Shows that Rabelais had three illegitimate children, not just one, and follows one to later disaster.

Marichal, Robert. "L'Attitude de Rabelais devant le néoplatonisme et l'italianisme. *Quart Livre*, ch. IX à XI." In *FR*, pp. 181–209.
Convincingly shows parody of both in these chapters.

———. "Commentaires du *Quart Livre*." In *ER* I (1956), pp. 151–202; "*Quart Livre*: Commentaires," in *ER* V (1964), pp. 65–162; "Notes pour le commentaire des œuvres de Rabelais." In *ER* VI (1965), pp. 89–112; "Le Quart Livre de 1548." In *ER* IX (1971), pp. 131–74.
Exhaustive treatments, mainly lexical and historical, of the *Fourth Book* and its background.

———. "Préface" to *ER* XI (1974), pp. vii–xv.
Judicious summary of theories on the dating of *Gargantua*.

Nykrog, Per. "Thélème, Panurge et la Dive Bouteille." *Revue d'Histoire Littéraire de la France* 65: 385–97, 1965.
In New Testament, Greek θέλημα was used for the will of God; used of man, it meant an unconsidered leaning.

Plattard, Jean. "L'Ecriture sainte et la littérature scripturaire dans l'œuvre de Rabelais." *RER* 8: 257–330, 1910.
Solid study, superseded on many points by Screech's work.

Romier, Lucien. "Notes critiques et documents sur le dernier voyage de Rabelais en Italie." *RER* 10: 113–42, 1912.
Strong, convincing treatment of a complex question.

Saulnier, V. L. "L'Enigme du Pantagruelion ou: du *Tiers* au *Quart Livre*." In *ER* I (1956), pp. 48–72.
Good review of theories of its meaning and presentation of his own—crypto-Evangelism.

———. "Médecins de Montpellier au temps de Rabelais." *BHR* 19: 425–79, 1957.
Solid study of the subject and of Rabelais's career at Montpellier.

———. "Pantagruel au large de Ganabin, ou La Peur de Panurge." *BHR* 16: 58–81, 1954.
Convincing demonstration that Ganabin represents the abode of the Parisian persecutors of the Evangelicals.

———. "Le Silence de Rabelais et le mythe des paroles gelées." In *FR*, pp. 233–47.
Persuasive argument for crypto-Evangelical reading of this episode.

Screech, M. A. "The Death of Pan and the Death of Heroes in the Fourth Book of Rabelais: A Study in Syncretism." *BHR* 17: 36–55, 1955.
Searching examination of religious and philosophical ideas in IV: 26–28.

———. "The Legal Comedy of Rabelais in the Trial of Bridoye in the *Tiers Livre* de Pantagruel." In *ER* V (1964), pp. 175–95.
Bridoye draws on old-fashioned commonplace books and usually misapplies his references.

———. "Some Stoic Elements in Rabelais's Religious Thought (The Will—Destiny—Active Virtue)." In *ER* I (1956), pp. 73–87.
Masterly study.

Spitzer, Leo. "Le Prétendu Réalisme de Rabelais." *Modern Philology* 37: 139–50, 1939–40.
Eloquent protest against treatment of Rabelais as a realist.

———. "Rabelais et les rabelaisants." *Studi Francesi* 12: 401–23, 1960.
Vigorous blast against Rabelais scholarship for underplaying his aesthetic side.

Telle, Emile V. "Thélème et le paulinisme matrimonial érasmien: le sens de l'énigme en prophétie (*Gargantua* chap. LVIII)." In *FR*, pp. 104–19.
Strong case for an Erasmian Thélème and prophecy.

Index
of Proper Names

INDEX OF PROPER NAMES